WINDOWS™ EDITION

Microsoft® VISUAL BASIC™ WORKSHOP

Microsoft® VISUAL BASIC™ WORKSHOP

Microsoft PRESS®

JOHN CLARK CRAIG

PUBLISHED BY
Microsoft Press
A Division of Microsoft Corporation
One Microsoft Way
Redmond, Washington 98052-6399

Copyright © 1993 by John Clark Craig

Library of Congress Cataloging-in-Publication Data
Craig, John Clark.
    Microsoft Visual Basic workshop, Windows edition / John Clark
  Craig.
       p. cm.
    Rev. ed. of: The Microsoft Visual Basic workshop, c1991.
    Includes index.
    ISBN 1-55615-512-3
    1. BASIC (Computer program language) 2. Microsoft Visual Basic
  for Windows.   I. Craig, John Clark.   Microsoft Visual Basic
  workshop. II. Title.
  QA76.73.M53C73 1993
  005.4'3--dc20   93-13650
                                                           CIP
Printed and bound in the United States of America.

  2 3 4 5 6 7 8 9 MLML 8 7 6 5 4 3

Distributed to the book trade in Canada by Macmillan of Canada, a division of Canad
Publishing Corporation.

Distributed to the book trade outside the United States and Canada by Penguin
Books Ltd.

Penguin Books Ltd., Harmondsworth, Middlesex, England
Penguin Books Australia Ltd., Ringwood, Victoria, Australia
Penguin Books N.Z. Ltd., 182-190 Wairau Road, Auckland 10, New Zealand

British Cataloging-in-Publication Data available.

Acquisitions Editor: Michael Halvorson
Project Editor: Laura Sackerman
Technical Editor: Dail Magee, Jr.

CONTENTS

Part III: Advanced Programming Concepts

ACKNOWLEDGMENTS

Once again, Microsoft has empowered us with a fantastic programming environment. They've listened to us programmers and have added to Visual Basic's already superb suite of features by providing database, OLE, and other capabilities to take us into the future of Windows-based computing. I applaud Microsoft for a great product!

It's been fun and exciting exploring these new features to create this book. I especially want to thank the many fine people at Microsoft Press for helping with this project. Laura Sackerman and Dail Magee, Jr., provided excellent editing and technical guidance on a tight schedule, and Michael Halvorson's guidance and suggestions were, as always, on target. My thanks also go out to the many other Microsoft Press people who helped make this book a reality and to Amy Ballensky for her artistic talents. I hope you enjoy Visual Basic for Windows 3 as much as I have.

INTRODUCTION

Visual Basic for Windows 3 is an exciting computer programming system. Visual Basic has been tremendously successful, and Microsoft put a lot of effort into upgrading it to version 3. Just about every complaint on the few shortcomings and limitations of the previous versions of Visual Basic was addressed. The power, flexibility, and speed of Visual Basic are now on a par with the C language, and when it comes to productivity, Visual Basic is clearly superior. This book provides information and ideas that enable you to quickly begin working with this revolutionary new way of creating full-featured applications for Windows.

I hope you have as much fun working with Visual Basic as I have. A programmer might need months to get up to speed programming for Windows by using the C language, but with Visual Basic you can develop applications for Windows after only a few hours of familiarizing yourself with the language. You'll be excited to see your first attempts at creating applications for Windows come to life more easily and more quickly than you thought possible.

This book is not intended to be a traditional tutorial; instead, you will learn to use Visual Basic as you step through examples. The text explains concepts, techniques, and tricks as it develops and demonstrates the example applications. Visual Basic is a highly interactive, hands-on programming language, which makes learning by example both enjoyable and productive.

The selection of application examples in this book covers subject areas that I hope will be of interest to just about everyone. You might enjoy expanding the capabilities of some of the applications as you gain experience with Visual Basic. In this edition of the book, I've made several changes at the suggestions of readers and the fine people at Microsoft. You'll find more comments in the code, for one thing. When you open the source code from the companion disk into the Visual Basic environment, the new color-coded comment lines make the code even easier to follow. And when a line of code is too long to fit on a page, you see a special character ($\rightarrow$) that indicates the statement continues in the following line.

I've spent considerable time enhancing several of the applications to make them more useful as stand-alone utilities and to demonstrate the powerful new features added to versions 2 and 3 of Visual Basic. I've also added new utilities to provide more value and to demonstrate features of Visual Basic that were not covered in the first edition of this book. For instance, the COLORBAR application in Chapter 10 demonstrates the drawing of graphics directly on the form rather than in a picture box; it's also a handy utility for adjusting your monitor's contrast and brightness. This book also contains new applications that demonstrate the advanced features of the Professional Edition of Visual Basic 3.

One of the primary goals of this book is to provide a source of timesaving forms that you can use in your own applications. (In Visual Basic's terminology, a *form* is a window and its associated controls, icons, graphics, and code.) For example, the GETFILE form presented in Chapter 6 lets the user select a file from any directory on any drive. This form closely mimics the File Open dialog box found in almost all the newer applications for Windows. Visual Basic 3 provides a control called Common Dialog that also provides these standard forms. However, the GETFILE example provides the source code, which you are free to modify to suit your own purposes.

This book includes a companion disk that contains all the forms and source code discussed in the coming chapters. (For more information, see the section "Using the Companion Disk," at the end of this Introduction.) The companion disk will save you hours of typing and will prevent typographic errors from ruining your day as you experiment with the forms in this book.

NOTE: If you're already up to speed with Visual Basic programming, you might want to skip the first few chapters of this book. If you're familiar with earlier versions of Basic and want to learn about the enhancements in Visual Basic, check out Chapter 2.

Part I gets you started programming in Visual Basic for Windows 3. Chapter 1 presents a short history of the Basic programming language to show how Visual Basic represents an evolutionary leap. Chapter 2 lists important features and advantages of Visual Basic, highlighting some of the recent changes to this language. Chapter 3 compares a very simple program in interpreted Basic syntax, in Microsoft QuickBasic syntax, and in Visual Basic syntax. Chapter 4 walks you through the steps of creating your first Visual Basic application, and Chapter 5 walks you through a larger application while introducing several more Visual Basic programming concepts.

Part II serves up a wide variety of Visual Basic forms and applications, so feel free to skip directly to the subjects that interest you. Chapter 6 presents some useful forms that solve common programming tasks. Many of these forms appear in other applications in the book. The applications in Chapter 7 are designed to help you learn more about Visual Basic's inner workings. For example, one program displays all the standard mouse cursors, and another program displays messages that describe each of the mouse events generated by mouse movements and button clicks. Chapter 8 explains in detail how to create your own screen savers for Windows, and it includes ready-to-run examples. Chapters 9 through 12 present a variety of Visual Basic applications: An advanced calculator, calendar functions, and file compression and decompression are only a few of the topics covered.

In Part III you'll learn about Visual Basic's advanced programming features. Chapter 13 provides examples of Dynamic Data Exchange (DDE), a way for Visual Basic applications to share data with other Windows-based applications. Chapter 14 provides a simple but complete example of Object Linking and Embedding (OLE). Chapter 15 demonstrates the new Data control and shows how to work with databases. In Chapter 16, you'll learn how to call Windows API (application programming interface) functions. Chapter 17 shows how to write and compile your own dynamic link libraries (DLLs), and Chapter 18 covers the creation of a simple custom control. Chapter 19 provides working examples of many of the controls in the Professional Edition of Visual Basic 3. The NISTTIME application has been improved, for example, so that it uses the new Communications control to dial up the National Institute of Standards and Technology and accurately set your system clock. One of the most important new controls lets you easily and efficiently interface with multimedia devices, and I've provided an example application that lets you scan through your directories to play WAV sound files.

Using the Companion Disk
Bound into the back of this book is a 1.44-MB companion disk that contains all the Visual Basic programming projects and applications described in this book. Whether you're a newcomer to Visual Basic or an experienced developer, these sample utilities and programming tools will help you make the most of Visual Basic for Windows 3. For specific information about how these programs are created, executed, and reused, see the relevant sections in this book.

Installing the Disk Files
To install the MICROSOFT VISUAL BASIC WORKSHOP companion disk files on your system:

1. Insert the companion disk in drive A.

2. Enter *a:install* at the MS-DOS prompt.

(continued)

continued

3. Follow the installation instructions on the screen. In a few minutes, the contents of the companion disk will be expanded and copied to the \WORKSHOP directory on drive C.

Exploring the Disk

You'll find the following items on the companion disk:

■ All the program code files, forms, message files, and project files described in the book. In all there are more than 50 sample programming projects, exploring diverse topics such as password protection and Dynamic Data Exchange (DDE).

■ Ready-to-run executable files for each programming project. Simply start the Windows File Manager and then double-click on the EXE files to try them out.

■ All the dynamic link library (DLL) files and custom control (VBX) files that you need to be able to run Visual Basic 3 applications without owning Visual Basic.

The MICROSOFT VISUAL BASIC WORKSHOP book-disk package has been designed to encourage fun and experimentation. As you read through the chapters, you'll learn how the special effects—which you can observe by using the disk's executable files—were accomplished. Soon you'll be creating innovative projects of your own!

## PART I

GETTING STARTED WITH VISUAL BASIC FOR WINDOWS

A SHORT HISTORY OF BASIC

The Basic programming language was created in 1963 by John Kemeny and Thomas Kurtz at Dartmouth College. They designed Basic to teach programming concepts, emphasizing program clarity at the expense of speed and efficiency. They accomplished this by doing away with the job control language and the compile/link steps required for creating programs in other programming languages, such as FORTRAN and assembly language. As a result, Basic was the first easy-to-use language that let the user concentrate on the methods and algorithms for solving programming tasks rather than requiring the user to concentrate on the methods and algorithms the computer hardware needed simply to build and debug programs.

Several characteristics of the earliest versions of Basic are notable. Each line of a program began with a line number, and statements were generally not indented (as is often done today to enhance readability and to clarify structure). All characters were entered and displayed in uppercase letters. All GOTO and GOSUB statements, which transfer program control to another part of the program, used line numbers as their destinations.

These characteristics tended to encourage the creation of hard-to-follow "spaghetti code"—so called because the logical flow of the program often wound and branched around, as do strands of limp spaghetti on a plate. Figure 1-1 on the following page shows a typical example of spaghetti code. Even in this short program, you can easily get lost trying to follow the code. Fortunately, Basic has come a long way since those days.

Early Basic gained the reputation of being a toy language that was not suitable for real-world programming tasks. Over the years, however, Basic evolved from a slow, unstructured, interpreted language into a fast, structured, compiled language suitable for creating a wide variety of applications. Hewlett-Packard Company, Microsoft Corporation, and several other companies have created enhanced versions of Basic that have highly advanced features. If you haven't used Basic for a while, it's time for you to take another look at the language.

```
10 REM - PRIME NUMBERS LESS THAN 100
20 N=N+1
30 IF N=100 THEN GOTO 120
40 I=1
50 I=I+1
60 J=N/I
70 IF INT(J)=J THEN GOTO 20
80 IF I>=SQR(N) THEN GOTO 100
90 GOTO 50
100 PRINT N,
110 GOTO 20
120 END
```

Figure 1-1.
An early Basic program that typifies spaghetti code.

Basic Marches On

The progress of Basic has closely followed the personal computer revolution. In the mid-1970s, Microsoft got its start by developing ROM-based interpreted Basic for the early microprocessor-based computers. The Radio Shack TRS-80, for example, introduced Basic (and the concept of personal computing) to many of us. This original version of Microsoft Basic is still with us today, without too many modifications, in the form of GW-BASIC, the interpreted Basic that shipped with versions 4.01 and earlier of the MS-DOS operating system.

Although GW-BASIC is a great tool for performing quick calculations and other simple tasks, it does pretty much fit the description of a toy language. No serious software developer today would consider marketing software written in GW-BASIC, for the same reasons that MS-DOS–based utilities are not written and marketed in the form of batch files. In both cases the programs are too slow, the source code must be provided to the user, and much better ways now exist to create such programs.

In 1982, Microsoft QuickBasic revolutionized Basic and legitimized it as a serious development language for the MS-DOS environment. QuickBasic effectively combined the interactive, productive nature of GW-BASIC with the power and speed of a compiled language. Line numbers were eliminated, and modern language features such as subprograms and user-defined, structured data types were added. Advanced graphics and sound capabilities provided QuickBasic programmers with power beyond that commonly available from C, Pascal, and FORTRAN. QuickBasic programs had another advantage: They could be run interactively, in interpreted mode, or be compiled into stand-alone, executable programs suitable for the marketplace. (Microsoft now ships QBasic, an interpreter-only version of QuickBasic, as part of MS-DOS.)

Visual Basic

Today the Microsoft Windows revolution is well under way, providing a powerful and standardized environment to take advantage of the capabilities of Intel Corporation's newest microprocessors. For the user, Windows was a breakthrough: It made personal computers more personal and user friendly. Programmers, however, had to retrain themselves and learn an entirely new set of programming concepts to achieve proficiency at developing applications for Windows. Visual Basic, the next great advance for the Basic language, changed all this. Learning how to create applications for Windows is now a breeze, and programming for Windows is now interactive, productive, and fun!

The Basic language has changed a lot over the last couple of decades, and Visual Basic for Windows 3 continues this trend. Thousands of full-featured Windows-based applications have been developed by using previous versions of Visual Basic, and many more will be developed by using Visual Basic 3, the most advanced version of this language. In the next chapter, we'll look at some of Visual Basic's unique features, so you'll begin to see what all the excitement is about.

FEATURES AND ADVANTAGES OF VISUAL BASIC FOR WINDOWS

Visual Basic for Windows has many features that make it an ideal language for developing applications for Microsoft Windows. These features increase productivity and provide all the tools and hooks needed to develop extremely sophisticated applications. This chapter highlights several of these features.

Beyond QuickBasic

Visual Basic for Windows retains most of the advanced features of Microsoft QuickBasic and has many enhancements for Windows-based software development. For example, graphics output can easily be directed to any part of a window or even to a printer. You select colors for the graphical objects from more than 16 million shades. (Windows will dither the pixels to approximate the shade you want, or it will create the exact shade if your hardware will support it. In either case, you don't have to worry about those details, now or in the future!)

Another enhancement over QuickBasic is the manner in which variables are scoped in Visual Basic. The rules are easier to understand and remember because they've been simplified and improved. Applications written in Visual Basic can include two types of files: forms, which contain both the visual representation of and the code for windows and dialog boxes; and modules, which contain only source code. Variables and constants declared in the general-declarations section of a form or module are accessible from any subprogram or function in that form or module. Variables and constants declared as Global in a module are accessible from any form or module in the project. Unless declared globally elsewhere, variables and constants in subprograms and functions are local to the routine in which they appear. (These rules will become obvious to you as you gain a little experience with Visual Basic.)

Figure 2-1 shows the code for an example application. When the mouse is clicked in the application's window, the application prints the following:

```
3.141593      6.283186
```

Notice that the constant PI is visible everywhere in this project, TWOPI is visible anywhere in Form1, and THREEPI is visible only in the Form_Load subprogram. (Beginning with Visual Basic 2, default variables are of type Variant. In the Form_Click routine below, THREEPI is interpreted as a null variant, which causes nothing to be printed for its value. In Visual Basic 1, a zero would have been printed.)

Don't worry if the code in Figure 2-1 looks a little strange to you; later you can come back to this example, and it'll make more sense. The important point to remember is that the visibility (or accessibility) of a constant or variable is easily determined by its location in a project.

One of the great advantages of Visual Basic is the short time required for a person to become a productive programmer. If you're already familiar with

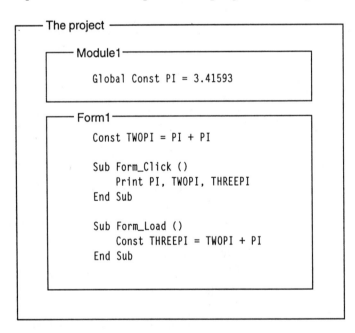

Figure 2-1.
An example of the scope of variables.

QuickBasic, you'll quickly feel right at home with Visual Basic. If you take a look at the amount of information that you need to digest and comprehend when learning to program applications for Windows by using C, you'll greatly appreciate the interactive and intuitive nature of Visual Basic. Learning to use Visual Basic is by far the quickest way to get up to speed in developing full-featured applications for Windows.

Even if you're a seasoned C language Windows developer, you'll appreciate the interactive interface-development cycle Visual Basic provides. The Basic language has always been superior for interactively trying out programming ideas. For example, it was often quicker and easier to use the GW-BASIC RUN command on a line or two of code to see how a statement worked than it was to look up the details in the documentation. This interactive development concept now applies to creating the Windows user interface for your application by using Visual Basic. Nothing compares to being able to get quick visual feedback as the interface design progresses. Unless you have the uncommon ability to hold in your mind all the details of an application's design, you'll find the interactive nature of Visual Basic to be a real time-saver.

Windows' Dynamic Link Libraries

Another advantage of Visual Basic is its extendability. Visual Basic for Windows applications run fast, but in some specialized cases optimized C language code can run faster. In Part II of this book, you'll find examples of Visual Basic applications calling optimized C language Windows functions that are provided in Windows' KERNEL, USER, and GDI dynamic link libraries (DLLs). These DLLs contain many powerful functions, and applications written in Visual Basic can easily access them. If you have a C compiler, it's also easy to create your own special-purpose DLLs.

If you have Windows, the power of these DLLs is available to you because they're an integral part of the Windows operating system. The Microsoft Windows Software Development Kit (SDK) describes the functions in these libraries in detail and provides the required prototype definitions for calling them from C. The Professional Edition of Visual Basic for Windows includes a special Help file that contains Visual Basic declarations for all the functions in the standard DLLs. If you've called these functions from Visual Basic 1, you'll understand how valuable these declarations can be and how much of a time saving they represent.

As I mentioned before, you can easily use the C language to create your own DLLs that contain executable code you can optimize for speed. By doing so, you get the incredibly fast interface-development capabilities of Visual

Basic combined with the highly optimized C compiler output. This is an important advantage of Visual Basic. Examples of this technique are found in Chapter 17 of this book. You'll need a C compiler to create your own DLLs; however, the sample DLL provided in this book is included on the floppy disk packaged with the book.

Other Features of Windows

Visual Basic for Windows 3 provides easy-to-use mechanisms for Dynamic Data Exchange (DDE) and Object Linking and Embedding (OLE) among any Windows-based applications that support these features. You'll see DDE and OLE in action increasingly in the future, as more Windows-based applications take advantage of these powerful features. Chapters 13 and 14 present Visual Basic programs that demonstrate how data and objects can be transferred or linked among separate Windows-based applications.

The Future

The applications that you develop today in Visual Basic will be around for a long time. The Windows operating system is designed to remain stable, even as the capabilities of computer hardware progress. For example, as the graphics resolutions and color capabilities of computer hardware increase, Windows-based applications will not require modification; they'll simply run better and faster.

## CHAPTER THREE

EVENT-DRIVEN PROGRAMMING

Visual Basic for Windows programs are *event driven,* a concept that's at the heart of all Microsoft Windows applications. After you do this type of programming, you'll never want to go back to the old ways. You'll discover a whole new level of creative, effective techniques for developing your applications.

Fortunately, the conceptual difference between event-driven code and procedural code isn't as drastic a leap as you might initially think. Much of the code you write for Visual Basic for Windows programs will be very familiar to you. To demonstrate, I've prepared three versions of a short program to show the progression from GW-BASIC code to Microsoft QuickBasic code and finally to Visual Basic code. You'll see that the Visual Basic example requires very little additional explanation yet provides a good example of an event-driven routine.

All three programs display *Testing... 1 2 3* at the top of the screen (or at the top of a window, for the Visual Basic version). Let's take a look at the GW-BASIC version first, good old line numbers and all:

```
10 REM - GW-BASIC Test Program
20 CLS
30 PRINT "Testing...";
40 FOR I = 1 TO 3
50 PRINT I;
60 NEXT I
70 PRINT
80 END
```

This program clears the screen, prints *Testing...* at the top of the display, and then enters a FOR loop to print the numbers 1, 2, and 3.

The QuickBasic program, presented next, displays exactly the same output. The program demonstrates a few of the improvements of QuickBasic over interpreted Basic, such as not needing line numbers.

```
' QuickBasic Test Program
CLS
PRINT "Testing...";
FOR i = 1 TO 3
    PRINT i;
NEXT i
PRINT
END
```

And now, here's what you've been waiting for...your first look at an event-driven application, written entirely in Visual Basic for Windows:

```
' Visual Basic for Windows Test Program
Sub Form_Click ()
    Print "Testing...";
    For i = 1 To 3
        Print i;
    Next i
End Sub
```

Notice how much of the Visual Basic code looks the same as the QuickBasic code. Keywords, such as *Print,* are now displayed with the first letter of the word uppercase and the rest of the letters lowercase, but the syntax remains the same. The major difference between this version of the program and its predecessor is that the code in the Visual Basic version has been placed in an event-driven subprogram called Form_Click.

N O T E: This example prints out the same in Visual Basic version 1, 2, or 3, but the source code is easier to work with in the two later versions because it is color coded on screen. Comment lines are green, keywords are blue, and variables are black. This is only one of the many nice touches Microsoft added to Visual Basic during its two major upgrades.

Why not put the code in the main part of the program? The answer to this question is very important, and it gets right to the heart of the Visual Basic programming philosophy: All executable code in a Visual Basic program exists in either a subprogram or a function. These subprograms and functions are activated by events (such as a mouse click, a command-button activation, or a change in the contents of a text box) or by calls from other routines (which can be traced back to some routine that was event activated). Because Visual Basic takes care of all the "housekeeping" chores, all your programs need to do is respond to events as they occur.

REMEMBER: In Visual Basic all executable code must exist inside a subprogram or a function block!

Visual Basic for Windows names event-driven subprograms for you by using the name of the object affected and the type of event that triggers the subprogram. The name Form_Click indicates that this subprogram runs when the user clicks the mouse in the form's window. It's really quite simple: When you run this program, a blank window appears; click the mouse anywhere in the window, and *Testing...1 2 3* appears in the window.

In this example, the mouse-click event activates a subprogram that displays the text. You could have just as easily placed the code in the Form_DblClick subprogram, in which case *Testing...1 2 3* would appear only after the user double-clicked the mouse anywhere in the form's window.

As you've probably guessed by now, you can use many other events to activate subprograms in Visual Basic for Windows. As you'll see in the sample applications throughout this book, this event-driven design is extremely powerful and greatly facilitates the development of applications for Windows.

YOUR FIRST VISUAL BASIC FOR WINDOWS APPLICATION

When people encounter Visual Basic for Windows for the first time, they often think, "OK, now just where do I start?" This chapter will help you get acclimated and will build your confidence by walking you through the process of developing a simple but complete application.

The WINDCHIL Application

The WINDCHIL application displays the windchill index for a given wind speed and air temperature. The windchill index is the air temperature that would produce an equivalent rate of heat loss from your skin if no wind were blowing. As wind speed increases and you lose heat more quickly, the windchill index decreases.

This application isn't large, yet it handily demonstrates several controls on a single form in a simple, easy-to-understand way. For example, one pair of option buttons lets the user select the type of temperature units to be used, either degrees Fahrenheit or degrees Celsius, and a scroll bar enables the user to efficiently select the wind speed.

We'll use the checklist on the following page to build the WINDCHIL application. While you're becoming familiar with the Visual Basic for Windows environment, you might find it useful to refer to this checklist to develop other single-form applications.

Single-Form Application Development Checklist

1. Begin a new project.

2. Design the form:

   ☐ Change the size and location of the form's window.

   ☐ Draw controls that have the sizes, shapes, and locations you want.

   ☐ Change other form and control properties as you like.

3. Add subprograms to the form for the events you want the program to handle.

4. Test the application, repeating the above steps as necessary.

5. Save the project on disk.

6. (Optional) Create an executable (EXE) file.

Beginning a New Project

Let's begin creating the WINDCHIL application. Start Visual Basic for Windows, or if it is already running, choose New Project from the File menu to start with a clean slate. Figure 4-1 shows the opening screen. (Some of the Visual Basic windows might be in different positions on your screen. You can move any of the windows to any position you want.)

Changing the Form's Caption Property

This project consists of a single form. A *form* is an application window that has associated code and controls that are necessary to perform one or more specific tasks. The default caption of the new form's window is *Form1*. To change the caption, select the Caption property in the Properties window of the new form, and type *Windchill Index*. (If you can't see the Properties window, click on the form, and then choose Properties from the Window menu or press F4.) As you type, you will see the caption change. Figure 4-2 shows the form after the change.

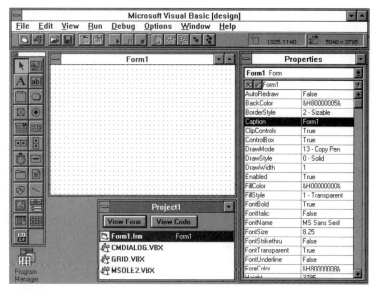

Figure 4-1.
The opening screen of the Visual Basic for Windows 3 program.

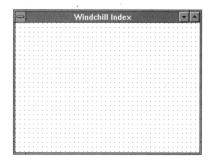

Figure 4-2.
The window of the new form after you change the Form1 *default caption to* Windchill Index.

Adding a Menu to the Form

To create a menu on the form, choose Menu Design from the Window menu. The Menu Design Window dialog box appears, similar to the one shown in Figure 4-3 on the following page. The Menu Design Window dialog box is the interface for designing and modifying menus for Visual Basic applications. Click in the Caption text box, and type *&Help*. This is the title of the WINDCHIL form's only menu. The ampersand (&) in &Help is optional; it causes the *H* to be underlined in the menu bar and allows the user to open the Help menu by pressing Alt-H. It's a good idea to get in the habit of using the ampersand when creating menu bar items; it adds a nice touch to your menus and provides keyboard-shortcut commands for users who prefer them to mouse clicking.

Press Tab to move to the Name text box, and type *menHelpTop*. Each menu title and menu item has a name, which is used in the code portion of the form to name the subprogram that activates when the user chooses that menu title or menu item. I've developed the habit of prefixing these menu names with *men*, which lets me immediately identify the parts of a program's code that are directly associated with menus.

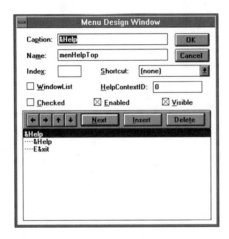

Figure 4-3.
The appearance of the Menu Design Window dialog box after you enter the menu information.

Click the Next button in the Menu Design Window dialog box to clear the dialog box's fields so that you can enter the next menu item. Indent the caption name you're about to enter by clicking the right arrow indentation button, which is in the group of buttons to the left of the Next button. Dashes appear in the highlighted line in the list box below. The dashes show the indentation that Visual Basic uses to nest menu items. The items in the first level of indentation are the main items in a drop-down menu. The items in the second level of indentation are placed in a submenu in the drop-down menu.

After you click the indentation button, enter *&Help* in the Caption text box and *menHelp* in the Name text box, for the first menu item. For the second menu item, enter *E&xit* in the Caption text box and *menExit* in the Name text box. (The *x* in *Exit* will be underlined because of the placement of the ampersand.) Notice that the second menu item retains the indentation of the item above it; you do not have to click the right arrow indentation button again. The table below illustrates how Menu Design Window dialog box entries are listed in this book.

WINDCHIL.FRM Menu Design Window Entries

Caption	Name	Indentation
&Help	menHelpTop	0
&Help	menHelp	1
E&xit	menExit	1

The menu for WINDCHIL is now complete. Click OK to exit the Menu Design Window dialog box. Immediately you'll see the Help menu on the menu bar of the form. Click on the form's new Help menu to see the Help menu items. Figure 4-4 shows the form with its Help menu open.

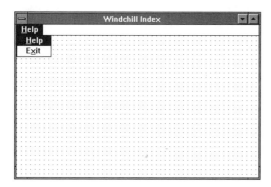

Figure 4-4.
The WINDCHIL form with its Help menu open.

Adding Controls to the Form

The next step is to add and modify the form's controls. *Controls* are buttons, labels, text fields, and other items that make up the user interface on the form. You select controls from the Toolbox. (See Figure 4-5 on the following page.) The selection and placement of controls on a form's window determine much of the functionality of the form. You can use controls to display text, provide user-alterable text input fields, define a rectangular graphics output region, display lists, toggle selections, and so on. Each type of control is described in detail in your Visual Basic for Windows manual.

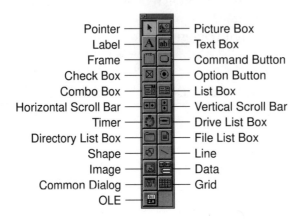

Pointer	Picture Box
Label	Text Box
Frame	Command Button
Check Box	Option Button
Combo Box	List Box
Horizontal Scroll Bar	Vertical Scroll Bar
Timer	Drive List Box
Directory List Box	File List Box
Shape	Line
Image	Data
Common Dialog	Grid
OLE	

Figure 4-5.
The Toolbox.

Figure 4-6 shows the WINDCHIL form with the controls in place. The following sections describe the controls and the process of placing them on the form.

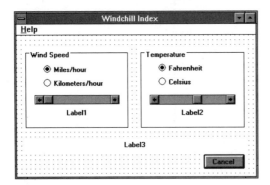

Figure 4-6.
The WINDCHIL form with controls in place.

Frames   In the Toolbox, click on the Frame button to select the Frame control. On the form, click near the upper left corner (under the Help menu) and drag to about the middle of the form to draw the first frame. This will be the Wind Speed frame on the left side of the finished form.

You can go back and resize or move this frame at any time to get the placement on the form exactly right, so don't worry about being too precise as you start. To resize an object, simply click on it to select it and then drag the sizing handles (the eight small black blocks around the object's perimeter) as needed. To move an object, select it and then drag it to its new location.

Click on the frame to select it. Then select the Caption property in the Properties window at the right side of the screen, and type *Wind Speed*. The frame's caption changes to *Wind Speed*. Follow the same steps to create the second frame, placing the new frame to the right of the first frame. Use the same height and width for this frame as you did for the first frame. (You can determine the frame's height and width by looking at the display at the right end of the toolbar.) Then enter *Temperature* for the new frame's Caption property.

Option Buttons Click on the Option button in the Toolbox to draw each of the option buttons on the form. First draw the two option buttons inside the Wind Speed frame, and then draw the two option buttons inside the Temperature frame. (It's important that you create the option buttons in this order.) You will need to click on the Option button in the Toolbox before you draw each option button on the form. Set each option button's Caption property to match Figure 4-6.

When you group option buttons inside a frame, Visual Basic allows only one option button in the frame to be selected at any given time. This is why you'll often see option buttons grouped in frames on Visual Basic forms. Set the Value property for the Miles/hour and Fahrenheit option buttons to *True* to make those buttons active when the application runs.

Scroll Bars You can now add the two Scroll Bar controls in a similar way. Click on the Horizontal Scroll Bar button in the Toolbox. Then move the mouse pointer to the form, and drag to draw the scroll bars inside each frame. Draw the scroll bar in the Wind Speed frame first. Refer to Figure 4-6 for placement. Now it's time to change five properties of these scroll bars. Click on the scroll bar inside the Wind Speed frame, select LargeChange in the Properties window, and set its value to *10*. In the same manner, change the values for the Max, Min, and Value properties to reflect the values shown in the table on the following page. We'll use the default value of *1* for the SmallChange property. Although you don't need to change the Name property for either scroll bar, I've included the default names so that you can easily identify which scroll bar I'm referring to.

WINDCHIL.FRM Form and Control Properties

Property	Value
Horizontal Scroll Bar	
LargeChange	10
Max	50
Min	5
Name	HScroll1
Value	5
Horizontal Scroll Bar	
LargeChange	10
Max	90
Min	-50
Name	HScroll2
Value	32

Labels Click on the Label button in the Toolbox, and draw two labels inside the frames. Then draw a third label on the form, below the frames, as shown in Figure 4-6. Change the Alignment property of all three labels to *2-Center.*

Command Button The last control to add is a command button. Click on the Command button in the Toolbox, and draw the button at the bottom right corner of the form, as shown in Figure 4-6. Change the button's Caption property to *Cancel,* and change the Cancel and Default properties to *True.* The Cancel property tells Visual Basic to choose this command button if the user presses the Esc key, and the Default property makes the button the default button when the form loads. (The default command button is chosen when the user presses the Enter key.)

Adding Code to Create Subprograms

The only task remaining in order to complete this application is to add some event-driven code that calculates and displays the windchill index. Double-click anywhere in the form's window, except on a control. The Visual Basic development environment interprets this double click to mean that you want to edit a subprogram for an event on the form. (If you double-click on a control, Visual Basic jumps to the subprograms that are connected to that control.) Visual Basic creates the following two lines in a code edit window:

```
Sub Form_Load ()

End Sub
```

You type code lines to build the subprogram between the beginning and ending lines that Visual Basic provides.

Visual Basic creates and names a subprogram for each event on each form, menu item, and control by using the Name property for that form, menu item, or control. All event-driven subprogram names have the same syntax: *Object_Event*. The *Object* portion is the name of the form, menu item, or control associated with the event designated in the *Event* portion. An underscore always separates the two parts of event-driven subprogram names. In this example, the subprogram is activated when Visual Basic loads the form—hence the name Form_Load.

You aren't required to add code to the Form_Load subprogram or to any other subprogram. If you want the application to respond to double clicks and not single clicks, for example, simply add code to the Form_DblClick subprogram and leave the Form_Click subprogram empty.

We'll start by adding code to the Form_Load subprogram. Add the following three lines to fill out the Form_Load subprogram.

NOTE: The disk packaged with this book includes the WINDCHIL application. If you'd like to avoid typing this program, open the File menu, choose the Open Project command, and type *C:\WORKSHOP\WINDCHIL.MAK*. I suggest, however, that you create this first program yourself so that you experience every step of developing an application.

```
Sub Form_Load ()
    'Force scroll bars to update
    HScroll1_Change
    HScroll2_Change
End Sub
```

All this code does is call two other event subprograms, the Change subprograms for the scroll bars. This ensures that the program's display is correct when it starts.

If you're used to the editing features of the Microsoft QuickBasic environment, you'll quickly adjust to the Visual Basic editor because many of the commands are the same. Figure 4-7, on the following page, shows what your code edit window looks like after you enter the Form_Load code.

Figure 4-7.
The Form_Load subprogram.

Now create the Command1_Click subprogram, the routine that activates when the user clicks the Cancel button. Select Command1 from the Object combo box at the top of the edit window, and select Click from the Proc combo box. Enter the following two lines to fill out this subprogram:

```
Sub Command1_Click ()
    'Cancel button clicked
    Unload Windchil
End Sub
```

In addition to subprograms associated with control events, Visual Basic lets you create other subprograms, with any names, to be called from inside a running program and not activated directly by an event. For example, the ChillOut subprogram is called from the HScroll1_Change subprogram to handle the task of updating the displayed windchill data. You can't select this subprogram from the Object and Proc combo boxes until it's been created. To create a brand-new subprogram such as ChillOut, choose New Procedure from the View menu. Enter the name of your new procedure in the dialog box that pops up, and Visual Basic creates the new procedure for you. Of course, it's up to you to fill out the routine with lines of code. Try your hand at creating the ChillOut subprogram now by adding the following lines of code:

```
Sub ChillOut ()
    'Get working values from scroll bars
    Wind = HScroll1.Value
    Temp = HScroll2.Value

    'Convert to MPH if KPH selected
    If Option2.Value = True Then
        Wind = Mph(Wind)
    End If
```

```
                    'Convert to Fahrenheit if Celsius selected
                    If Option4.Value = True Then
                        Temp = Fahrenheit(Temp)
                    End If

                    'Calculate windchill index
                    X = .303439 * Sqr(Wind) - .0202886 * Wind
                    Chill = Int(91.9 - (91.4 - Temp) * (X + .474266))

                    'Convert back to Celsius if selected
                    If Option4.Value = True Then
                        Chill = Celsius(Chill)
                    End If

                    'Display windchill index
                    Y$ = "Windchill Index is " + Str$(CInt(Chill))
                    If Option3.Value = True Then
                        Label3.Caption = Y$ + " F"
                    Else
                        Label3.Caption = Y$ + " C"
                    End If
                End Sub
```

Throughout the rest of this book, the source-code listings for each form are presented in a continuous block. Following is the code for WINDCHIL in its entirety, including the subprograms you have already entered. Use this listing to enter the code for the rest of the routines in this application. You enter the first few comment lines in the general-declarations area of the form. To display this area, choose (general) from the Object combo box and (declarations) from the Proc combo box.

Source code for the windchill index program

```
' WINDCHIL
' Calculates windchill index

Function Celsius (F)
    'Convert Fahrenheit to Celsius
    Celsius = (F + 40) * 5 / 9 - 40
End Function

Sub ChillOut ()
    'Get working values from scroll bars
    Wind = HScroll1.Value
    Temp = HScroll2.Value
```

(continued)

25

Windchill index program *continued*

```
        'Convert to MPH if KPH selected
        If Option2.Value = True Then
            Wind = Mph(Wind)
        End If

        'Convert to Fahrenheit if Celsius selected
        If Option4.Value = True Then
            Temp = Fahrenheit(Temp)
        End If

        'Calculate windchill index
        X = .303439 * Sqr(Wind) - .0202886 * Wind
        Chill = Int(91.9 - (91.4 - Temp) * (X + .474266))

        'Convert back to Celsius if selected
        If Option4.Value = True Then
            Chill = Celsius(Chill)
        End If

        'Display windchill index
        Y$ = "Windchill Index is " + Str$(CInt(Chill))
        If Option3.Value = True Then
            Label3.Caption = Y$ + " F"
        Else
            Label3.Caption = Y$ + " C"
        End If
End Sub

Sub Command1_Click ()
    'Cancel button clicked
    Unload Windchil
End Sub

Function Fahrenheit (C)
    'Convert Celsius to Fahrenheit
    Fahrenheit = (C + 40) * 9 / 5 - 40
End Function

Sub Form_Load ()
    'Force scroll bars to update
    HScroll1_Change
    HScroll2_Change
End Sub
```

(continued)

Windchill index program *continued*

```
Sub HScroll1_Change ()
    'Get wind speed
    Tmp = HScroll1.Value

    'Display using selected units
    If Option2.Value = True Then
        Label1.Caption = Tmp + " KPH"
    Else
        Label1.Caption = Tmp + " MPH"
    End If

    'Calculate windchill index
    ChillOut
End Sub

Sub HScroll1_Scroll ()
    'Update when scroll box moves
    HScroll1_Change
End Sub

Sub HScroll2_Change ()
    'Get temperature
    Tmp = HScroll2.Value

    'Display using selected units
    If Option4.Value = True Then
        Label2.Caption = Tmp + " C"
    Else
        Label2.Caption = Tmp + " F"
    End If

    'Calculate windchill index
    ChillOut
End Sub

Sub HScroll2_Scroll ()
    'Update when scroll box moves
    HScroll2_Change
End Sub

Function Kph (M)
    'Convert MPH to KPH
    Kph = M * 1.609344
End Function
```

(continued)

Windchill index program *continued*

```
Sub menExit_Click ()
    'Menu Exit clicked
    Unload Windchil
End Sub

Sub menHelp_Click ()
    'Build Help message
    Msg$ = "Use the scroll bars to select wind speed and" + CHR$(10)
    Msg$ = Msg$ + "air temperature.  The calculated Windchill"↴
     + CHR$(10)
    Msg$ = Msg$ + "Index is displayed below.  You may select"↴
     + CHR$(10)
    Msg$ = Msg$ + "metric units if desired." + CHR$(10)

    'Display Help message
    MsgBox Msg$
End Sub

Function Mph (K)
    'Convert KPH to MPH
    Mph = K / 1.609344
End Function

Sub Option1_Click ()
    'Convert current wind speed to MPH
    X% = Mph(CSng(HScroll1.Value))

    'Reset scroll bar for MPH
    HScroll1.Min = 5
    HScroll1.Max = 50
    HScroll1.Value = X%
End Sub

Sub Option2_Click ()
    'Convert current wind speed to KPH
    X% = Kph(CSng(HScroll1.Value))

    'Reset scroll bar for KPH
    HScroll1.Min = 8
    HScroll1.Max = 80
    HScroll1.Value = X%
End Sub
```

(continued)

Windchill index program *continued*

```
Sub Option3_Click ()
    'Convert current temperature to Fahrenheit
    X% = Fahrenheit(CSng(HScroll2.Value))
    If X% < -50 Then X% = -50

    'Reset scroll bar for Fahrenheit
    HScroll2.Min = -50
    HScroll2.Max = 90
    HScroll2.Value = X%
End Sub

Sub Option4_Click ()
    'Convert current temperature to Celsius
    X% = Celsius(CSng(HScroll2.Value))
    If X% < -45 Then X% = -45

    'Reset scroll bar for Celsius
    HScroll2.Min = -45
    HScroll2.Max = 32
    HScroll2.Value = X%
End Sub
```

Testing the Application

The WINDCHIL application is now ready to run! Open the Run menu, and choose the Start command; alternatively, press the F5 key or click the Run button in the toolbar. The Windchill Index window appears, displaying a default wind speed, air temperature, and calculated windchill index, similar to Figure 4-8.

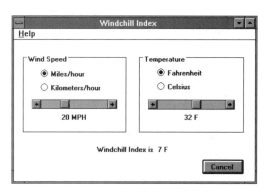

Figure 4-8.
The WINDCHIL application in action.

Use the scroll bars to change the wind speed and air temperature settings. You can click to the left or right of the scroll box to move the scroll box in large increments, and you can click on the scroll arrows to move the scroll box in small increments. You can also drag the scroll box to the position you want. The application's calculation of the windchill index is valid over a prescribed range of wind speeds and air temperatures. Your setting of the Max and Min values of the scroll bars to these range limits in the program code serves as a convenient way to guarantee that the user can't enter data outside the range limits for these values.

If you prefer to use metric units, click the appropriate option buttons. The scroll bar ranges and current values all change to reflect the new units.

Arranging Application Help

In this application, the Help message text is embedded directly in the menHelp_Click subprogram. This is an effective technique only when short Help messages are displayed. Most of the programs in this book use a more flexible approach to displaying Help messages, storing them in separate text files that are loaded and displayed when the user asks for Help. See the FILEMSG application in Chapter 6 for more information.

Saving a Project on Disk

Now that you've created your first Visual Basic for Windows application, you should save it on disk. Open the File menu, and then choose Save Project. Two files will be saved: WINDCHIL.MAK, which defines the overall project, and WINDCHIL.FRM, which contains the single form we built for this application. When you save a project for the first time, Visual Basic notes this fact, and it prompts you for new filenames for each part of the project. For this example, type *WINDCHIL* each time. Visual Basic adds the correct extensions.

As you have seen, the WINDCHIL project is saved in only two files. Visual Basic saves each form and each source-code module in a separate file, and it keeps track of the associated files in the project's MAK file. In later chapters we'll take a look at larger projects, some of which require three or more files for all their parts.

Creating an EXE File

The last step in the development checklist is to create an executable (EXE) file for the application. (This step is optional.) You can reload a project at any time into the Visual Basic environment and run it from there. However, if you want to run the application from outside the Visual Basic environment (for example, directly from Windows' File Manager), you will need to create an EXE file for the application. Open the File menu and choose the Make EXE File command to generate an executable file. The EXE file that Visual Basic compiles includes an icon that is used when the application's window is minimized or when the application is added to the Program Manager. By default, the icon is the one associated with the Icon property in the application's first form. You can change the startup form's icon by modifying the Icon property's setting in the Visual Basic environment, or you can change the project's icon in the Make EXE File dialog box.

The executable file is what you would ship to a customer. The code is compiled and cannot easily be tampered with, and all the forms and modules of the application are combined into one EXE file for convenience. Customers do not need Visual Basic for Windows to run the executable file, but they do need the Visual Basic runtime dynamic link library named VBRUN300.DLL. Microsoft Corporation allows you to ship this file—along with your application—to your customers. Depending on your application, you might have to ship additional DLL and VBX files that are provided with Visual Basic 3. (See the Visual Basic manual for more information about this.)

This chapter provided an example of creating a simple Windows-based application in Visual Basic. In the following chapter, I cover additional concepts that can be applied to larger, more complex projects.

THE PHASE-OF-THE-MOON APPLICATION

Now that your feet are wet, it's time for you to start swimming! In this chapter, the development of an application named MOON is described in detail. It uses additional Visual Basic for Windows features, such as graphics output and program manipulation of form properties. As you follow the steps for building and running this application, you learn several new Visual Basic programming concepts.

The disk packaged with this book contains the files for the MOON application. You might want to create the application yourself as a learning exercise, by following the instructions in this chapter, and then compare the results to the packaged version. However, if you'd prefer to save time and avoid typing errors, load the application into Visual Basic by opening the File menu, choosing the Open Project command, and entering the filename *C:\WORKSHOP\MOON.MAK*.

The MOON application graphically shows the phase of the moon for any date from the year 100 through the year 9999, which is the range of valid dates for Visual Basic's calendar-related functions. The moon's elliptical orbit and the tilt of its path around the earth are quite complicated, so the simple calculation presented here is accurate to only about plus or minus one day. However, this should be accurate enough for planting potatoes, planning fishing trips, or demonstrating some interesting Visual Basic graphics.

Begin by opening the File menu and choosing the New Project command. Size the form to be nearly square—Width and Height properties of *4710* and *5160* work well—so that the moon image will appear round instead of elliptical. The location of the form during development is not critical because we'll put instructions in the program to center the form on the screen when the form loads.

Before we enter code to fill out the subprograms, let's create a menu bar, add a label field, and set all the properties that define the appearance of the application. Open the Window menu, and choose the Menu Design command. The MOON application has one menu-bar item, called Options, that opens a drop-down menu of two selections: New Date and Exit. Create the menu bar by using the information in the following menu design window entries table.

MOON.FRM Menu Design Window Entries

Caption	Name	Indentation
&Options	menOptMoon	0
&New Date	menDateMoon	1
E&xit	menExitMoon	1

The MOON application uses only one control item: a label field to display the date and state of the moon (whether the moon is waxing or waning, heading toward or away from the full moon). Click the Label button (the large uppercase *A*) in the Toolbox, and draw the label field so that it's centered near the top of the form. To correctly display the text, change the label's Width property to *1935* and its Height property to *375*.

We will now set several more properties of the form and label. Click on the label to select it, and then set its Alignment property to *2 - Center*. Next set the label's BackColor property to *&H00400000&* to set the background color to dark blue. (You can also set the background color by selecting BackColor and then clicking the ellipsis at the right of the property value entry field. This opens a window that contains a variety of colors from which to choose. Simply click on the preferred color.) Set the label's ForeColor property to yellow by typing *&H0000FFFF&*.

Set the form's Caption property to *Phase of the Moon,* its Name property to *Moon,* and its BorderStyle property to *0 - None*. Set the BackColor property to match that of the label, *&H00400000&,* and set ForeColor to *&H0080FFFF&*. Finally, set the MaxButton property to *False*. All other properties of the form and the label should be left at their default settings.

The following table summarizes the changed properties for the MOON form. Figure 5-1 shows the MOON application's form during development.

MOON.FRM Form and Control Properties

Property	Value
Form	
BackColor	&H00400000&
BorderStyle	0 - None
Caption	Phase of the Moon
ForeColor	&H0080FFFF&
MaxButton	False
Name	Moon
Label	
Alignment	2 - Center
BackColor	&H00400000&
ForeColor	&H0000FFFF&
Height	375
Name	Label1
Width	1935

Figure 5-1.
The MOON application's form during development.

The last task is to add code to the appropriate subprograms. One constant and two variables that are global to the form are declared in the general-declarations section of the code. Type the following three lines:

```
Const NUMSTARS = 1000

Dim Phase
Dim MoonDate$
```

Five subprograms make up the rest of this application. Add the following code to the Form_Load subprogram:

```
Sub Form_Load ()
    'Center form on screen
    Left = (Screen.Width - Width) / 2
    Top = (Screen.Height - Height) / 2

    'Get date from user
    GetMoonDate

    'Shuffle random numbers for displaying stars
    Randomize Timer
End Sub
```

As mentioned in Chapter 4, the Form_Load subprogram is activated once—when the application starts and the form is loaded. Centering the form's window, getting the initial date from the user, and shuffling the random numbers are all tasks that need not be done more than once during the course of the program—and these are precisely the types of tasks that are appropriate for putting in the Form_Load subprogram.

The Form_Paint subprogram is activated immediately after the form loads, whenever Windows decides that the form should be repainted, and whenever the Form_Paint subprogram is called from elsewhere in the application's code. In the MOON application, Form_Paint is called from the menDateMoon_Click subprogram, which is in turn activated when you choose New Date from the Options menu. Select Paint from the Proc combo box. Then type the following code to build the Form_Paint subprogram:

```
Sub Form_Paint ()
    'Update label and clear the graphics
    If Phase < .5 Then
        Label1.Caption = "The waning moon on " + MoonDate$
    Else
        Label1.Caption = "The waxing moon on " + MoonDate$
    End If
    Cls
```

```
        'Determine number of pixel lines
        ScaleMode = 3
        Pixels% = ScaleHeight + 1

        'Scale for convenient scattering of a few stars
        Scale (0, 0)-(1, 1)
        For i% = 1 To NUMSTARS
            PSet (Rnd, Rnd)
        Next i%

        'Scale for centering moon with radius of 1
        Scale (-2, -2)-(2, 2)

        'Draw visible part of moon
        For y = 0 To 1 Step 4 / Pixels%
            x = Sqr(1 - y * y)

            'Black out any stars behind moon
            Line (-x, y)-(x, y), 0
            Line (-x, -y)-(x, -y), 0

            'Determine edges of lit portion
            r = 2 * x
            If Phase < .5 Then
                x1 = -x
                x2 = r - 2 * Phase * r - x
            Else
                x1 = x
                x2 = x - 2 * Phase * r + r
            End If

            'Draw lit portion of moon
            Line (x1, y)-(x2, y)
            Line (x1, -y)-(x2, -y)
        Next y
End Sub
```

As mentioned before, choosing New Date from the Options menu activates a subprogram called menDateMoon_Click. Select menDateMoon from the Object combo box and Click from the Proc combo box. Then add the following comment line and two lines of code:

```
Sub menDateMoon_Click ()
    'Get new date from user
    GetMoonDate
    Form_Paint
End Sub
```

The GetMoonDate subprogram is called once from within Form_Load; it is also called from within menDateMoon_Click each time the user selects a new date. Select New Procedure from the View menu, and then enter the name *GetMoonDate* to create this subprogram. Now add the rest of the code to the subprogram.

```
Sub GetMoonDate ()
    'Get current date the first time
    Static NotFirstTimeFlag As Integer

TryAgain:

    'Don't ask user for date the first time
    If NotFirstTimeFlag = True Then

        'Set up parameters for InputBox$
        Prompt$ = "Enter a date in this format... mm-dd-yyyy"
        Title$ = "Phase of the Moon"
        Default$ = Date$

        'Ask user for date
        MoonDate$ = InputBox$(Prompt$, Title$, Default$)

    Else

        'Use current date the first time
        MoonDate$ = Date$

        NotFirstTimeFlag = True

    End If

    'Check for Cancel
    If MoonDate$ = "" Then
        MoonDate$ = Date$
    End If

    'Extract date numbers from string
    MonthNum = Val(Left$(MoonDate$, 2))
    DayNum = Val(Mid$(MoonDate$, 4, 2))
    YearNum = Val(Mid$(MoonDate$, 7, 4))

    'Get serial number for entered date
    On Error GoTo ErrorTrap
    SerialNum = DateSerial(YearNum, MonthNum, DayNum)
```

```
'Extract date numbers from serial number
MTst = Month(SerialNum)
DTst = Day(SerialNum)
YTst = Year(SerialNum)

'Calculate astronomical Julian day number
Julian = SerialNum + 2415019

'Calculate approximate phase of moon
Phase = (Julian + 4.867) / 29.53059
Phase = Phase - Int(Phase)

'Verify entered date
If MTst <> MonthNum Or DTst <> DayNum Or YTst <> YearNum Then
    Error 1
End If

Exit Sub

ErrorTrap:

Beep
MsgBox "Invalid date... " + MoonDate$, 48, "Moon"
Resume TryAgain
End Sub
```

One more subprogram needs a little code. Choosing Exit from the Options menu activates the menExitMoon_Click subprogram, which should be filled in as follows:

```
Sub menExitMoon_Click ()
    'All done
    Unload Moon
End Sub
```

The MOON application is now ready to run. Following is the complete source-code listing for this application. Open the Run menu and choose the Start command, or press F5. Stars sprinkle randomly across the dark blue form, and the moon appears in the correct phase for the current date. Open the Options menu, and then choose New Date to enter a different date. When you enter a new date, the graphics are updated to show the moon's phase for the new date. For example, Figure 5-2, on page 43, shows the moon on the evening of July 4, 1776.

Source code for MOON.FRM

```
Const NUMSTARS = 1000

Dim Phase
Dim MoonDate$

Sub Form_Load ()
    'Center form on screen
    Left = (Screen.Width - Width) / 2
    Top = (Screen.Height - Height) / 2

    'Get date from user
    GetMoonDate

    'Shuffle random numbers for displaying stars
    Randomize Timer
End Sub

Sub Form_Paint ()
    'Update label and clear the graphics
    If Phase < .5 Then
        Label1.Caption = "The waning moon on " + MoonDate$
    Else
        Label1.Caption = "The waxing moon on " + MoonDate$
    End If
    Cls

    'Determine number of pixel lines
    ScaleMode = 3
    Pixels% = ScaleHeight + 1

    'Scale for convenient scattering of a few stars
    Scale (0, 0)-(1, 1)
    For i% = 1 To NUMSTARS
        PSet (Rnd, Rnd)
    Next i%

    'Scale for centering moon with radius of 1
    Scale (-2, -2)-(2, 2)

    'Draw visible part of moon
    For y = 0 To 1 Step 4 / Pixels%
        x = Sqr(1 - y * y)
```

(continued)

40

MOON.FRM *continued*

```
        'Black out any stars behind moon
        Line (-x, y)-(x, y), 0
        Line (-x, -y)-(x, -y), 0

        'Determine edges of lit portion
        r = 2 * x
        If Phase < .5 Then
            x1 = -x
            x2 = r - 2 * Phase * r - x
        Else
            x1 = x
            x2 = x - 2 * Phase * r + r
        End If

        'Draw lit portion of moon
        Line (x1, y)-(x2, y)
        Line (x1, -y)-(x2, -y)
    Next y
End Sub

Sub GetMoonDate ()
    'Get current date the first time
    Static NotFirstTimeFlag As Integer

TryAgain:

    'Don't ask user for date the first time
    If NotFirstTimeFlag = True Then

        'Set up parameters for InputBox$
        Prompt$ = "Enter a date in this format... mm-dd-yyyy"
        Title$ = "Phase of the Moon"
        Default$ = Date$

        'Ask user for date
        MoonDate$ = InputBox$(Prompt$, Title$, Default$)

    Else

        'Use current date the first time
        MoonDate$ = Date$

        NotFirstTimeFlag = True

    End If
```

(continued)

MOON.FRM *continued*

```
        'Check for Cancel
        If MoonDate$ = "" Then
            MoonDate$ = Date$
        End If

        'Extract date numbers from string
        MonthNum = Val(Left$(MoonDate$, 2))
        DayNum = Val(Mid$(MoonDate$, 4, 2))
        YearNum = Val(Mid$(MoonDate$, 7, 4))

        'Get serial number for entered date
        On Error GoTo ErrorTrap
        SerialNum = DateSerial(YearNum, MonthNum, DayNum)

        'Extract date numbers from serial number
        MTst = Month(SerialNum)
        DTst = Day(SerialNum)
        YTst = Year(SerialNum)

        'Calculate astronomical Julian day number
        Julian = SerialNum + 2415019

        'Calculate approximate phase of moon
        Phase = (Julian + 4.867) / 29.53059
        Phase = Phase - Int(Phase)

        'Verify entered date
        If MTst <> MonthNum Or DTst <> DayNum Or YTst <> YearNum Then
            Error 1
        End If

        Exit Sub

ErrorTrap:

        Beep
        MsgBox "Invalid date... " + MoonDate$, 48, "Moon"
        Resume TryAgain
    End Sub

Sub menDateMoon_Click ()
        'Get new date from user
        GetMoonDate
        Form_Paint
    End Sub
```

(continued)

MOON.FRM *continued*

```
Sub menExitMoon_Click ()
    'All done
    Unload Moon
End Sub
```

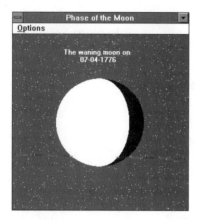

Figure 5-2.
The moon as it appeared on July 4, 1776.

Program Notes

The GetMoonDate subprogram includes error-trapping code. In Visual Basic, the *On Error GoTo* statement is active only while the subprogram containing it is active. The error trapping returns to the default state as soon as the *Exit Sub* statement is encountered. Details of error-trapping techniques are explained in the Visual Basic for Windows manual and in the online Help facility. In the MOON application, error trapping is used to detect an incorrectly entered date and to initiate action.

The first two executable lines in the Form_Load subprogram demonstrate a useful technique for centering a form on the screen. Normally a form is loaded at the same location on the screen where it appeared during program development. Often this location is as good as any other, but sometimes it's nice to place the form smack-dab in the middle. The *Screen.Width* and *Screen.Height* references to properties provide the dimensions of the entire background screen, which might change from computer to computer, based on the graphics resolution of the hardware. The *Moon.Width* and *Moon.Height* references to properties of the application's form are used, along with the

43

screen's dimensions, to calculate and set the position of the upper left corner of the form to center it.

NOTE: Because this code exists in the Moon form, the unqualified references *Width* and *Height* are equivalent to *Moon.Width* and *Moon.Height*.

Each row of pixels that is part of the face of the moon is drawn by using the *Line* method. In the middle of the Form_Paint subprogram is *ScaleMode = 3*, a statement that sets the units of the form to pixels, correct for whatever graphics hardware Windows is running on. Later on, the statement *Scale (-2, -2)-(2, 2)* rescales the form to make it convenient for creating the disk of the moon with a radius of 1. Take a look at *ScaleMode* in the Visual Basic for Windows online Help facility for information about other units you can use for scaling graphics output. This flexible scaling is one of the features that sets Visual Basic apart from previous versions of Basic.

Visual Basic has several functions for calendar and time calculations. The *DateSerial, Month, Day,* and *Year* functions, in particular, are powerful and easy to use. The GetMoonDate subprogram calls these functions to verify user-entered dates and to calculate the astronomical Julian-calendar day number for determining the phase of the moon.

Two important and related functions are used in GetMoonDate. The *InputBox$* function displays a dialog box that prompts the user for a new date, and the *MsgBox* function displays the "Invalid date" message during error trapping. These two functions can be thought of as enhanced versions of the INPUT and PRINT statements in previous versions of Basic. For simple, quick input and output of strings, they can't be beat.

The MOON application uses considerably more of Visual Basic's features than did the WINDCHIL application in the previous chapter. You've seen how multiple event-driven subprograms can work together to accomplish a task and how several graphics output techniques are used.

The applications presented in Part II of this book employ the techniques you've learned in Chapter 4 and in this chapter (and several other techniques) to help you learn more about Visual Basic for Windows and to add interesting and useful forms to your bag of tricks.

VISUAL BASIC FOR WINDOWS FORMS AND APPLICATIONS

## CHAPTER SIX

SOME OFTEN-USED FORMS

This chapter presents some common forms you might want to incorporate in the applications you write in Visual Basic for Windows, including an About dialog box, a Help information form, a File Open dialog box, a Save As dialog box, and many others.

The ABOUTDEM Application

The ABOUTDEM application demonstrates the ABOUT form, which is used by most of the applications in this book to display a standard About dialog box.

The ABOUTDEM project is composed of four files: CONSTANT.TXT, ABOUTDEM.MAK, ABOUT.FRM, and ABOUTDEM.FRM. The file CONSTANT.TXT comes with Visual Basic for Windows; the disk that is packaged with this book contains the other three files. To load all of them into Visual Basic, choose the Open Project command from the File menu, and then type *C:\WORKSHOP\ABOUTDEM.MAK*. I'll describe each of the project's files and provide instructions for creating them so that when you want to create a similar application, you'll know the steps to follow.

The CONSTANT.TXT File

The CONSTANT.TXT file contains constants and declarations that are provided by Microsoft in the Visual Basic for Windows 3 package. This is the only file in this project that is not created from scratch. You'll notice that this file is loaded into the projects for most of the applications in this book. If you take a look at the contents of CONSTANT.TXT, you'll see many standard constants defined, such as constants for key codes, variant types, and system colors. Perhaps the most commonly used constant in the programs in this book is MODAL, which is a parameter to the form *Show* command. I've used the form *Show* command in many applications to display the About dialog box. You might want to add CONSTANT.TXT to your AUTOLOAD.MAK file so that it will load whenever you start a new project. (The AUTOLOAD.MAK file feature was introduced in Visual Basic 2.)

The ABOUTDEM.MAK File

The ABOUTDEM.MAK file is the project file; it contains the names of all the forms and modules that make up the project. With Visual Basic 3 (and Visual Basic 2) you can save all files, including the project file, in ASCII format. This means that you can load ABOUTDEM.MAK into Notepad and make some sense of the contents, which are shown below. The Visual Basic environment maintains the contents of the MAK file for you, so don't worry about the some-what cryptic lines for *ProjWinSize* and *ProjWinShow*. Notice, however, that the forms and modules that make up the ABOUTDEM project are clearly listed in the first few lines.

Contents of the ABOUTDEM.MAK file

```
ABOUTDEM.FRM
C:\VB\CONSTANT.TXT
ABOUT.FRM
ProjWinSize=362,394,246,118
ProjWinShow=2
IconForm="AboutDem"
Title="AboutDem"
ExeName="ABOUTDEM.EXE"
```

Compare the contents of ABOUTDEM.MAK with what's displayed in the project window, which is shown in Figure 6-1.

Figure 6-1.
The project window for the ABOUTDEM project.

The ABOUT.FRM File

The ABOUT.FRM file is the form that this application demonstrates. This form is loaded into many of the projects in this book to provide a common About dialog box. The form displays informational lines about the current program, a copyright notice, and a happy face icon. I've added a bit of animation in this edition of the book by switching between two happy face icons every few seconds. Watch for the wink when you select About from the menu!

The ABOUTDEM.FRM File

The ABOUTDEM.FRM file is the startup form for this application. A short explanatory message is displayed on the form, and you can choose an option from the menu to activate the About form.

Editing the ABOUT Form

You can edit the ABOUTDEM and ABOUT forms in any order. To edit the ABOUT form, you can use Figure 6-2 and the following table as guides.

Figure 6-2.
ABOUT.FRM during development.

ABOUT.FRM Form and Control Properties

Property	Value
Form	
BorderStyle	3 - Fixed Double
Caption	About
ControlBox	False
MaxButton	False
MinButton	False
Name	About
Timer	
Interval	2000
Name	Timer1

(continued)

ABOUT.FRM Form and Control Properties *continued*

Property	Value
Command Button	
Caption	OK
Cancel	True
Default	True
Name	Command1
Image	
Name	Image1
Picture	c:\vb\icons\misc\face03.ico
Image	
Name	Image2
Picture	c:\workshop\facewink.ico
Line	
Name	Line1
X1	480
X2	4680
Y1	1440
Y2	1440
Label	
Alignment	2 - Center
Caption	Label1
FontBold	False
FontSize	18
ForeColor	&H00008000&
Name	Label1
Label	
Alignment	2 - Center
Caption	Microsoft Visual Basic Workshop
FontSize	12
Name	Label2

(continued)

ABOUT.FRM Form and Control Properties *continued*

Property	Value
Label	
Alignment	2 - Center
Caption	For Microsoft Visual Basic for Windows 3
Name	Label3
Label	
Alignment	2 - Center
Caption	Copyright © 1993 John Clark Craig
Name	Label4

The BorderStyle property of the form is set to *3 - Fixed Double*. This causes the form to look slightly different than it does with the default setting of *2 - Sizable*. In particular, the sizing handles are gone, and the size of the form can't be altered when the program is running. There's no reason to let the user adjust the size of the About dialog box because the appearance would only degrade, so the form's only interaction with the user is the OK button used to unload the form.

FontSize and FontBold, as well as other settings for the font properties of labels, were introduced in Visual Basic 2. You adjust the appearance of the characters in the labels by changing these property values. A good way to experiment with the various font settings is to select one of the labels and then select alternative settings for the font-related properties. The displayed text is changed immediately to reflect the new settings.

All the labels have their Alignment property set to *2 - Center*. This setting centers any text strings placed in the labels. The default setting (*0 - Left Justify*) causes the text to align flush left in the label area, which means that the text begins at the left edge of the label area. It's often advantageous to center the text or to align it with the right edge (flush right).

The Caption property of the fourth label contains the copyright announcement. To enter the copyright symbol (ANSI value 169), turn on the Num Lock key, hold down the Alt key, and type *0169* on the numeric keypad.

The Default and Cancel properties for the Command1 control are both set to *True* to allow the Enter and Esc keys to function as shortcuts for clicking the OK button. If both of these properties are left set to *False*, you must use the mouse to click the OK button. The Default and Cancel properties are handy in forms that have multiple buttons. Any button can be designated as the default, which means that pressing the Enter key is equivalent to choosing the button; and any button can be designated as the Cancel button, which means that pressing Esc has the same effect as choosing the button.

The Picture property of Image1 is loaded from the icon file named FACE03.ICO, one of many icons shipped with Visual Basic. (The ICONVIEW application presented in Chapter 12 lets you browse through the icons.) The path to FACE03.ICO listed in the ABOUT.FRM form and control properties table specifies where this file can normally be found, but its location depends on how Visual Basic was installed. You might have to specify a different subdirectory. After this icon is installed, the information in the property line in ABOUT.FRM is different from that shown in the table. Visual Basic for Windows 3 stores loaded icons, bitmaps, and other embedded files in a special data file that has the same name as the form but has the extension FRX. The line in ABOUT.FRM then appears as follows:

```
Picture          =    ABOUT.FRX:0302
```

Image2 is loaded with the icon file C:\WORKSHOP\FACEWINK.ICO, which is an icon I created by editing FACE03.ICO. The only change from the original happy face icon is the winking eye. The Timer1_Timer subprogram temporarily swaps these two icon images to cause the winking animation.

You can create icons for your programs by using the ICONWRKS application shipped with Visual Basic. If you haven't done so, be sure to take a look at this excellent full-blown application for Windows. It provides a good example of what can be done with the power of Visual Basic, and it's an excellent way to add creative, unique icons to your projects.

The final step required for completion of the ABOUT form is to add code to three of the control events. The following code is added to the Form_Load, Command1_Click, and Timer1_Timer subprograms.

Source code for ABOUT.FRM

```
Sub Form_Load ()
    'Center form
    Left = (Screen.Width - Width) / 2
    Top = (Screen.Height - Height) / 2

    'Place both happy faces
    Image1.Left = 840
    Image1.Top = 840
    Image2.Left = 840
    Image2.Top = 840
```

(continued)

52

ABOUT.FRM *continued*

```
        'Make first face visible
        Image1.ZOrder
    End Sub

    Sub Command1_Click ()
        'Cancel About form
        Unload About
    End Sub

    Sub Timer1_Timer ()
        'Wink
        If Timer1.Interval <> 200 Then
            Timer1.Interval = 200
            Image2.ZOrder
        'Undo wink
        Else
            Timer1.Interval = 5000
            Image2.ZOrder 1
            Image1.ZOrder
        End If
    End Sub
```

Editing the ABOUTDEM Form

As previously mentioned, when the ABOUTDEM application is run, it first
loads the ABOUTDEM.FRM form. (See Figure 6-3.) To edit this form, double-
click on ABOUTDEM.FRM in the project list. To create the menu, use the
following table and Figure 6-4, on the following page, as guides.

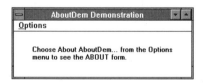

Figure 6-3.
Opening screen of the ABOUTDEM application.

ABOUTDEM.FRM Menu Design Window Entries

Caption	Name	Indentation
&Options	menOptAboutDem	0
&About AboutDem...	menAboutAboutDem	1
E&xit	menExitAboutDem	1

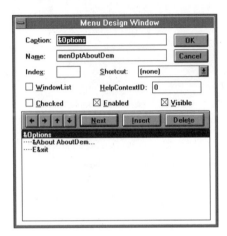

Figure 6-4.
Menu Design Window for ABOUTDEM.FRM.

If you are creating this form from scratch, add a label, and edit the form and label properties to match those shown in Figure 6-5 and in the following table.

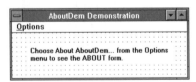

Figure 6-5.
ABOUTDEM.FRM during development.

ABOUTDEM.FRM Form and Control Properties

Property	Value
Form	
Caption	AboutDem Demonstration
Icon	c:\vb\icons\misc\face02.ico
Name	AboutDem
Label	
Caption	Choose About AboutDem... from the Options menu to see the ABOUT form.
Name	Label1

An icon slightly different from those in the ABOUT form is loaded into the Icon property for the ABOUTDEM form. (The smile is a little less pronounced in FACE02.ICO than in FACE03.ICO and FACEWINK.ICO.) This icon appears when you minimize the completed, running application. If you install the executable version of this application in a Program Manager group, this icon also shows up there.

You enter the long line of text in the Caption field of Label1 all on one line. The size of the label field on the form causes the text to wrap to a second line. Ensure that the label field is tall enough for both lines of text.

You add the following code to the form to complete the project.

Source code for ABOUTDEM.FRM

```
Sub menAboutAboutDem_Click ()
    'Display About form
    About.Label1.Caption = "ABOUTDEM"
    About.Show MODAL
End Sub

Sub menExitAboutDem_Click ()
    'Quit program
    Unload AboutDem
End Sub
```

Save the project, and then choose the Start command from the Run menu to start the demonstration. Figure 6-6, on the following page, shows the ABOUTDEM application when running.

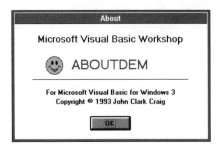

Figure 6-6.
ABOUTDEM.FRM in action.

The ABOUT.FRM module is loaded into many of the applications in this book. Adding it to a project requires a couple of steps. You choose the Add File command from Visual Basic's File menu to add a file to a project. You can use this command to add ABOUT.FRM to the current project list. You pass the name of the project to the ABOUT form by directly setting the name in the *About.Label1.Caption* property. The menAboutAboutDem_Click subprogram listing uses the *Show* method to load the ABOUT form. The parameter MODAL specifies that the user can switch to a different window in the application only after clicking the OK button or choosing the Close option from the system menu.

Whenever you use the *Show MODAL* command in an application, you must declare the constant MODAL for proper operation. You can declare MODAL in the general-declarations section of the form's code, or you can load the declaration file Microsoft supplies with Visual Basic for Windows 3 into your project. I strongly suggest you do the latter. I've developed the habit of loading C:\VB\CONSTANT.TXT into all my projects, to use the standard and useful constants declared in it.

The FILEMSG Application

The FILEMSG application demonstrates the FILEMSG.BAS module, which most of the applications in this book use to display Help information. The FileMsg subprogram in this module uses the *MsgBox* statement to display lines from a specially formatted text file. You can use FILEMSG effectively to display Help information or any other blocks of informational text.

You can embed Help text directly in a form's code, but the FileMsg technique works better. Perhaps the biggest advantage of this technique is that you can edit the lines of Help text by using Notepad (or any ASCII text editor) with much greater ease than if the lines were enclosed in quotation marks and assigned to variables in the form's code. The Help information can be edited independently of the application, even after the application has been compiled to create an executable module.

The files for the FILEMSG application are included on the disk packaged with this book. To load these files into the Visual Basic environment, choose the Open Project option from the File menu, and then type *C:\WORKSHOP\FILEMSG.MAK*. Figure 6-7 shows the project list for the FILEMSG application. FILEMSG.FRM is the startup form that demonstrates the FILEMSG.BAS module. The ABOUT.FRM and CONSTANT.TXT files are described in the ABOUTDEM application, earlier in this chapter. They are used here to add the About dialog box to the FILEMSG application. No change to the ABOUT form or its code is required for use by the FILEMSG application. Simply choose the Add File command from the File menu to add these modules to the current project list.

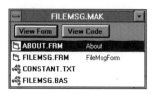

Figure 6-7.
FILEMSG project list.

Figure 6-8 shows the FILEMSG.FRM form, which is loaded when the application starts, and Figure 6-9, on the following page, shows the Options menu's selections. You can use the following table and Figure 6-10, on the following page, to build the Options menu.

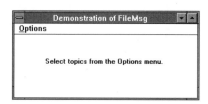

Figure 6-8.
FILEMSG.FRM in action.

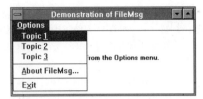

Figure 6-9.
Selections on FILEMSG.FRM's Options menu.

FILEMSG.FRM Menu Design Window Entries

Caption	Name	Indentation
&Options	menOptions	0
Topic &1	menTopic1	1
Topic &2	menTopic2	1
Topic &3	menTopic3	1
-	menSep1	1
&About FileMsg...	menAboutFileMsg	1
-	menSep2	1
E&xit	menExitFileMsg	1

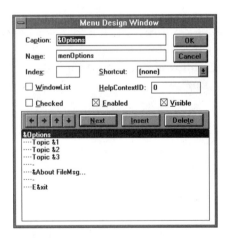

Figure 6-10.
Menu Design Window for FILEMSG.FRM's Options menu.

Notice that the fifth and seventh lines of the menu items begin with a dash. These dashes cause separator lines to appear in the menu, as shown in Figure 6-9. Every menu caption must have an associated name, so *menSep1* and *menSep2* provide generic, dummy names that are never used. This technique makes it easy to add separator lines to a menu.

The form contains only one control—a label—and only a couple of its properties require changes from the defaults. The form and label properties are set as shown in the following table.

FILEMSG.FRM Form and Control Properties

Property	Value
Form	
Caption	Demonstration of FileMsg
Name	FileMsgForm
Label	
Alignment	2 - Center
Caption	Select topics from the Options menu.
Name	Label1

You add the following code to FILEMSG.FRM to complete the form.

Source code for FILEMSG.FRM

```
Sub Form_Load ()
    'Display form toward upper left
    FileMsgForm.Left = (Screen.Width - FileMsgForm.Width) / 5
    FileMsgForm.Top = (Screen.Height - FileMsgForm.Height) / 5

    'Show form before first message box appears
    Show

    'Display first block of message file text
    FileMsg "FILEMSG.MSG", 1
End Sub
```

(continued)

FILEMSG.FRM *continued*

```
Sub menAboutFileMsg_Click ()
    'Display About form
    About.Label1.Caption = "FILEMSG"
    About.Show MODAL
End Sub

Sub menExitFileMsg_Click ()
    'Quit program
    Unload FileMsgForm
End Sub

Sub menTopic1_Click ()
    'Display first topic
    FileMsg "FILEMSG.MSG", 2
End Sub

Sub menTopic2_Click ()
    'Display second topic
    FileMsg "FILEMSG.MSG", 3
End Sub

Sub menTopic3_Click ()
    'Display third topic
    FileMsg "FILEMSG.MSG", 4
End Sub
```

Most of these subprograms call the FileMsg subprogram to open and display a particular section of text from the FILEMSG.MSG text file. One message box is displayed when the form is loaded, and other sections of text are displayed when each of the menu topic items is chosen. This gives you a hint of the many ways the FILEMSG.BAS module can be used to display Help text or other informational text.

You must also create the text file FILEMSG.MSG to enable this program to run correctly. You can use Notepad or any other text editor to create this file, but be sure to save the file in unformatted, ASCII text mode. The following listing shows the contents of FILEMSG.MSG, which is included on the disk packaged with this book.

Contents of FILEMSG.MSG

These first few lines of text are never displayed by the
FileMsg subprogram because they lack the special line that
marks each message section. These lines are handy for
documenting (adding comments to) the message file.

The line that marks each section begins with the greater-
than (>) character, which is followed by the block number,
the MsgBox type number, and the MsgBox title string.
Commas must separate these parameters; spaces are simply
ignored. Message lines end when another line that starts
with > is found, or at the end of the file.

> 1, 0, FILEMSG.MSG
This program demonstrates how FileMsg can be
used to display several lines of text in a message
box. The text is loaded from an ASCII file, which
you can easily create and edit by using Notepad.

When FILEMSG runs, it uses the FILEMSG.BAS
module to display the message you are now reading.
You can select Help from the menu bar to display
other sections of text from the same message file.

> 2, 0, FILEMSG.MSG - Topic 1
This is the second section of text from the
FILEMSG.MSG file, representing the Options,
Topic 1 menu selection.

A program can display many different message
blocks, all loaded from the same file.

> 3, 64, FILEMSG.MSG - Topic 2
This is the third message block loaded
from FILEMSG.MSG. This message is
activated when Options, Topic 2 is
selected.

Look at FILEMSG.MSG to see how the
MsgBox type, title, and lines of text
are indicated.

(continued)

61

FILEMSG.MSG *continued*

```
Take a look at FILEMSG.FRM and
FILEMSG.BAS to see how message file
contents are accessed and displayed.

> 4, 0, Sequential messages - Topic 3

This demonstrates how sequential message blocks
can be displayed.  Click OK to proceed to the next
message block.
>
This is the second message for Options, Topic 3.
Sections of a single message block are separated
with a > character.

One more section follows this one...
>
This is the last section of text for the
Options, Topic 3 message block.
```

Lines that begin with the > character provide formatting information to the FileMsg subprogram. The rules for creating this formatting information are simple, and they're easy to remember as you enter text to create your own message files. After the > character is the block number for the lines of text that follow. The end of the block of lines occurs at the start of another block or at the end of the file, whichever is encountered first. Following the block number is a number for the *type* parameter in a *MsgBox* statement, and the line ends with the title string to be displayed in the title bar of the message box.

Often, 0 is given for the *type* parameter, to create a plain vanilla message box without icons; however, any of the legal *type* values can be used here. For example, message block 3 in FILEMSG.MSG has a *type* value of 64, which causes the small *i* (information) icon to appear in the left part of the message box. Visual Basic's online Help facility describes the *type* parameter of the *MsgBox* statement in detail.

If a > character appears on a line by itself, the text lines that follow are continuation lines for the current block of text. This means that the lines before the > character are displayed in a message box, and when the user clicks the OK button, the lines that follow pop up in a new message box. Text block 4, above, is broken into three sequentially displayed message boxes by using this technique.

The FILEMSG.BAS module is included in most of the applications in this book. This module is not a form; it contains only Visual Basic code. In particular, this module contains the subprogram FileMsg. FileMsg does not interact with the Windows environment through forms; it creates standard message boxes by using the *MsgBox* statement.

The following code details the contents of FILEMSG.BAS.

Source code for FILEMSG.BAS

```
Sub FileMsg (FileName$, Section%)
    'Determine path for message file
    MsgFile$ = App.Path + "\" + FileName$

    'Be sure file exists
    Fil$ = Dir$(MsgFile$)
    If Fil$ = "" Then
        Msg$ = "File " + MsgFile$ + " not found"
        MsgBox Msg$, 48, "FILEMSG"
        Exit Sub
    End If

    'Create newline string
    NL$ = Chr$(13) + Chr$(10)

    'Open message file for reading
    NumFile% = FreeFile
    Open MsgFile$ For Input As #NumFile%

    'Find specified section
    Do Until EOF(NumFile%)
        Line Input #NumFile%, FileTxt$
            If Left$(FileTxt$, 1) = ">" Then
            If Val(Mid$(FileTxt$, 2)) = Section Then
                Exit Do
            End If
        End If
    Loop

    'Did we reach end of file during search?
    If EOF(NumFile%) Then
        Msg$ = "Message section" + Str$(Section) + " not found"
        MsgBox Msg$
        Exit Sub
    End If
```

(continued)

63

FILEMSG.BAS *continued*

```
        'Extract message box type and title
        FileTxt$ = RTrim$(LTrim$(Mid$(FileTxt$, 2)))
        FileTxt$ = Mid$(FileTxt$, InStr(FileTxt$, ",") + 1)
        TypeNum% = Val(FileTxt$)
        Title$ = LTrim$(Mid$(FileTxt$, InStr(FileTxt$, ",") + 1))

        'Loop through all sections of block
        Do

            'Clear message string
            Msg$ = ""

            'Read message section
            Do Until EOF(NumFile%)
                Line Input #NumFile%, FileTxt$
                If Left$(FileTxt$, 1) = ">" Then
                    Exit Do
                End If
                Msg$ = Msg$ + FileTxt$ + NL$
            Loop

            'Chop off any ending blank lines
            Do While Right$(Msg$, 4) = NL$ + NL$
                Msg$ = Left$(Msg$, Len(Msg$) - 2)
            Loop

            'Display message block
            If Msg$ <> "" Then
                MsgBox Msg$, TypeNum%, Title$
            End If

        'Continue block if > was by itself
        Loop While LTrim$(RTrim$(FileTxt$)) = ">"

        'We've finished with file
        Close NumFile%
    End Sub
```

The first executable line of this code uses a feature that was introduced in Visual Basic 2. The property *App.Path* contains the path to the application's directory—a convenient and safe place from which to read the application's MSG files. You can put the MSG files in any subdirectory, but be sure to change this path declaration to match. If the indicated file is not located, the application displays a special message box to let you know.

To use FileMsg in one of your own programs, add FILEMSG.BAS to the project list, create an MSG text file, and call FileMsg from your program, as shown in the source code for FILEMSG.FRM.

The GETFILE Application

One of the most commonly used standard forms in applications for Windows is the dialog box that appears after you choose the Open command from an application's File menu. To cite only one example, consider the Open Project dialog box that is part of the Visual Basic development environment; you can use this dialog box to select a project from any subdirectory on any drive. The GETFILE.FRM module is designed to provide this feature for any program you build.

Visual Basic provides three controls that greatly facilitate the building of the GETFILE form:

- The file list box displays a list of files for a given directory.

- The directory list box displays a list of available directories.

- The drive list box displays a list of available disk drives.

When these list boxes are combined on one form, with code to connect the interactive properties of these controls correctly, a complete file-selection dialog box results.

The GETFILE application, which tests the GETFILE form, is included on the disk packaged with this book. To load the files for the application into the Visual Basic environment, choose Open Project from the File menu, and then type *C:\WORKSHOP\GETFILE.MAK.*

Figure 6-11 shows the project list for the GETFILE project. All but two of these modules are described earlier in this chapter. You simply choose the Add File command from the File menu to add the ABOUT.FRM, FILEMSG.BAS, and C:\VB\CONSTANT.TXT files to the project list.

Figure 6-11.
GETFILE project list.

The GETTEST Form

GETTEST is the startup form that demonstrates the GETFILE form. GETTEST is mostly simply a menu that lets you access Help, the About dialog box, and the GETFILE form. One label displays a starting prompt and then displays the full path and filename of any file you select by using the GETFILE form. The Menu Design Window entries for GETTEST.FRM are listed in the following table.

GETTEST.FRM Menu Design Window Entries

Caption	Name	Indentation
&File	menFileTop	0
&File Select...	menFileSelect	1
-	menSep1	1
E&xit	menExitGetFile	1
&Help	menHelpTop	0
&Help on GetFile	menHelpGetFile	1
&About GetFile...	menAboutGetFile	1

The few property settings that are changed from their defaults in the GETTEST form are listed in the following table, and the form is shown in Figure 6-12.

GETTEST.FRM Form and Control Properties

Property	Value
Form	
Caption	GETFILE.FRM Demonstration
Name	GetTest
Label	
Alignment	2 - Center
Caption	Choose File Select from the File menu.
Name	Label1

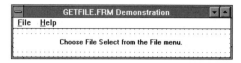

Figure 6-12.
GETTEST.FRM during development.

The contents of the FileTypes combo box in GETFILE determine the default files to list when the form is loaded. If you want to use GETFILE in an application that expects filenames to have a given extension, use *AddItem* to set up the list. For example, if your application commonly works with TXT files, as Notepad does, the following command prepares the form for displaying TXT files. Compare the string added to the list with the file types listed in Notepad's Open dialog box.

```
GetFile.FileTypes.AddItem "Text Files (*.TXT)"
```

In GETTEST, the list is initialized with three types of files so that you can experiment with selecting different file types from the list. A similar statement prepares the title at the top of the GETFILE form, if you want a title other than the default:

```
GetFile.Caption = "File Open (Demonstration Only)"
```

These lines are in GETTEST's subprogram menFileSelect_Click, along with the line that shows the GETFILE form. The following listing contains all the code for the GETTEST form.

Source code for GETTEST.FRM

```
Sub Form_Load ()
    'Place form toward upper left corner of screen
    Left = (Screen.Width - Width) / 7
    Top = (Screen.Height - Height) / 7
End Sub

Sub Form_Unload (Cancel As Integer)
    'All done
    Unload GetFile
End Sub
```

(continued)

GETTEST.FRM *continued*

```
Sub menAboutGetFile_Click ()
    'Display About dialog box
    About.Label1.Caption = "GETFILE"
    About.Show MODAL
End Sub

Sub menExitGetFile_Click ()
    'All done
    Unload GetTest
End Sub

Sub menFileSelect_Click ()
    'Set GetFile caption as desired
    GetFile.Caption = "File Open (Demonstration Only)"

    'Create list of patterns
    GetFile.FileTypes.AddItem "All Files (*.*)"
    GetFile.FileTypes.AddItem "Project Files (*.MAK)"
    GetFile.FileTypes.AddItem "Executable (*.EXE;*.COM)"

    'Just do it
    GetFile.Show MODAL

    'Here's the selected file
    Label1.Caption = GetFile.FullPath.Text

    '...unless Cancel was clicked
    If Label1.Caption = "" Then
        Label1.Caption = "File not selected"
    End If
End Sub

Sub menHelpGetTest_Click ()
    'Display some Help text
    FileMsg "GETTEST.MSG", 1
End Sub
```

The GETFILE Form

As mentioned previously, the GETFILE application is designed to demonstrate the GETFILE form, which is the form that will be loaded into other projects. Figure 6-13 shows the GETFILE form during development.

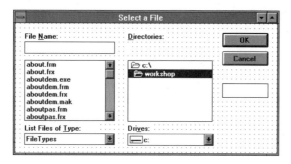

Figure 6-13.
GETFILE.FRM during development.

This form contains quite a few controls. The following table lists the form and control properties.

GETFILE.FRM Form and Control Properties

Property	Value
Form	
BorderStyle	3 - Fixed Double
Caption	Select a File
KeyPreview	True
MinButton	False
Name	GetFile
Text Box	
Visible	False
Name	FullPath
Combo Box	
Name	FileTypes
Style	2 - Dropdown List
Command Button	
Caption	OK
Default	True
Name	Command1

(continued)

GETFILE.FRM Form and Control Properties *continued*

Property	Value
Command Button	
Caption	Cancel
Cancel	True
Name	Command2
Label	
Caption	List Files of &Type:
Name	Label3
Label	
AutoSize	True
Caption	File &Name:
Name	Label2
Label	
AutoSize	True
Name	Label1
Label	
AutoSize	True
Caption	&Directories:
Name	Label4
Label	
AutoSize	True
Caption	Dri&ves:
Name	Label5

One of the label fields is difficult to see, as is evident in Figure 6-13. It's the blank label below the Directories label, and it's used to display the currently selected path. You can find it by looking closely for the two missing dots on the background grid.

The Text property of the FullPath text box in the GETFILE form contains the name of the file selected by the user, or it contains an empty string if the user canceled the dialog box. This property also keeps track of the last selected drive and directory so that GETFILE can restore these selections when it is activated multiple times. Because the Visible property of the FullPath Text Box control is set to *False*, you won't see this control when the form runs, but it still works behind the scenes. During development, you can see the FullPath Text Box control just below the Cancel button on the right side of the form.

The following code completes the GETFILE form. Figure 6-14 shows the form when running.

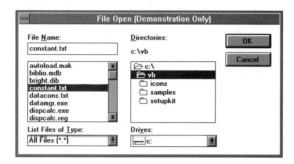

Figure 6-14.
GETFILE.FRM in action.

Source code for GETFILE.FRM

```
'Declarations for GETFILE.FRM

Const TEXTFLAG = 0
Const FILEFLAG = 1
Const DIRFLAG = 2

Dim SelectFlag As Integer

Sub Command1_Click ()
    'OK button; some errors can happen
    On Error GoTo ErrorTrap

    'Was the last change to the filename in Text1?
    If SelectFlag = TEXTFLAG Then
        File1.FileName = Text1.Text

        'We're done if FullPath was set
        If FullPath <> "" Then
            On Error GoTo 0
            ExitForm
        End If
```

(continued)

71

GETFILE.FRM *continued*

```
        'Update directory list
        Dir1.Path = File1.Path

    'Was user only selecting a new directory?
    ElseIf SelectFlag = DIRFLAG Then
        Dir1.Path = Dir1.List(Dir1.ListIndex)
        Dir1_Change

    'Set FullPath to selected file
    Else
        If Right$(Dir1.Path, 1) = "\" Then
            FullPath.Text = Dir1.Path + Text1.Text
        Else
            FullPath.Text = Dir1.Path + "\" + Text1.Text
        End If

        'All done
        ExitForm
    End If

    Exit Sub

ErrorTrap:
    Beep
    Resume Next
End Sub

Sub Command2_Click ()
    'Cancel button; indicate by erasing FullPath
    FullPath = ""

    'All done
    ExitForm
End Sub

Sub Dir1_Change ()
    'User selected new subdirectory
    FillLabel1

    'Update filename
    File1.FileName = Dir1.Path + "\" + File1.Pattern

    'Update drive list
    Drive1.Drive = Dir1.Path
```

(continued)

GETFILE.FRM *continued*

```
     'Update name of file
     Text1.Text = File1.Pattern

     'Set last change to directory
     SelectFlag = DIRFLAG
End Sub

Sub Dir1_Click ()
     'User clicked on new subdirectory
     SelectFlag = DIRFLAG
End Sub

Sub Drive1_Change ()
     'User changed drive; update directory
     Dir1.Path = Drive1.Drive

     'Display current pattern
     Text1.Text = File1.Pattern

     'Set last change to directory
     SelectFlag = DIRFLAG
End Sub

Sub ExitForm ()
     'User might want different patterns next time
     FileTypes.Clear

     'Don't unload, simply hide
     GetFile.Hide
End Sub

Sub File1_Click ()
     'User clicked on new filename
     Text1.Text = File1.FileName

     'Set last change to filename
     SelectFlag = FILEFLAG
End Sub

Sub File1_DblClick ()
     'User double-clicked on a filename
     Command1_Click
End Sub
```

(continued)

GETFILE.FRM *continued*

```
Sub FileTypes_Click ()
    'User selected new pattern from combo box
    File1.Pattern = GetFileType$()

    'Display pattern until a file is selected
    Text1.Text = File1.Pattern
End Sub

Sub FillLabel1 ()
    'Display directory part of path
    Label1.Caption = Dir1.Path

    'If directory string is too long, squish it down
    If Label1.Width > 2200 Then

        'Extract drive part
        a$ = Left$(Dir1.Path, 3)
        b$ = Mid$(Dir1.Path, 4)

        'Extract last subdirectory part
        Do While InStr(b$, "\")
            b$ = Mid$(b$, InStr(b$, "\") + 1)
        Loop

        'Squish out middle part
        Label1.Caption = a$ + "...\" + b$
    End If
End Sub

Sub Form_Activate ()
    'Don't select any filename at first
    File1.ListIndex = -1

    'If no pattern list, default to *.*
    If FileTypes.ListCount = 0 Then
        FileTypes.AddItem "All Files (*.*)"
    End If

    'Default to first pattern in list
    FileTypes.ListIndex = 0

    'If no previous path, use application's path
    If FullPath.Text = "" Then
        FullPath.Text = App.Path + "\"
    End If
```

(continued)

GETFILE.FRM *continued*

```
        'Update lists and labels
        File1.Pattern = GetFileType$()
        Text1.Text = File1.Pattern
        Dir1.Path = File1.Path
        FillLabel1
        SelectFlag = DIRFLAG
        FullPath = ""
End Sub

Sub Form_KeyUp (KeyCode As Integer, Shift As Integer)
        'Watch only for Alt plus N, D, T, or V key
        If Shift = 4 Then
                Select Case KeyCode

                'Alt-N
                Case 78
                        Text1.SetFocus

                'Alt-D
                Case 68
                        Dir1.SetFocus

                'Alt-T
                Case 84
                        FileTypes.SetFocus

                'Alt-V
                Case 86
                        Drive1.SetFocus

                End Select
        End If
End Sub

Sub Form_Load ()
        'Center form on screen
        GetFile.Left = (Screen.Width - GetFile.Width) / 2
        GetFile.Top = (Screen.Height - GetFile.Height) / 2
End Sub

Function GetFileType$ ()
        'Get pattern description from combo box
        Tmp$ = FileTypes.Text
```

(continued)

GETFILE.FRM *continued*

```
    'Find position of parentheses
    p1 = InStr(Tmp$, "(") + 1
    p2 = InStr(Tmp$, ")")

    'Return part between parentheses
    If p1 > 0 And p2 > p1 Then
        GetFileType$ = LCase$(Mid$(Tmp$, p1, p2 - p1))
    Else
        GetFileType$ = "*.*"
    End If
End Function

Sub Text1_Change ()
    'Set last change to File Name field
    SelectFlag = TEXTFLAG
End Sub
```

Toward the end of the code listing is a subprogram named FillLabel1. This routine is not activated by an event; rather, it is called by one or more of the other subprograms. In this case, both the Form_Load and Dir1_Change subprograms call FillLabel1 during their activation. FillLabel1 squeezes long path strings by replacing the middle of the path with an ellipsis (...) if the path is too long to fit in the field.

The KeyPreview property was introduced in Visual Basic version 2. This form property is set to *True* in GETFILE to let the Form_KeyUp subprogram intercept all keystrokes before they are sent to whichever control on the form currently has the focus. The Form_KeyUp routine checks for Alt-N, Alt-D, Alt-T, and Alt-V keypresses, and it sets the focus appropriately. Notice the under-lined letters in the labels on the form and how they correlate to where the focus is sent when the indicated keys are pressed.

For this demonstration to run properly, GETTEST.FRM must be the startup form—the form that is loaded when the application starts. If you create GETFILE.FRM first, Visual Basic considers it to be the startup form. To change this situation, open the Options menu, choose Project, and change the Start Up Form entry to GetTest.

To add the GetFile dialog box to a project, add the GETFILE.FRM mod-ule to the project list. Ensure that the CONSTANT.TXT file is included in your project; add it to the project list if it isn't already there. Set up the GETFILE form properties, and then make the call to GETFILE, as shown in the menFileSelect_Click subprogram in GETTEST.FRM.

Figures 6-15 and 6-16 show GETTEST in operation, during the selection of a file by using the GETFILE form.

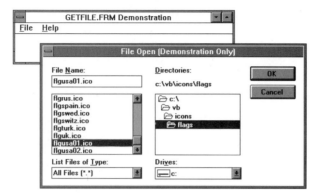

Figure 6-15.
GETTEST.FRM in action.

Figure 6-16.
Selecting a file by using the GETFILE form.

The SAVEFILE Application

The SAVEFILE form provides the Save As dialog box that's found in many applications for Windows. This form is similar in design and appearance to GETFILE.FRM; the greatest difference is that the file list box entries are grayed on the SAVEFILE form.

The SAVEFILE application, which tests this form, is included on the disk packaged with this book. To load the files for the application into the Visual Basic environment, choose Open Project from the File menu, and then type *C:\WORKSHOP\SAVEFILE.MAK*. Figure 6-17, which appears on the following page, shows the project list for the SAVEFILE application. The ABOUT.FRM, CONSTANT.TXT, and FILEMSG.BAS files in the list are those described earlier in this chapter.

Figure 6-17.
SAVEFILE project list.

You add the SAVEFILE.FRM form to the project lists of applications that require the Save As dialog box. Figure 6-18 shows SAVEFILE.FRM during development.

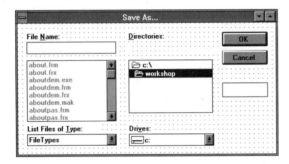

Figure 6-18.
SAVEFILE.FRM during development.

The form and control properties of SAVEFILE.FRM are listed in the following table.

SAVEFILE.FRM Form and Control Properties

Property	Value
Form	
BorderStyle	3 - Fixed Double
Caption	Save As...
KeyPreview	True
MinButton	False
Name	SaveFile

(continued)

SAVEFILE.FRM Form and Control Properties *continued*

Property	Value
Text Box	
Visible	False
Name	FullPath
Combo Box	
Name	FileTypes
Style	2 - Dropdown List
Command Button	
Caption	OK
Default	True
Name	Command1
Command Button	
Caption	Cancel
Cancel	True
Name	Command2
File List Box	
ForeColor	&H00C0C0C0&
Name	File1
Label	
Caption	List Files of &Type:
Name	Label3
Label	
AutoSize	True
Caption	File &Name:
Name	Label2
Label	
AutoSize	True
Name	Label1

(continued)

SAVEFILE.FRM Form and Control Properties *continued*

Property	Value
Label	
AutoSize	True
Caption	&Directories:
Name	Label4
Label	
AutoSize	True
Caption	Dri&ves:
Name	Label5

The ForeColor property of the File List Box control is changed to *&H00C0C0C0&*, which is light gray. This gives the file list the appearance of being disabled, although it actually is enabled. This matches the way the Save File As dialog box works in newer applications for Windows, including the Visual Basic for Windows environment itself.

The following code completes the form. This code can be found in the file SAVEFILE.FRM, which is included on the disk packaged with this book.

Source code for SAVEFILE.FRM

```
'Declarations for SAVEFILE.FRM

Const TEXTFLAG = 0
Const FILEFLAG = 1
Const DIRFLAG = 2

Dim SelectFlag As Integer

Sub Command1_Click ()
    'OK button; some errors can happen
    On Error GoTo ErrorTrap

    'Was user only selecting a new directory?
    If SelectFlag = DIRFLAG Then
        Dir1.Path = Dir1.List(Dir1.ListIndex)
        Dir1_Change
        SelectFlag = TEXTFLAG
```

(continued)

SAVEFILE.FRM *continued*

```
'Try to return indicated filename
ElseIf InStr(Text1.Text, "\") Then
    Tmp$ = Text1.Text

    'Trim back to last \
    Do Until Right$(Tmp$, 1) = "\"
        Tmp$ = Left$(Tmp$, Len(Tmp$) - 1)
    Loop

    'Trim off \ if not root directory
    If Len(Tmp$) > 3 Then
        Tmp$ = Left$(Tmp$, Len(Tmp$) - 1)
    End If

    'Set indicated directory
    Dir1.Path = Tmp$

    'Trim path off left of filename
    Do
        p1 = InStr(Text1.Text, "\")
        Text1.Text = Mid$(Text1.Text, p1)
    Loop While InStr(Text1.Text, "\")

'Filename shown with no user-entered path
Else

    'Get working copy of filename
    Tmp$ = Trim$(Text1.Text)

    'First character must be alphabetic
    If Not Left$(Tmp$, 1) Like "[a-zA-Z]" Then
        Tmp$ = ""
    End If

    'Check for position of period
    p1 = InStr(Tmp$, ".")
    If p1 > 0 Then
        If Len(Tmp$) - p1 > 3 Then Tmp$ = ""
        If p1 > 9 Then Tmp$ = ""
    Else
        If Len(Tmp$) > 9 Then Tmp$ = ""
    End If
```

(continued)

SAVEFILE.FRM *continued*

```
            'Proceed only if filename seems OK
            If Tmp$ <> "" Then

                'Build full path to file
                If Right$(Dir1.Path, 1) = "\" Then
                    FullPath = Dir1.Path + Tmp$
                Else
                    FullPath = Dir1.Path + "\" + Tmp$
                End If

                'Return full path
                ExitForm

            'Not a good filename
            Else
                Beep
                Text1.SetFocus
            End If

        End If

        Exit Sub

ErrorTrap:
        Beep
        Resume Next
End Sub

Sub Command2_Click ()
        'Cancel button; indicate by erasing FullPath
        FullPath = ""

        'All done
        ExitForm
End Sub

Sub Dir1_Change ()
        'User selected new subdirectory
        FillLabel1

        'Update filename
        File1.FileName = Dir1.Path + "\" + File1.Pattern
```

(continued)

SAVEFILE.FRM *continued*

```
        'Update drive list
        Drive1.Drive = Dir1.Path

        'Update name of file
        Text1.Text = File1.Pattern

        'Set last change to directory
        SelectFlag = DIRFLAG
    End Sub

    Sub Dir1_Click ()
        'User clicked on new subdirectory
        SelectFlag = DIRFLAG
    End Sub

    Sub Drive1_Change ()
        'User changed drive; update directory
        Dir1.Path = Drive1.Drive

        'Display current pattern
        Text1.Text = File1.Pattern

        'Set last change to directory
        SelectFlag = DIRFLAG
    End Sub

    Sub ExitForm ()
        'User might want different patterns next time
        FileTypes.Clear

        'Don't unload, simply hide
        SaveFile.Hide
    End Sub

    Sub File1_Click ()
        'User clicked on new filename
        If File1.ListIndex <> -1 Then
            Tmp$ = File1.FileName
            File1.ListIndex = -1
            Text1.Text = Tmp$
        End If

        'Set last change to filename
        SelectFlag = FILEFLAG
    End Sub
```

(continued)

SAVEFILE.FRM *continued*

```
Sub File1_DblClick ()
    'User double-clicked on a filename
    Command1_Click
End Sub

Sub FileTypes_Click ()
    'User selected new pattern from combo box
    File1.Pattern = SaveFileType$()

    'Display pattern until a file is selected
    Text1.Text = File1.Pattern
End Sub

Sub FillLabel1 ()
    'Display directory part of path
    Label1.Caption = Dir1.Path

    'If directory string is too long, squish it down
    If Label1.Width > 2200 Then

        'Extract drive part
        a$ = Left$(Dir1.Path, 3)
        b$ = Mid$(Dir1.Path, 4)

        'Extract last subdirectory part
        Do While InStr(b$, "\")
            b$ = Mid$(b$, InStr(b$, "\") + 1)
        Loop

        'Squish out middle part
        Label1.Caption = a$ + "...\" + b$
    End If
End Sub

Sub Form_Activate ()
    'Don't select any filename at first
    File1.ListIndex = -1

    'If no pattern list, default to *.*
    If FileTypes.ListCount = 0 Then
        FileTypes.AddItem "All Files(*.*)"
    End If
```

(continued)

84

SAVEFILE.FRM *continued*

```
    'Default to first pattern in list
    FileTypes.ListIndex = 0

    'If no previous path, use application's path
    If FullPath.Text = "" Then
        FullPath.Text = App.Path + "\"
    End If

    'Update lists and labels
    File1.Pattern = SaveFileType$()
    Text1.Text = File1.Pattern
    Dir1.Path = File1.Path
    FillLabel1
    SelectFlag = DIRFLAG
    FullPath = ""

    'Set focus to File Name text field
    Text1.SetFocus

    'Select all of the filename
    Text1.SelStart = 0
    Text1.SelLength = Len(Text1.Text)
End Sub

Sub Form_KeyUp (KeyCode As Integer, Shift As Integer)
    'Watch only for Alt plus N, D, T, or V key
    If Shift = 4 Then
        Select Case KeyCode

        'Alt-N
        Case 78
            Text1.SetFocus

        'Alt-D
        Case 68
            Dir1.SetFocus

        'Alt-T
        Case 84
            FileTypes.SetFocus
```

(continued)

SAVEFILE.FRM *continued*

```
            'Alt-V
            Case 86
                Drive1.SetFocus

            End Select
        End If
End Sub

Sub Form_Load ()
    'Center form on screen
    SaveFile.Left = (Screen.Width - SaveFile.Width) / 2
    SaveFile.Top = (Screen.Height - SaveFile.Height) / 2
End Sub

Function SaveFileType$ ()
    'Get pattern description from combo box
    Tmp$ = FileTypes.Text

    'Find position of parentheses
    p1 = InStr(Tmp$, "(") + 1
    p2 = InStr(Tmp$, ")")

    'Return part between parentheses
    If p1 > 0 And p2 > p1 Then
        SaveFileType$ = LCase$(Mid$(Tmp$, p1, p2 - p1))
    Else
        SaveFileType$ = "*.*"
    End If
End Function

Sub Text1_Change ()
    'Set last change to File Name field
    SelectFlag = TEXTFLAG
End Sub
```

SAVEFILE's invisible Text Box control, FullPath, is assigned a string containing the full path to the named file. This works the same way as in the GETFILE form, which is described earlier in this chapter. Unlike the GETFILE form, however, the SAVEFILE form lets the user type a new filename rather than demanding that the file already exist.

The SAVETEST.FRM module is the startup form that demonstrates the SAVEFILE.FRM form. Figure 6-19 shows the SAVETEST.FRM form during development.

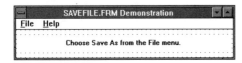

Figure 6-19.
SAVETEST.FRM during development.

The SAVETEST.FRM menu contains seven items. You can create the menu by using the following table and Figure 6-20.

SAVETEST.FRM Menu Design Window Entries

Caption	Name	Indentation
&File	menFile	0
Save &As...	menSaveAs	1
-	menSep1	1
E&xit	menExit	1
&Help	menHelp	0
&Help on SaveFile	menHelpSaveFile	1
&About SaveFile...	menAboutSaveFile	1

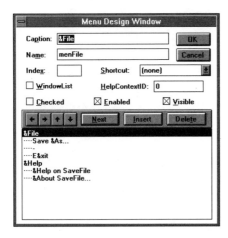

Figure 6-20.
Menu Design Window for SAVETEST.FRM.

The following table lists the nondefault settings for the SAVETEST form and Label control properties.

SAVETEST.FRM Form and Control Properties

Property	Value
Form	
Caption	SAVEFILE.FRM Demonstration
Name	SaveTest
Label	
Alignment	2 - Center
Caption	Choose Save As from the File menu.
Name	Label1

The following code fills out the SAVETEST form.

Source code for SAVETEST.FRM

```
Sub Form_Load ()
    'Place form toward upper left corner of screen
    Left = (Screen.Width - Width) / 7
    Top = (Screen.Height - Height) / 7
End Sub


Sub Form_Unload (Cancel As Integer)
    'All done
    Unload SaveFile
End Sub


Sub menAboutSaveFile_Click ()
    'Display About dialog box
    About.Label1.Caption = "SAVEFILE"
    About.Show MODAL
End Sub


Sub menExit_Click ()
    'All done
    Unload SaveTest
End Sub
```

(continued)

SAVETEST.FRM *continued*

```
Sub menHelpSaveTest_Click ()
    'Display some Help text
    FileMsg "SAVETEST.MSG", 1
End Sub

Sub menSaveAs_Click ()
    'Set SaveFile caption as desired
    SaveFile.Caption = "Save As... (Demonstration Only)"

    'Create list of patterns
    SaveFile.FileTypes.AddItem "All Files (*.*)"
    SaveFile.FileTypes.AddItem "Project Files (*.MAK)"
    SaveFile.FileTypes.AddItem "Executable (*.EXE;*.COM)"

    'Just do it
    SaveFile.Show MODAL

    'Here's the selected file
    Label1.Caption = SaveFile.FullPath.Text

    '...unless Cancel was clicked
    If Label1.Caption = "" Then
        Label1.Caption = "File not selected"
    End If
End Sub
```

Figure 6-21 shows the SAVEFILE form as executed by the SAVETEST module. After you select a filename, the full path to the file is displayed in the SAVETEST form, as shown in Figure 6-22 on the following page.

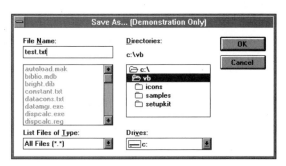

Figure 6-21.
SAVEFILE.FRM as executed by the SAVETEST module.

Figure 6-22.
SAVETEST.FRM after a filename is selected.

The FILESHOW Application

The FILESHOW application demonstrates FILEVIEW.FRM, a useful form that displays the contents of a text file in a window that can be scrolled quickly.

The GETFILE form is used to select a file, and the path and filename of the file are returned in *GetFile.FullPath.Text*. FILEVIEW uses this filename during the Form_Load event to open the indicated file. FILEVIEW reads the lines of text from the file and concatenates the lines to form a single string. Carriage-return and linefeed characters are inserted at the end of each line. Visual Basic for Windows 3 provides plenty of string space (memory for storing strings), but the size of a single string is still limited. Because of this, the application loads only the first 32,000 bytes of a large file into the string.

You can display a multiline string in Visual Basic in several ways. After doing some experimentation, I found that a Text Box control is well suited to this task. Text boxes have the ScrollBars property, which means that you can interact with the text. In addition, scrolling the text by using the scroll bars is considerably faster than using the *Print* method to update the text.

Before you run the application, the text box in the FILEVIEW form is smaller than the form. The Form_Resize subprogram, which is activated whenever the FILEVIEW form is resized, contains statements that also resize the Text Box control. The control is sized to match the internal dimensions of the form so that it fills the entire window. You can change the size of the form at any time while using it to view a file, and the text box instantly resizes with it.

Whenever FILESHOW is repainted (such as immediately after it loads), instructions to the user are printed on the form. The main body of the FILESHOW form is not used for any other purpose, so this technique works well in this case. Most applications in this book display Help information when you choose a command from the Help menu, but this application shows one of the alternative approaches for displaying this information.

To use FILEVIEW.FRM in one of your own applications, load it and CONSTANT.TXT into the project. The subprogram menOpen_Click in FILESHOW.FRM shows how to activate the FILEVIEW form to show a file. These two lines from that subprogram tell FILEVIEW which file to load, and they launch the form into action:

```
FileView.FullPath.Text = GetFile.FullPath.Text
FileView.Show MODAL
```

The files for this application are included on the disk packaged with this book. To load the files into the Visual Basic environment, choose Open Project from the File menu, and then type *C:\WORKSHOP\FILESHOW.MAK*. This opens the project and enables you to view and modify the forms and code. The following figures, tables, and code give the details of the application's creation.

Figure 6-23.
FILESHOW project list.

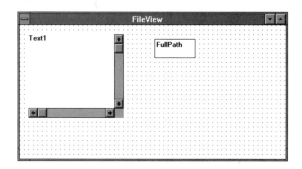

Figure 6-24.
FILEVIEW.FRM during development.

FILEVIEW.FRM Form and Control Properties

Property	Value
Form	
Caption	FileView
Name	FileView

(continued)

91

FILEVIEW.FRM Form and Control Properties *continued*

Property	Value
Text Box	
Name	FullPath
Text	FullPath
Visible	False
Text Box	
BorderStyle	0 - None
MultiLine	True
Name	Text1
ScrollBars	3 - Both

Source code for FILEVIEW.FRM

```
Sub Form_Activate ()
    'Force Text1 to fill form
    Form_Resize

    'Initialization
    NL$ = Chr$(13) + Chr$(10)
    T$ = Space$(32000)
    Ndx& = 1

    'Load file to be displayed
    Open FullPath.Text For Input As #1

    'Load file up to 32,000 bytes
    Do Until EOF(1)
        Line Input #1, A$
        A$ = Space$(2) + A$ + NL$
        If Ndx& + Len(A$) >= 32000 Then
            Exit Do
        Else
            Mid$(T$, Ndx&, Len(A$)) = A$
            Ndx& = Ndx& + Len(A$)
        End If
    Loop
```

(continued)

FILEVIEW.FRM *continued*

```
    'Close file
    Close #1

    'Set caption of this form based on file listed
    Caption = FullPath.Text

    'Display file contents in text box
    Text1.Text = RTrim$(T$)
End Sub

Sub Form_Resize ()
    'Size text box in form window
    Text1.Move 0, 0, ScaleWidth, ScaleHeight
End Sub
```

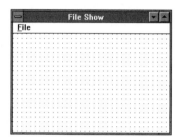

Figure 6-25.
FILESHOW.FRM during development.

FILESHOW.FRM Form Properties

Property	Value
Form	
Caption	FileShow
Name	FileShow

FILESHOW.FRM Menu Design Window Entries

Caption	Name	Indentation
&File	menFileTop	0
&Open...	menOpen	1
-	menSep	1
E&xit	menExit	1

Source code for FILESHOW.FRM

```
Sub Form_Paint ()
    Cls
    Print
    Print " This program demonstrates FILEVIEW.FRM,"
    Print " a form that displays ASCII files."
    Print
    Print " Choose File Open, and then select a readable"
    Print " (ASCII) file from the dialog box.  If the file is"
    Print " large, only the first 32 KB, approximately, are"
    Print " displayed."
    Print
    Print " Use the scroll bars to browse the file."
    Print
    Print " The FILEVIEW form can be resized."
End Sub

Sub Form_Unload (Cancel As Integer)
    'Also unload GetFile form
    Unload GetFile
End Sub

Sub menExit_Click ()
    'All done
    Unload FileShow
End Sub

Sub menOpen_Click ()
    'Set caption for GetFile form
    GetFile.Caption = "Select a file to view"
```

(continued)

94

FILESHOW.FRM *continued*

```
    'Get filename from user
    GetFile.Show MODAL

    'Display file contents
    If GetFile.FullPath.Text <> "" Then
        FileView.FullPath.Text = GetFile.FullPath.Text
        FileView.Show MODAL
    End If
End Sub
```

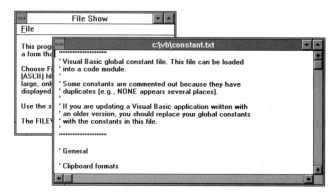

Figure 6-26.
FILESHOW.FRM in action.

The PASSWORD Application

The PASSWORD application demonstrates how to set up a Text Box control for entering a password. You set a password character in the PasswordChar property of the text box, and the password character is displayed as each character is entered. This prevents a casual observer from reading the password. For this example, as each character is typed, an *X* is displayed at the cursor and a second text box displays the entry in normal text. Normally, of course, the password is not displayed in a second text box in this way, but this demonstration displays it to show you what's happening behind the scenes.

This application uses its own About dialog box rather than the standard ABOUT.FRM module that I've loaded into most of the projects in this book. The new form is named ABOUTPAS.FRM, and it's simply a modified copy of ABOUT.FRM. A couple of icons are displayed at the sides of the application title—icons more appropriate to the security flavor of the PASSWORD program. The timer-driven animation of the icons in ABOUT.FRM has been removed, which makes this a slightly simpler form of the About dialog box.

The AutoSize property for the IconPic Picture Box control enables the control to adjust in size to completely display whichever image file is loaded into it. This is a convenient feature for loading icons or other image files into Picture Box controls, especially when the exact dimensions of the image files are not known in advance.

The files for the PASSWORD application are included on the disk packaged with this book. To load the files into the Visual Basic environment, choose the Open Project option from the File menu, and then type *C:\WORKSHOP\PASSWORD.MAK*. This opens the project and enables you to view and modify the forms and code. The following figures, tables, and code give the details of the application's creation.

Figure 6-27.
PASSWORD project list.

ABOUTPAS.FRM Form and Control Properties

Property	Value
Form	
BorderStyle	3 - Fixed Double
Caption	About
MaxButton	False
MinButton	False
Name	AboutPas
Picture Box	
AutoSize	True
BorderStyle	0 - None
Name	Picture1
Picture	c:\vb\icons\misc\secur03.ico

(continued)

96

ABOUTPAS.FRM Form and Control Properties *continued*

Property	Value
Picture Box	
AutoSize	True
BorderStyle	0 - None
Name	IconPic
Picture	c:\vb\icons\misc\secur08.ico
Command Button	
Caption	OK
Name	Command1
Label	
Alignment	2 - Center
Caption	Microsoft Visual Basic Workshop
FontBold	True
FontSize	12
Name	Label2
Label	
Alignment	2 - Center
Caption	PASSWORD
FontBold	True
FontSize	12
FontUnderline	True
ForeColor	&H00008000&
Name	Label1
Label	
Alignment	2 - Center
Caption	For Microsoft Visual Basic for Windows 3
Name	Label3
Label	
Alignment	2 - Center
Caption	Copyright © 1993 John Clark Craig
Name	Label4

Source code for ABOUTPAS.FRM

```
Sub Command1_Click ()
    'Quit showing this About dialog box
    Unload AboutPas
End Sub

Sub Form_Load ()
    'Center form
    Left = (Screen.Width - Width) / 2
    Top = (Screen.Height - Height) / 2
End Sub
```

Figure 6-28.
ABOUTPAS.FRM in action.

PASSWORD.FRM Menu Design Window Entries

Caption	Name	Indentation
&Help	menHelpTop	0
&Help on Password	menHelpPassword	1
&About Password...	menAboutPassword	1
-	menSep	1
E&xit	menExitPassword	1

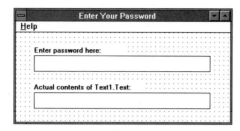

Figure 6-29.
PASSWORD.FRM during development.

PASSWORD.FRM Form and Control Properties

Property	Value
Form	
BorderStyle	1 - Fixed Single
Caption	Enter Your Password
Icon	c:\vb\icons\misc\secur03.ico
MaxButton	False
Name	Password
Text Box	
Alignment	2 - Center
FontName	Courier New
FontSize	12
Name	Text2
Text Box	
Alignment	2 - Center
FontName	Courier New
FontSize	12
PasswordChar	X
Name	Text1

(continued)

PASSWORD.FRM Form and Control Properties *continued*

Property	Value
Label	
Caption	Actual contents of Text1.Text:
Name	Label2
Label	
Caption	Enter password here:
Name	Label1

Source code for PASSWORD.FRM

```
Sub Form_Load ()
    'Place form toward upper left part of screen
    Password.Left = (Screen.Width - Password.Width) * .2
    Password.Top = (Screen.Height - Password.Height) * .3
End Sub

Sub menAboutPassword_Click ()
    'Display About dialog box
    AboutPas.Show MODAL
End Sub

Sub menExitPassword_Click ()
    'All done
    Unload Password
End Sub

Sub menHelpPassword_Click ()
    'Display some Help information
    FileMsg "PASSWORD.MSG", 1
End Sub

Sub Text1_Change ()
    'Update other text box
    Text2.Text = Text1.Text
End Sub
```

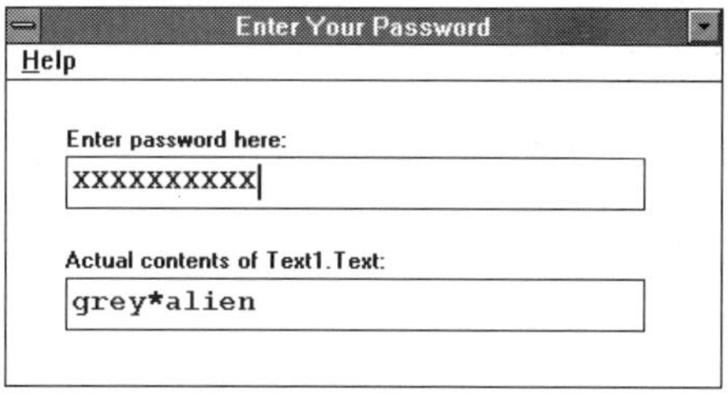

Figure 6-30.
PASSWORD.FRM in action.

The PROFILE Application

The PROFILE application demonstrates how to write and read private profile strings. *Profile strings* are lines of text stored in an INI (initialization) file; they're usually used to save information about an application's state and configuration from run to run. For example, Windows saves its changes in WIN.INI, and Visual Basic saves its information in VB.INI. The contents of a typical VB.INI file, which determine the exact appearance of the Visual Basic environment each time it's run, are shown in the following code.

Contents of a typical VB.INI file

```
[Visual Basic]
DataAccess=1
DebugWindow=402 375 400 226 0
MainWindow=0 0 799 72 1
ToolBar=0
ProjectWindow=290 395 243 162 9
ToolBox=4 76 0 0 1
PropertiesWindow=591 72 207 484 9
ColorPalette=69 375 0 0 0
CustomColors=16777215 16777215 16777215 16777215 16777215 16777215
16777215 16777215 16777215 16777215 16777215 16777215 16777215
16777215 16777215 16777215
RecentFile1=C:\WORKSHOP\PASSWORD.MAK
RecentFile2=C:\WORKSHOP\FILESHOW.MAK
RecentFile3=C:\WORKSHOP\SAVEFILE.MAK
RecentFile4=C:\WORKSHOP\GETFILE.MAK
TabStops=4
InsOptExplicit=0
SyntaxChecking=1
DefSaveFormat=0
SaveBeforeRun=0
```

(continued)

101

VB.INI *continued*

```
SelectText=15
SelectBkground=1
NextStatementText=0
NextStatementBkground=15
BreakPtText=15
BreakPtBkground=4
CommentText=2
CommentBkground=15
KeywordText=1
KeywordBkground=15
IdentifiersText=0
IdentifiersBkground=15
CodeWinText=0
CodeWinBkground=15
DebugWinText=0
DebugWinBkground=15
GridWidth=120
GridHeight=120
ShowGrid=1
AlignToGrid=1
ReportDesign=1

[Installable ISAMs]
Btrieve=C:\WINDOWS\SYSTEM\btrv110.dll
FoxPro 2.0=C:\WINDOWS\SYSTEM\xbs110.dll
dBASE III=C:\WINDOWS\SYSTEM\xbs110.dll
dBASE IV=C:\WINDOWS\SYSTEM\xbs110.dll
Paradox 3.X=C:\WINDOWS\SYSTEM\pdx110.dll
FoxPro 2.5=C:\WINDOWS\SYSTEM\xbs110.dll

[dBase ISAM]
Deleted=On
```

Each profile string begins with a keyword, which is followed by an equal-sign character and a string associated with the keyword. A string can contain any alphanumeric information.

This is the first application in this book that calls functions in Windows' dynamic link libraries (DLLs). The KERNEL.DLL, USER.DLL, and GDI.DLL libraries, which are provided as part of the Windows environment, contain almost 500 functions for programming applications for Windows. Visual Basic directly provides much of the functionality of these functions; however, some handy routines that extend Visual Basic's capabilities are available.

The *GetPrivateProfileString* and *WritePrivateProfileString* functions, which are located in KERNEL.DLL, make it easy to read and write profile strings. The declarations for these functions are shown in the following code. These declarations were copied and pasted directly from the Windows 3.1 API (application programming interface) Help file provided with the Professional Edition of Visual Basic for Windows 3.

```
Declare Function GetPrivateProfileString Lib "Kernel"→
 (ByVal lpApplicationName As String, ByVal lpKeyName As String,→
 ByVal lpDefault As String, ByVal lpReturnedString As String,→
 ByVal nSize As Integer, ByVal lpFileName As String) As Integer

Declare Function WritePrivateProfileString Lib "Kernel"→
 (ByVal lpApplicationName As String, ByVal lpKeyName As String,→
 (ByVal lpString As String, ByVal lplFileName As String) As Integer
```

When you want to use these functions, you should enter their declarations in a global module for the project or in the general-declarations area of the form in which they are used. In this case, you should enter these declarations in PROFILE.BAS.

As you can see, some of these declarations are quite long. Because Visual Basic does not have a line-continuation character, each declaration should be on one line, not continued on multiple lines as shown above.

The following two declarations are equivalent to the two above—and they're much shorter. However, it's a good idea to copy the declarations directly from the Windows 3.1 API Help file to save time and effort and to prevent typographic errors. These shortened versions are presented here to show that there are ways to condense the long declarations in a pinch.

```
Declare Function GetPrivateProfileString% Lib "Kernel"→
 (ByVal AppName$, ByVal KeyName$, ByVal Default$, ByVal RetStr$,→
 ByVal Size%, ByVal FileName$)

Declare Function WritePrivateProfileString% Lib "Kernel"→
 (ByVal AppName$, ByVal KeyName$, ByVal String$, ByVal FileName$)
```

This brings up an important point about the API declarations: The functions listed are unforgiving. If you make a mistake in the *Declare* statement, it's quite possible that your system will hang and you will have to reboot your computer. Therefore, you should follow a few simple rules to keep out of trouble:

■ Save your work often.

■ Copy the *Declare* lines from the Windows 3.1 API Help file instead of creating them yourself.

■ Save your work often.

■ Be as knowledgeable as possible about the functions called and how they work.

■ And don't forget—save your work often!

It's beyond the scope of this book to describe all the standard API functions. The Microsoft Windows Software Development Kit (SDK) is the best source of information; utility packages from Microsoft Corporation, Borland International, and other sources also provide good information. Applications in this book do demonstrate several of the functions, however, which provides a good introduction to using the standard API functions.

The PROFILE application updates a file named PROFILE.INI (or creates it, if it doesn't exist). PROFILE.INI can be found in the same directory where the PROFILE application exists. This file is made up of two lines: One line consists of the application name (PROFILE), surrounded by brackets, and the other line contains a date-and-time string associated with the keyname string of *LastRun.* This string is read and then updated when a command button on the PROFILE form is clicked. Here are the contents of PROFILE.INI:

Contents of PROFILE.INI

```
[PROFILE]
LastRun=09-28-1993 18:30:07
```

Applications can use the profile string technique this program demonstrates to store settings users select for colors, sizes, locations, and so on. Other possible uses include storing passwords, logging elapsed time, and logging the number of times an application is run.

The files for the PROFILE application are included on the disk packaged with this book. To load these files into the Visual Basic environment, choose the Open Project option from the File menu, and then type *C:\WORKSHOP\PROFILE.MAK.* This opens the project and enables you to view and modify the forms and code. The following figures, tables, and code give the details of the application's creation.

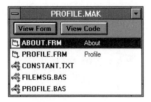

Figure 6-31.
PROFILE project list.

Source code for PROFILE.BAS

```
'Global declarations for PROFILE.FRM

Declare Function GetPrivateProfileString Lib "Kernel"↵
  (ByVal lpApplicationName As String, ByVal lpKeyName As String,↵
  ByVal lpDefault As String, ByVal lpReturnedString As String,↵
  ByVal nSize As Integer, ByVal lpFileName As String) As Integer

Declare Function WritePrivateProfileString Lib "Kernel"↵
  (ByVal lpApplicationName As String, ByVal lpKeyName As String,↵
  ByVal lpString As String, ByVal lplFileName As String) As Integer
```

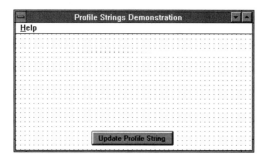

Figure 6-32.
PROFILE.FRM during development.

PROFILE.FRM Menu Design Window Entries

Caption	Name	Indentation
&Help	menHelpTop	0
&Help on Profile	menHelpProfile	1
&About Profile...	menAboutProfile	1
-	menSep	1
E&xit	menExit	1

PROFILE.FRM Form and Control Properties

Property	Value
Form	
AutoRedraw	True
Caption	Profile Strings Demonstration
Name	Profile
Command Button	
Caption	Update Profile String
Name	Command1

Source code for PROFILE.FRM

```
Sub Command1_Click ()
    'Set up parameters for reading and writing profile strings
    lpApplicationName$ = "PROFILE"
    lpKeyName$ = "LastRun"
    lpDefault$ = Date$ + " " + Time$
    lpReturnedString$ = Space$(81)
    nSize = 81

    'INI file is in application's directory
    lpFileName$ = App.Path + "\PROFILE.INI"

    'Read profile string
    n% = GetPrivateProfileString%(lpApplicationName$, lpKeyName$,
     lpDefault$, lpReturnedString$, nSize, lpFileName$)

    'Trim string at terminating 0 byte
    lpReturnedString$ = Left$(lpReturnedString$,
     InStr(lpReturnedString$, Chr$(0)) - 1)

    'Display string
    Print "Date and time this program was last run:",
    Print lpReturnedString$

    'Update string for writing to PROFILE.INI
    lpReturnedString$ = Date$ + " " + Time$
    Print "Current date and time (new profile string):",
    Print lpReturnedString$
    Print
```

(continued)

PROFILE.FRM *continued*

```
        'Replacecontinuedcontinuedstring in file
        Result% = WritePrivateProfileString%(lpApplicationName$,→
        lpKeyName$, lpReturnedString$, lpFileName$)
        If Result% = 0 Then
            Print "Error while writing profile string"
        End If
End Sub

Sub menAboutProfile_Click ()
        'Display About dialog box
        About.Label1.Caption = "PROFILE"
        About.Show MODAL
End Sub

Sub menExit_Click ()
        'All done
        Unload Profile
End Sub

Sub menHelpProfile_Click ()
        'Display some Help information
        FileMsg "PROFILE.MSG", 1
End Sub
```

Figure 6-33.
PROFILE.FRM in action.

The PCTBAR Application

Any application that performs a time-consuming task can use the PCTBAR
form to keep the user informed of the progress of the task. The form displays
a horizontal bar that is filled from left to right with solid blue representing the
percentage of the task that is completed. (This is similar to the blue bar displayed during the installation of Visual Basic.)

The application continuously updates a label named PctDone with a number from 0 through 100, indicating the percentage-completed value. A timer event in PCTBAR.FRM reads *PctDone.Caption* once each second and updates the amount of blue displayed in the picture box on the form. (Your application can override the update interval by changing the value of *PctDone.Timer1.Interval.*) When 100 percent completion is reached, PCTBAR unloads itself.

The PCTTEST form demonstrates the PCTBAR form by loading it when the user clicks the Begin command button. Notice that the *Show* method for activating PCTBAR uses MODELESS (a constant that is defined in the CONSTANT.TXT file), whereas most applications in this book use MODAL with the *Show* method. When MODELESS is used, the calling form's code continues to run while the called form is running. In this example application, if MODAL were used instead of MODELESS, the PCTTEST program would not update the value of *PctDone*, and the blue bar would remain at the 0 percent completion point.

The *PctDone* label is made invisible by setting its Visible property to *False*, but the numeric value of *PctDone.Caption* is displayed near the edge of the expanding blue bar. If this value is less than 50 percent, the number is displayed to the right of the blue bar; if this value is 50 percent or more, the number is displayed to the left of the blue bar. This keeps the displayed number inside the picture box in all cases.

To add PCTBAR.FRM to one of your applications, add PCTBAR.FRM to the project list, and ensure that CONSTANT.TXT is loaded into the project. Ensure that your calling program shows PCTBAR by using MODELESS and that it updates the *PctBar.PctDone.Caption* property on a regular basis, such as once per second.

The files for the PCTBAR application, which demonstrates the PCTBAR form, are included on the disk packaged with this book. To load the files into the Visual Basic environment, choose Open Project from the File menu, and then type *C:\WORKSHOP\PCTBAR.MAK.* This opens the project and enables you to view and modify the forms and code. The following figures, tables, and code give the details of the application's creation.

Figure 6-34.
PCTBAR project list.

Figure 6-35.
PCTBAR.FRM during development.

PCTBAR.FRM Form and Control Properties

Property	Value
Form	
BorderStyle	3 - Fixed Double
Caption	Percentage Completed
ControlBox	False
MaxButton	False
MinButton	False
Name	PctBar
Timer	
Interval	1000
Name	Timer1
Picture Box	
Name	Picture1
ScaleHeight	1
ScaleMode	0 - User
ScaleWidth	100
Label	
Caption	PctDone
Name	PctDone
Visible	False

Source code for PCTBAR.FRM

```
Sub Form_Load ()
    'Center form
    Left = (Screen.Width - Width) / 2
    Top = (Screen.Height - Height) / 2
End Sub

Sub Timer1_Timer ()
    'Fill right part of bar with white
    Picture1.Line (PctDone, 0)-(100, 1), RGB(255, 255, 255), BF

    'Fill left part of bar with blue
    Picture1.Line (0, 0)-(PctDone, 1), RGB(0, 0, 255), BF

    'Format percentage done for display in bar
    Pct$ = Format$(PctDone, " ##\% ")

    'If less than half done, display percentage on white part
    If PctDone < 50 Then
        Picture1.CurrentX = PctDone
        Picture1.ForeColor = RGB(0, 0, 255)

    'If more than half done, display percentage on blue part
    Else
        Picture1.CurrentX = PctDone - Picture1.TextWidth(Pct$)
        Picture1.ForeColor = RGB(255, 255, 255)
    End If

    'Position percentage in bar
    Picture1.CurrentY = (1 - Picture1.TextHeight(Pct$)) / 2

    'Display percentage-done number
    Picture1.Print Pct$

    'Quit when percentage done reaches 100
    If PctDone >= 100 Then
        Unload PctBar
    End If
End Sub
```

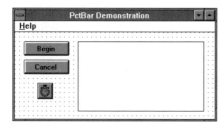

Figure 6-36.
PCTTEST.FRM during development.

PCTTEST.FRM Menu Design Window Entries

Caption	Name	Indentation
&Help	menHelpTop	0
&Help on PctBar	menHelpPctBar	1
&About PctBar...	menAboutPctBar	1

PCTTEST.FRM Form and Control Properties

Property	Value
Form	
Caption	PctBar Demonstration
Name	PctTest
Picture Box	
AutoRedraw	True
Name	Picture1
Timer	
Enabled	False
Interval	50
Command Button	
Caption	Begin
Name	Command1

(continued)

PCTTEST.FRM Form and Control Properties *continued*

Property	Value
Command Button	
Caption	Cancel
Name	Command2

Source code for PCTTEST.FRM

```
Dim Angle

Sub Command1_Click ()
    'Initialize percentage-done amount
    PctBar.PctDone.Caption = "0"

    'Set percentage-done update interval
    PctBar.Timer1.Interval = 500

    'Initialize line angle
    Angle = 0

    'Start up percentage-done bar
    PctBar.Show MODELESS

    'Scale picture box for drawing some lines
    Picture1.Scale (-1, -1)-(1, 1)

    'Erase picture box
    Picture1.Cls

    'Start drawing lines at regular intervals
    Timer1.Enabled = True
End Sub

Sub Command2_Click ()
    'All done
    Unload PctTest
End Sub

Sub Form_Load ()
```

(continued)

PCTTEST.FRM *continued*

```
    'Place form toward upper left
    Left = (Screen.Width - Width) / 6
    Top = (Screen.Height - Height) / 4
End Sub

Sub Form_Unload (Cancel As Integer)
    'Force PctBar to finish
    PctBar.PctDone.Caption = "100"
End Sub

Sub menAboutPctBar_Click ()
    'Display About dialog box
    About.Label1.Caption = "PCTBAR"
    About.Show MODAL
End Sub

Sub menHelpPct_Click ()
    'Display some Help text
    FileMsg "PCTBAR.MSG", 1
End Sub

Sub Timer1_Timer ()
    'Increment line angle by 2 degrees
    Angle = Angle + 2

    'Convert angle to radians
    Radians = Angle * 3.141593 / 180

    'Draw line at given angle
    LineColor = RGB(255, 0, 0)
    x = Cos(Radians)
    y = Sin(Radians)
    Picture1.Line (0, 0)-(x, -y), LineColor

    'Update percentage done
    PctBar.PctDone.Caption = Str$(Angle / 3.6)

    'Quit when 100 percent done
    If Val(PctBar.PctDone.Caption) >= 100 Then
        Timer1.Enabled = False
    End If
End Sub
```

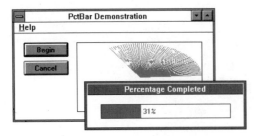

Figure 6-37.
PCTTEST.FRM and PCTBAR.FRM in action.

The NUMPAD Application

The NUMPAD application lets a user enter a numeric value by using the mouse to click on numbered buttons. This application can also provide a good starting point for creating your own calculator application.

The 16 command buttons on NUMPAD.FRM are configured as an array. Each command button has an Index property that uniquely identifies that button. A click on any of these buttons activates the same subprogram, Button_Click, and a *Select Case* statement then determines which of the 16 buttons was clicked. This method results in much less code than if each button had a unique Name property, which would require a lot of duplicate code.

Because Visual Basic for Windows 3 provides the KeyPreview property for forms, I was able easily to add code to process keypresses so that numbers can be entered by using the keyboard. Take a look at the subprogram Form_KeyPress in NUMPAD.FRM to see how this was accomplished.

The *NumPad.Text1.Text* property holds the entered number and provides the returned number to the calling form. When NUMPAD is shown, the current value of *NumPad.Text1.Text* is displayed. This is handy for situations in which a given number is to be altered or replaced by the user. To always start with 0 showing, be sure to assign 0 to *NumPad.Text1.Text* before NUMPAD is loaded.

The NUMPAD1 form demonstrates the use of NUMPAD.FRM. Click the Enter New Number or Edit Previous Number button to activate the NUMPAD form. When the user clicks Enter, the number returned is displayed in a label on NUMPAD1.FRM.

The files for the NUMPAD application are included on the disk packaged with this book. To load the files into the Visual Basic environment, choose the Open Project option from the File menu, and then type *C:\WORKSHOP\NUMPAD.MAK*. This opens the project and enables you to view and modify the forms and code. The following figures, tables, and code give the details of the application's creation.

Figure 6-38.
NUMPAD project list.

Figure 6-39.
NUMPAD.FRM during development.

NUMPAD.FRM Form and Control Properties

Property	Value
Form	
Caption	Number Entry Pad
KeyPreview	True
Name	NumPad
Text Box	
Index	6
Name	Text1
Text	0
Command Button	
Caption	1
Index	1
Name	Button

(continued)

NUMPAD.FRM Form and Control Properties *continued*

Property	Value
Command Button	
Caption	2
Index	2
Name	Button
Command Button	
Caption	3
Index	3
Name	Button
Command Button	
Caption	<-
Index	12
Name	Button
Command Button	
Caption	4
Index	4
Name	Button
Command Button	
Caption	5
Index	5
Name	Button
Command Button	
Caption	6
Index	6
Name	Button
Command Button	
Caption	CE
Index	13
Name	Button

(continued)

NUMPAD.FRM Form and Control Properties *continued*

Property	Value
Command Button	
Caption	7
Index	7
Name	Button
Command Button	
Caption	8
Index	8
Name	Button
Command Button	
Caption	9
Index	9
Name	Button
Command Button	
Caption	Cancel
Index	14
Name	Button
Command Button	
Caption	0
Index	0
Name	Button
Command Button	
Caption	+/-
Index	10
Name	Button
Command Button	
Caption	.
Index	11
Name	Button

(continued)

NUMPAD.FRM Form and Control Properties *continued*

Property	Value
Command Button	
Caption	Enter
Index	15
Name	Button

Source code for NUMPAD.FRM

```
Dim Temp As Double

Sub Button_Click (Index As Integer)
    'Process each of the 16 buttons
    Select Case Index

    'One of the 10 digits
    Case 0 To 9
        Text1.Text = Str$(Val(Text1.Text + Chr$(48 + Index)))

    'Change sign
    Case 10
        Text1.Text = Str$(-Val(Text1.Text))

    'Decimal point
    Case 11
        If InStr(Text1.Text, ".") = 0 Then
            Text1.Text = Text1.Text + "."
        End If

    'Backspace
    Case 12
        If Len(Text1.Text) > 2 Then
            Text1.Text = Left$(Text1.Text, Len(Text1.Text) - 1)
        Else
            Text1.Text = " 0"
        End If

    'Clear entry
    Case 13
        Text1.Text = " 0"
```

(continued)

NUMPAD.FRM *continued*

```
    'Cancel current entry
    Case 14
        Text1.Text = Str$(Temp)

    'Enter button
    Case 15
        Hide
    End Select

    'Set focus back to Enter button
    If Index <> 15 Then Button(15).SetFocus
End Sub

Sub Form_Activate ()
    'Record starting value
    Temp = Val(Text1.Text)
End Sub

Sub Form_KeyPress (KeyAscii As Integer)
    'Process only some of the keys
    Select Case KeyAscii
    Case 48 To 57   'Digit
        Button_Click KeyAscii - 48
    Case 8          'Backspace
        Button_Click 12
    Case 46         'Decimal point
        Button_Click 11
    Case 45         'Negative sign
        Button_Click 10
    Case 27         'Escape key
        Button_Click 14
    End Select

    'Disable any further key processing
    KeyAscii = 0
End Sub

Sub Text1_GotFocus ()
    'Keep focus on Enter button
    Button(15).SetFocus
End Sub
```

Figure 6-40.
NUMPAD1.FRM during development.

NUMPAD1.FRM Menu Design Window Entries

Caption	Name	Indentation
&Help	menHelpTop	0
&Help on NumPad	menHelpNumPad	1
&About NumPad...	menAboutNumPad	1
-	menSep	1
E&xit	menExit	1

NUMPAD1.FRM Form and Control Properties

Property	Value
Form	
Caption	NumPad Test
Name	NumPadTest
Command Button	
Caption	Edit Previous Number
Name	Command2
Command Button	
Caption	Enter New Number
Name	Command1
Label	
Alignment	2 - Center
BorderStyle	1 - Fixed Single
Caption	0
Name	Label1

Source code for **NUMPAD1.FRM**

```
Sub Command1_Click ()
    'Zero current number pad value
    NumPad.Text1.Text = " 0"

    'Start NumPad form
    NumPad.Show MODAL

    'Display entered number
    Label1.Caption = NumPad.Text1.Text
End Sub

Sub Command2_Click ()
    'Start NumPad form
    NumPad.Show MODAL

    'Display entered number
    Label1.Caption = NumPad.Text1.Text
End Sub

Sub Form_Unload (Cancel As Integer)
    'Also unload NumPad form
    Unload NumPad
End Sub

Sub menAboutNumPad_Click ()
    'Display About dialog box
    About.Label1.Caption = "NUMPAD"
    About.Show MODAL
End Sub

Sub menExit_Click ()
    'All done
    Unload NumPadTest
End Sub

Sub menHelpNumPad_Click ()
    'Display some Help text
    FileMsg "NUMPAD.MSG", 1
End Sub
```

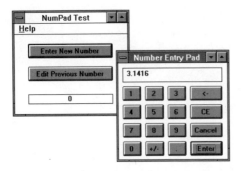

Figure 6-41.
NUMPAD1.FRM and NUMPAD.FRM in action.

The EDITBOX Application

The *InputBox$* function is handy for single-line input by the user, but multiline text input and editing is also often needed. Users can use the EDITBOX form to edit text lines exactly as they would use Notepad. Scroll bars allow a lot of text to be edited, and the standard cut, copy, and paste functions are available. In fact, because the Clipboard is used for these functions, text can be copied and pasted between this and most other applications.

All the editing is performed in a single Text Box control. The ScrollBars attribute is set to *3 - Both* to allow scrolling horizontally and vertically through the lines of text. The SelStart, SelLength, and SelText properties of the text box (which can be set only while the application is running) provide the information for determining where and how much to cut and copy when text is marked.

All the lines of text exist in a single string variable, the Text property of the text box. The carriage-return and linefeed characters (Chr$(13) and Chr$(10)) are inserted in the string wherever a line break is wanted, which gives the appearance of multiple strings.

The Align property for picture boxes was introduced in Visual Basic 2. This property is handy for creating toolbars. A Picture Box control can be aligned at the top of the form, as in EDITBOX, or at the bottom. When aligned, the picture box stretches from left to right to fit exactly inside the form, and it hugs the top (or bottom) of the form, maintaining its original height as it was defined during development. In EDITBOX, the Picture1 control is aligned at the top, and the BackColor property is set to gray. Command buttons drawn on this picture box complete the toolbar.

The toolbar functions are identical to those in the drop-down menu. If you have the Professional Edition of Visual Basic for Windows, you might consider substituting one of the types of buttons that were introduced in Visual Basic 2 for the toolbar command buttons. The 3D Command Button and Animated Button controls, for example, let you put a bit-mapped image, instead of a text caption, on a button.

To use the EDITBOX form in an application, add the EDITBOX.FRM file to the application's project list, and ensure that the CONSTANT.TXT file is loaded into the project. Set and read the *EditBox.Text1.Text* property to access the edited text string.

For this demonstration, the startup form is EDITTEST.BAS. This form assigns *EditBox.Text1.Text* a few lines of text and then shows the EDITBOX form for editing. When the editing is completed, the contents of *EditBox.Text1.Text* are displayed in a local text box for review.

The files for the EDITBOX application are included on the disk packaged with this book. To load the files into the Visual Basic environment, choose the Open Project option from the File menu, and then type *C:\WORKSHOP\EDITBOX.MAK.* This opens the project and enables you to view and modify the forms and code. The following figures, tables, and code give the details of the application's creation.

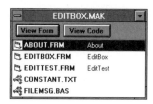

Figure 6-42.
EDITBOX project list.

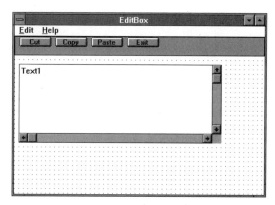

Figure 6-43.
EDITBOX.FRM during development.

EDITBOX.FRM Menu Design Window Entries

Caption	Name	Indentation
&Edit	menEditTop	0
Cu&t	menCut	1
&Copy	menCopy	1
&Paste	menPaste	1
-	menSep	1
E&xit	menExitEditBox	1
&Help	menHelpTop	0
&Help on EditBox	menHelpEditBox	1
&About EditBox...	menAboutEditBox	1

EDITBOX.FRM Form and Control Properties

Property	Value
Form	
Caption	EditBox
Name	EditBox
Picture Box	
Align	1 - Align Top
BackColor	&H00C0C0C0&
Height	495
Name	Picture1
Command Button	
Caption	Exit
Height	255
Name	cmdExit
Command Button	
Caption	Paste
Height	255
Name	cmdPaste

(continued)

EDITBOX.FRM Form and Control Properties *continued*

Property	Value
Command Button	
Caption	Copy
Height	255
Name	cmdCopy
Command Button	
Caption	Cut
Height	255
Name	cmdCut
Text Box	
MultiLine	True
Name	Text1
ScrollBars	3 - Both

Source code for EDITBOX.FRM

```
Sub cmdCopy_Click ()
    'Use equivalent menu code
    menCopy_Click

    'Set focus back to text box
    Text1.SetFocus
End Sub

Sub cmdCut_Click ()
    'Use equivalent menu code
    menCut_Click

    'Set focus back to text box
    Text1.SetFocus
End Sub

Sub cmdExit_Click ()
    'Use equivalent menu code
    menExitEditBox_Click
End Sub
```

(continued)

125

EDITBOX.FRM *continued*

```
Sub cmdPaste_Click ()
    'Use equivalent menu code
    menPaste_Click

    'Set focus back to text box
    Text1.SetFocus
End Sub

Sub Form_Activate ()
    'Set focus on text box
    Text1.SetFocus
End Sub

Sub Form_Load ()
    'Force a form resize event
    Form_Resize
End Sub

Sub Form_Resize ()
    'Prevent an error if form gets sized too short
    If ScaleHeight < cmdCut.Height Then
        Exit Sub
    End If

    'Size picture box to fit buttons
    Picture1.Height = cmdCut.Height + 25

    'Size text box to exactly fill form
    Text1.Move 0, Picture1.Height, ScaleWidth, ↴
     ScaleHeight - Picture1.Height

    'Snug command buttons end to end
    cmdCut.Left = 0
    cmdCopy.Left = cmdCut.Width
    cmdPaste.Left = cmdCopy.Left + cmdCopy.Width

    'Snug Exit button to the right
    cmdExit.Left = ScaleWidth - cmdExit.Width - 25

    'Move command buttons to top row
    cmdCut.Top = 0
    cmdCopy.Top = 0
```

(continued)

EDITBOX.FRM *continued*

```
    cmdPaste.Top = 0
    cmdExit.Top = 0
End Sub

Sub menAboutEditBox_Click ()
    'Display About dialog box
    About.Label1.Caption = "EDITBOX"
    About.Show MODAL
End Sub

Sub menCopy_Click ()
    'Copy cut text to Clipboard
    Clipboard.SetText Text1.SelText
End Sub

Sub menCut_Click ()
    'Get working parameters
    Work$ = Text1.Text
    Wstart% = Text1.SelStart
    Wlength% = Text1.SelLength

    'Copy cut text to Clipboard
    Clipboard.SetText Mid$(Work$, Wstart% + 1, Wlength%)

    'Cut out text
    Work$ = Left$(Work$, Wstart%) +⬎
     Mid$(Work$, Wstart% + Wlength% + 1)
    Text1.Text = Work$

    'Position edit cursor
    Text1.SelStart = Wstart%
End Sub

Sub menExitEditBox_Click ()
    'All done for now
    Hide
End Sub

Sub menHelpEditBox_Click ()
    'Display some Help text
    FileMsg "EDITBOX.MSG", 1
End Sub
```

(continued)

127

EDITBOX.FRM *continued*

```
Sub menPaste_Click ()
    'Get working parameters
    Work$ = Text1.Text
    Wstart% = Text1.SelStart
    Wlength% = Text1.SelLength

    'Cut out text, if any, and insert Clipboard text
    Work$ = Left$(Work$, Wstart%) + Clipboard.GetText() +⌐
     Mid$(Work$, Wstart% + Wlength% + 1)
    Text1.Text = Work$

    'Position edit cursor
    Text1.SelStart = Wstart%
End Sub
```

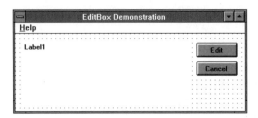

Figure 6-44.
EDITTEST.FRM during development.

EDITTEST.FRM Menu Design Window Entries

Caption	Name	Indentation
&Help	menHelp	0
&Help on EditBox	menHelpEditBox	1
&About EditBox...	menAboutEditBox	1
-	menSep	1
E&xit	menExit	1

EDITTEST.FRM Form and Control Properties

Property	Value
Form	
Caption	EditBox Demonstration
Name	EditTest
Command Button	
Caption	Cancel
Name	Command2
Command Button	
Caption	Edit
Name	Command1
Label	
Caption	Label1
Name	Label1

Source code for EDITTEST.FRM

```
Sub Command1_Click ()
    'Set up text to be edited
    EditBox.Text1.Text = Label1.Caption

    'Let user do some editing
    EditBox.Show MODAL

    'Show results
    Label1.Caption = EditBox.Text1.Text
End Sub

Sub Command2_Click ()
    'All done
    Unload EditTest
End Sub
```

(continued)

EDITTEST.FRM *continued*

```
Sub Form_Load ()
    'Build newline (CR/LF) string
    NL$ = Chr$(13) + Chr$(10)

    'Build string for editing
    A$ = "The EditBox form lets you edit text" + NL$
    A$ = A$ + "in a way similar to Notepad.  For this" + NL$
    A$ = A$ + "example, you can edit the lines you" + NL$
    A$ = A$ + "are now reading."

    'Let user edit this string
    Label1.Caption = A$
End Sub

Sub Form_Unload (Cancel As Integer)
    'Also unload EditBox form
    Unload EditBox
End Sub

Sub menAboutEditBox_Click ()
    'Display About dialog box
    About.Label1.Caption = "EDITTEST"
    About.Show MODAL
End Sub

Sub menExit_Click ()
    'All done
    Unload EditTest
End Sub

Sub menHelpEditBox_Click ()
    'Display some Help text
    FileMsg "EDITTEST.MSG", 1
End Sub
```

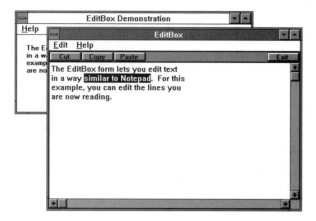

Figure 6-45.
EDITTEST.FRM and EDITBOX.FRM in action.

APPLICATIONS FOR EXPLORING VISUAL BASIC FOR WINDOWS

This chapter presents applications that help you explore the inner workings of Visual Basic for Windows. These applications introduce several ideas and new techniques. For example, the RGBHSV application provides a working example of using scroll bars on a form. In addition, the running applications provide working references to the parameters and operations of several Visual Basic commands and methods. For example, the MSGBOXES application lets you interactively explore the *MsgBox* function by creating and displaying message boxes that have any combination of possible parameters.

The RGBHSV Application

Scroll bars on the RGBHSV form enable the user to select any possible Windows environment color. Six scroll bars are displayed: three for selecting colors by using red, green, and blue values and three for selecting colors by using hue, saturation, and value values. All six scroll bars are updated as you adjust any one scroll bar, which helps you get a feel for how the two color schemes work. Changes to the scroll bars cause immediate changes in the form's picture box, which displays the defined color. Between the two sets of scroll bars, the hexadecimal long-integer number for the color is displayed; this number can be given as the color parameter in many graphics commands.

The Max and Min properties of the Red, Green, and Blue scroll bars are set so that the scroll bar ranges match the 0 through 255 range for standard color values. Hue values range from 0 through 360, representing the angles around a circle. Saturation and value values are percentages, so their scroll bar ranges have been set to 0 through 100.

The *HsvToRgb* and *RgbToHsv* functions in this form can be useful in other applications. Many people find the hue-saturation-value color system more intuitive and better suited for some color selection tasks than the red-green-blue color system. For example, let's say that the user is painting an artistic scene and wants to select from a variety of shades of red for a sunset. Setting the hue to red and sweeping through the saturation and value settings might be a better approach than tweaking green and blue values. Of course, the HSV values must be converted to RGB values because Windows' graphics functions can use only the RGB system for color designation. You can copy the *HsvToRgb* and *RgbToHsv* functions into any application in which HSV color designation is useful.

On many computers, Windows creates the full range of possible colors by using a technique called *dithering*. Take a close look at the displayed color as you manipulate the scroll bars. If you see a pattern of multicolored dots, the graphics-display driver for Windows is blending different-colored pixels to create the color. Dithering allows applications for Windows to use any of 16,777,216 possible colors (256 x 256 x 256). If your graphics board and Windows driver provide 256-color mode or better, many of these colors are displayed without dithering, which improves the appearance of your Visual Basic applications without requiring any changes to them.

The files for the RGBHSV application, which demonstrates the RGBHSV form, are included on the disk packaged with this book. To load the files into the Visual Basic environment, choose Open Project from the File menu, and then type *C:\WORKSHOP\RGBHSV.MAK*. This opens the project and enables you to view and modify the forms and code. The following figures, tables, and code give the details of the application's creation.

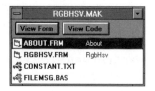

Figure 7-1.
RGBHSV project list.

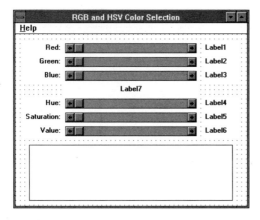

Figure 7-2.
RGBHSV.FRM during development.

RGBHSV.FRM Menu Design Window Entries

Caption	Name	Indentation
&Help	menHelpTop	0
&Help on RGBHSV	menHelpRGBHSV	1
&About RGBHSV...	menAboutRGBHSV	1
-	menSep	1
E&xit	menExit	1

RGBHSV.FRM Form and Control Properties

Property	Value
Form	
BorderStyle	1 - Fixed Single
Caption	RGB and HSV Color Selection
Name	RgbHsv
Picture Box	
Name	Picture1

(continued)

RGBHSV.FRM Form and Control Properties *continued*

Property	Value
Horizontal Scroll Bar	
LargeChange	20
Max	100
Name	HScroll6
Horizontal Scroll Bar	
LargeChange	20
Max	100
Name	HScroll5
Horizontal Scroll Bar	
LargeChange	20
Max	360
Name	HScroll4
Horizontal Scroll Bar	
LargeChange	20
Max	255
Name	HScroll3
Horizontal Scroll Bar	
LargeChange	20
Max	255
Name	HScroll2
Horizontal Scroll Bar	
LargeChange	20
Max	255
Name	HScroll1
Label	
Alignment	2 - Center
Caption	Label7
Name	Label7

(continued)

RGBHSV.FRM Form and Control Properties *continued*

Property	Value
Label	
Caption	Label6
Name	Label6
Label	
Caption	Label5
Name	Label5
Label	
Caption	Label4
Name	Label4
Label	
Caption	Label3
Name	Label3
Label	
Caption	Label2
Name	Label2
Label	
Caption	Label1
Name	Label1
Label	
Alignment	1 - Right Justify
Caption	Value:
Name	Label13
Label	
Alignment	1 - Right Justify
Caption	Saturation:
Name	Label12

(continued)

RGBHSV.FRM Form and Control Properties *continued*

Property	Value
Label	
Alignment	1 - Right Justify
Caption	Hue:
Name	Label11
Label	
Alignment	1 - Right Justify
Caption	Blue:
Name	Label10
Label	
Alignment	1 - Right Justify
Caption	Green:
Name	Label9
Label	
Alignment	1 - Right Justify
Caption	Red:
Name	Label8

Source code for RGBHSV.FRM

```
Dim FlagA, FlagB As Integer

Sub Form_Load ()
    'Initialize to random color
    Randomize Timer
    HScroll1.Value = Rnd * 255
    HScroll2.Value = Rnd * 255
    HScroll3.Value = Rnd * 255

    'Center form on screen
    Left = (Screen.Width - Width) / 2
    Top = (Screen.Height - Height) / 2
```

(continued)

RGBHSV.FRM *continued*

```
    'Initialize flags
    FlagA = 1
    FlagB = 1
    ShowColor
End Sub

Sub HScroll1_Change ()
    Label1.Caption = HScroll1.Value
    FlagA = 1
    ShowColor
End Sub

Sub HScroll1_GotFocus ()
    FlagB = 1
End Sub

Sub HScroll1_Scroll ()
    HScroll1_Change
End Sub

Sub HScroll2_Change ()
    Label2.Caption = HScroll2.Value
    FlagA = 2
    ShowColor
End Sub

Sub HScroll2_GotFocus ()
    FlagB = 2
End Sub

Sub HScroll2_Scroll ()
    HScroll2_Change
End Sub

Sub HScroll3_Change ()
    Label3.Caption = HScroll3.Value
    FlagA = 3
    ShowColor
End Sub

Sub HScroll3_GotFocus ()
    FlagB = 3
End Sub
```

(continued)

RGBHSV.FRM *continued*

```
Sub HScroll3_Scroll ()
    HScroll3_Change
End Sub

Sub HScroll4_Change ()
    Label4.Caption = HScroll4.Value
    FlagA = 4
    ShowColor
End Sub

Sub HScroll4_GotFocus ()
    FlagB = 4
End Sub

Sub HScroll4_Scroll ()
    HScroll4_Change
End Sub

Sub HScroll5_Change ()
    Label5.Caption = HScroll5.Value
    FlagA = 5
    ShowColor
End Sub

Sub HScroll5_GotFocus ()
    FlagB = 5
End Sub

Sub HScroll5_Scroll ()
    HScroll5_Change
End Sub

Sub HScroll6_Change ()
    Label6.Caption = HScroll6.Value
    FlagA = 6
    ShowColor
End Sub

Sub HScroll6_GotFocus ()
    FlagB = 6
End Sub

Sub HScroll6_Scroll ()
    HScroll6_Change
End Sub
```

(continued)

RGBHSV.FRM *continued*

```
Sub HsvToRgb (H, S, V, R, G, B)
    Sa = S / 100
    Va = V / 100
    If S = 0 Then
        R = Va
        G = Va
        B = Va
    Else
        Hue = H / 60
        If Hue = 6 Then Hue = 0
        i = Int(Hue)
        f = Hue - i
        p = Va * (1 - Sa)
        q = Va * (1 - (Sa * f))
        t = Va * (1 - (Sa * (1 - f)))
        Select Case i
        Case 0
            R = Va
            G = t
            B = p
        Case 1
            R = q
            G = Va
            B = p
        Case 2
            R = p
            G = Va
            B = t
        Case 3
            R = p
            G = q
            B = Va
        Case 4
            R = t
            G = p
            B = Va
        Case 5
            R = Va
            G = p
            B = q
        End Select
    End If

    R = Int(255.9999 * R)
    G = Int(255.9999 * G)
```

(continued)

RGBHSV.FRM *continued*

```
    B = Int(255.9999 * B)
End Sub

Sub menAboutRGBHSV_Click ()
    'Display About dialog box
    About.Label1.Caption = "RGBHSV"
    About.Show MODAL
End Sub

Sub menExit_Click ()
    'All done
    Unload RgbHsv
End Sub

Sub menHelpRGBHSV_Click ()
    'Display some Help text
    FileMsg "RGBHSV.MSG", 1
End Sub

Sub RgbToHsv (R, G, B, H, S, V)
    vRed = R / 255
    vGreen = G / 255
    vBlue = B / 255

    Mx = vRed
    If vGreen > Mx Then Mx = vGreen
    If vBlue > Mx Then Mx = vBlue

    Mn = vRed
    If vGreen < Mn Then Mn = vGreen
    If vBlue < Mn Then Mn = vBlue

    Va = Mx
    If Mx Then
        Sa = (Mx - Mn) / Mx
    Else
        Sa = 0
    End If
    If Sa = 0 Then
        H = 0
    Else
        rc = (Mx - vRed) / (Mx - Mn)
        gc = (Mx - vGreen) / (Mx - Mn)
        bc = (Mx - vBlue) / (Mx - Mn)
```

(continued)

RGBHSV.FRM *continued*

```
        Select Case Mx
        Case vRed
            H = bc - gc
        Case vGreen
            H = 2 + rc - bc
        Case vBlue
            H = 4 + gc - rc
        End Select
        H = H * 60
        If H < 0 Then H = H + 360
    End If

    S = Sa * 100
    V = Va * 100
End Sub

Sub SetHSV ()
    'Get current RGB scroll bar values
    R = HScroll1.Value
    G = HScroll2.Value
    B = HScroll3.Value

    'Convert RGB to HSV
    RgbToHsv R, G, B, H, S, V

    'Set HSV scroll bars
    HScroll4.Value = H
    HScroll5.Value = S
    HScroll6.Value = V
End Sub

Sub SetRGB ()
    'Get current HSV scroll bar values
    H = HScroll4.Value
    S = HScroll5.Value
    V = HScroll6.Value

    'Convert HSV to RGB
    HsvToRgb H, S, V, R, G, B

    'Set RGB scroll bars
    HScroll1.Value = R
    HScroll2.Value = G
```

(continued)

RGBHSV.FRM *continued*

```
      HScroll3.Value = B
   End Sub

   Sub ShowColor ()
      'Be sure scroll bars are coordinated
      If FlagA > 0 And FlagA = FlagB Then
          If FlagA < 4 Then
              SetHSV
          Else
              SetRGB
          End If
      End If

      'Get RGB scroll bar values
      R = HScroll1.Value
      G = HScroll2.Value
      B = HScroll3.Value

      'Convert R, G, and B values to long color value
      RgbVal& = RGB(R, G, B)

      'Display color in picture box
      Picture1.BackColor = RgbVal&

      'Display long color value
      Label7.Caption = "H" + Hex$(RgbVal&)
   End Sub
```

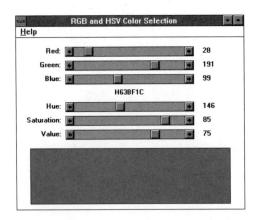

Figure 7-3.
RGBHSV.FRM in action.

The MOUSEPTR Application

Each form and most objects have a property named MousePointer. The default value for MousePointer is *0 - Default,* which causes the mouse pointer to be its default shape when it is positioned over a form or an object. However, MousePointer can be set to any of 13 values, resulting in different pointer shapes. For example, assigning *11 - Hourglass* to MousePointer causes the standard hourglass pointer to be displayed.

The MOUSEPTR application displays all the available mouse pointers. You click the option buttons to change the value of the MousePointer property. The mouse pointer changes immediately to reflect the new value.

At first, mouse pointers 0 and 1 appear the same when you select them because the default pointer usually appears as the same standard arrow that is displayed when MousePointer is set to *1 - Arrow.* You can move the pointer over the text box on the form to see the difference between these two settings. When MousePointer is set to *0 - Default,* the default pointer over the text box is an I-beam; when it's set to *1 - Arrow,* the standard arrow that points up and to the left is always displayed.

The constants for the various MousePointer settings are defined in CONSTANT.TXT for easy use. These descriptive constants are easier than integers to understand in source code. For example, *MousePointer = HOURGLASS* is easier to understand than *MousePointer = 11.*

The files for the MOUSEPTR application are included on the disk packaged with this book. To load the files into the Visual Basic environment, choose the Open Project option from the File menu, and then enter the filename *C:\WORKSHOP\MOUSEPTR.MAK.* This opens the project and enables you to view and modify the forms and code. The following figures, tables, and code give the details of the application's creation.

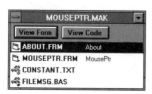

Figure 7-4.
MOUSEPTR project list.

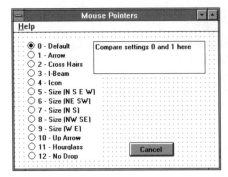

Figure 7-5.
MOUSEPTR.FRM during development.

MOUSEPTR.FRM Menu Design Window Entries

Caption	Name	Indentation
&Help	menHelpTop	0
&Help on MousePtr	menHelpMousePtr	1
&About MousePtr...	menAboutMousePtr	1
-	menSep	1
E&xit	menExit	1

MOUSEPTR.FRM Form and Control Properties

Property	Value
Form	
Caption	Mouse Pointers
Name	MousePtr
Command Button	
Caption	Cancel
Name	Command1
Option Button	
Caption	12 - No Drop
Index	12
Name	Option1

(continued)

MOUSEPTR.FRM Form and Control Properties *continued*

Property	Value
Option Button	
Caption	11 - Hourglass
Index	11
Name	Option1
Option Button	
Caption	10 - Up Arrow
Index	10
Name	Option1
Option Button	
Caption	9 - Size (W E)
Index	9
Name	Option1
Option Button	
Caption	8 - Size (NW SE)
Index	8
Name	Option1
Option Button	
Caption	7 - Size (N S)
Index	7
Name	Option1
Option Button	
Caption	6 - Size (NE SW)
Index	6
Name	Option1
Option Button	
Caption	5 - Size (N S E W)
Index	5
Name	Option1

(continued)

MOUSEPTR.FRM Form and Control Properties *continued*

Property	Value
Option Button	
Caption	4 - Icon
Index	4
Name	Option1
Option Button	
Caption	3 - I-Beam
Index	3
Name	Option1
Option Button	
Caption	2 - Cross Hairs
Index	2
Name	Option1
Option Button	
Caption	1 - Arrow
Index	1
Name	Option1
Option Button	
Caption	0 - Default
Index	0
Name	Option1
Text Box	
Text	Compare settings 0 and 1 here
Name	Text1

Source code for MOUSEPTR.FRM

```
Sub Command1_Click ()
    'Another way to end the program
    menExit_Click
End Sub
```

(continued)

MOUSEPTR.FRM *continued*

```
Sub Form_Load ()
    'Move focus off text box and onto option buttons
    Show
    Option1(0).SetFocus
End Sub

Sub menAboutMousePtr_Click ()
    'Show About dialog box
    About.Label1.Caption = "MOUSEPTR"
    About.Show MODAL
End Sub

Sub menExit_Click ()
    'All done
    Unload MousePtr
End Sub

Sub menHelpMousePtr_Click ()
    'Display some Help text
    FileMsg "MOUSEPTR.MSG", 1
End Sub

Sub Option1_Click (Index As Integer)
    'Set selected mouse pointer
    MousePtr.MousePointer = Index
End Sub
```

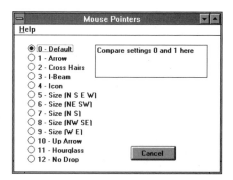

Figure 7-6.
MOUSEPTR.FRM in action.

The MOUSEVNT Application

The MOUSEVNT application demonstrates the mouse events that are generated by mouse movement and button clicks. The MOUSEVNT form handles five different mouse events; each causes a message to be printed on the form. The Form_MouseMove subprogram, which handles mouse movement events, is activated most often—whenever the mouse is moved on the form. The MouseDown, MouseUp, and Click events occur whenever one or both mouse buttons are clicked. The DblClick event occurs when a button is double-clicked.

Each message for a MouseMove, MouseDown, or MouseUp event indicates which mouse button is pressed (0 for neither, 1 for left, 2 for right, or 3 for both) and whether any of the shift keys are pressed down (0 for none, 1 for Shift, 2 for Ctrl, and 4 for Alt). If more than one button or shift key is down, the numbers for each button or key are added together; for example, *Shift: 5* means that both the Shift key and the Alt key are down. The messages also show the coordinates of the mouse pointer relative to the form.

Several controls appear on the form. Their only purpose is to show that mouse events for the form do not occur when the pointer is over these controls; mouse events for these controls are separate from those for the form. To cause a program to act on mouse events for these controls, you must create a similar but unique set of subprograms for each control.

The MOUSEVNT form is shorter during development than when the application is running because the Form_Load subprogram contains the following statement:

```
Height = .8 * Screen.Height
```

This statement changes the size of the form at load time to 80 percent of the full screen height. Other statements in Form_Load center the form on the screen.

The files for the MOUSEVNT application are included on the disk packaged with this book. To load the files into the Visual Basic environment, choose the Open Project option from the File menu, and then enter the filename *C:\WORKSHOP\MOUSEVNT.MAK*. This opens the project and enables you to view and modify the forms and code. The following figures, tables, and code give the details of the application's creation.

Figure 7-7.
MOUSEVNT project list.

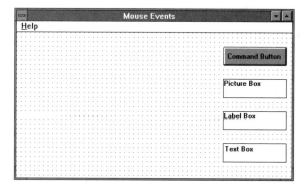

Figure 7-8.
MOUSEVNT.FRM during development.

MOUSEVNT.FRM Menu Design Window Entries

Caption	Name	Indentation
&Help	menHelpTop	0
&Help on MousEvnt	menHelpMousEvnt	1
&About MousEvnt...	menAboutMousEvnt	1
-	menSep	1
E&xit	menExit	1

MOUSEVNT.FRM Form and Control Properties

Property	Value
Form	
Caption	Mouse Events
Name	MousEvnt
Command Button	
Caption	Command Button
Name	Command1
Picture Box	
Name	Picture1
Label	
Caption	Picture Box
Name	Label1
Label	
BorderStyle	1 - Fixed Single
Caption	Label Box
Text Box	
Name	Text1
Text	Text Box

Source code for MOUSEVNT.FRM

```
Sub CheckFormBottom ()
    'Keep event messages on form
    If CurrentY > ScaleHeight Then
        Cls
    End If
End Sub

Sub Form_Click ()
    'Mouse clicked on form
    Print "Click"
    CheckFormBottom
End Sub
```

(continued)

MOUSEVNT.FRM *continued*

```
Sub Form_DblClick ()
    'Double click occurred
    Print "DblClick"
    CheckFormBottom
End Sub

Sub Form_Load ()
    'Make form 80% as tall as screen
    Height = .8 * Screen.Height

    'Center form on screen
    Left = (Screen.Width - Width) / 2
    Top = (Screen.Height - Height) / 2
End Sub

Sub Form_MouseDown (Button As Integer, Shift As Integer,
 X As Single, Y As Single)
    'Mouse button pressed
    Print "MouseDown",
    Print "Button:"; Button,
    Print "Shift:"; Shift,
    Print "X:"; X; "Y:"; Y
    CheckFormBottom
End Sub

Sub Form_MouseMove (Button As Integer, Shift As Integer,
 X As Single, Y As Single)
    'Mouse has moved across form
    Print "MouseMove",
    Print "Button:"; Button,
    Print "Shift:"; Shift,
    Print "X:"; X; "Y:"; Y
    CheckFormBottom
End Sub

Sub Form_MouseUp (Button As Integer, Shift As Integer,
 X As Single, Y As Single)
    'Mouse button has been released
    Print "MouseUp",
    Print "Button:"; Button,
    Print "Shift:"; Shift,
    Print "X:"; X; "Y:"; Y
    CheckFormBottom
End Sub
```

(continued)

MOUSEVNT.FRM *continued*

```
Sub menAboutMousEvnt_Click ()
    'Show About dialog box
    About.Label1.Caption = "MOUSEVNT"
    About.Show MODAL
End Sub

Sub menExit_Click ()
    'All done
    Unload MousEvnt
End Sub

Sub menHelpMousEvnt_Click ()
    'Display some Help text
    FileMsg "MOUSEVNT.MSG", 1
End Sub
```

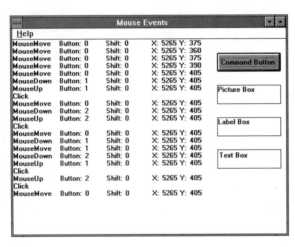

Figure 7-9.
MOUSEVNT.FRM in action.

The KEYEVNTS Application

The KEYEVNTS application interactively demonstrates how various keyboard events take place. It is similar to the MOUSEVNT application, but it monitors keyboard events instead of mouse events.

Three keyboard events are monitored: KeyDown, KeyPress, and KeyUp. When you are creating an application, you normally need to attach code for only one, or perhaps two, of these events. Here you'll see how all three events occur each time a key is pressed.

The KeyPress event occurs whenever a character key is pressed. For many applications, this is the only event you need to handle. However, special-purpose keys (such as the function and shift keys) do not generate KeyPress events. To catch all keyboard activity, you must also attach code to the KeyDown or KeyUp event. Each KeyDown event, for example, provides a KeyCode parameter that uniquely identifies a key on the keyboard.

Run this application, and press some keys to see how the various events are generated. You'll notice that holding down a key generates a series of KeyDown and KeyPress events but generates only one KeyUp event—when the key is finally released.

If you click the KeyPreview check box, you can see how keyboard events are intercepted first by the form, even when the command button or the check box has the focus.

The files for the KEYEVNTS application are included on the disk packaged with this book. To load the files into the Visual Basic environment, choose the Open Project option from the File menu, and then type *C:\WORKSHOP\KEYEVNTS.MAK*. This opens the project and enables you to view and modify the forms and code. The following figures, tables, and code give the details of the application's creation.

Figure 7-10.
KEYEVNTS project list.

Figure 7-11.
KEYEVNTS.FRM during development.

KEYEVNTS.FRM Menu Design Window Entries

Caption	Name	Indentation
&Help	menHelpTop	0
&Help on KeyEvnts	menHelpKeyEvnts	1
&About KeyEvnts...	menAboutKeyEvnts	1
-	menSep	1
E&xit	menExit	1

KEYEVNTS.FRM Form and Control Properties

Property	Value
Form	
AutoRedraw	True
Caption	Key Events
KeyPreview	True
Name	KeyEvnts
Check Box	
Caption	KeyPreview
Name	Check1
Value	1 - Checked
Command Button	
Caption	Command1
Name	Command1

Source code for KEYEVNTS.FRM

```
Sub Check1_Click ()
    'Toggle form's KeyPreview property
    If Check1.Value = CHECKED Then
        KeyPreview = True
    Else
        KeyPreview = False
    End If
End Sub
```

(continued)

156

KEYEVNTS.FRM *continued*

```
Sub Form_KeyDown (KeyCode As Integer, Shift As Integer)
    'A key has been pressed
    Print "KeyDown", KeyCode; Shift
    Position
End Sub

Sub Form_KeyPress (KeyAscii As Integer)
    'An ANSI key has been pressed and released
    Print "KeyPress", KeyAscii; Chr$(KeyAscii)
    Position
End Sub

Sub Form_KeyUp (KeyCode As Integer, Shift As Integer)
    'A key has been released
    Print "KeyUp", KeyCode; Shift
    Position
End Sub

Sub Form_Load ()
    'Make form 80% of screen height
    KeyEvnts.Height = Screen.Height * .8

    'Center form vertically on screen
    Top = (Screen.Height - Height) / 2

    'Place form 10% from left
    Left = Screen.Width * .1
End Sub

Sub menAboutKeyEvnts_Click ()
    'Display About dialog box
    About.Label1.Caption = "KEYEVNTS"
    About.Show MODAL
End Sub

Sub menExit_Click ()
    'All done
    Unload KeyEvnts
End Sub

Sub menHelpKeyEvnts_Click ()
    'Display some Help text
    FileMsg "KEYEVNTS.MSG", 1
End Sub
```

(continued)

157

KEYEVNTS.FRM *continued*

```
Sub Position ()
        'Keep displayed data on visible form
        If CurrentY > ScaleHeight Then
            Cls
        End If
End Sub
```

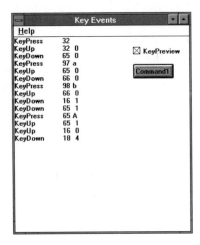

Figure 7-12.
KEYEVNTS.FRM in action.

The MSGBOXES Application

Message boxes are easy to use, and they are useful for Visual Basic programming. In previous versions of Basic, the PRINT statement was the workhorse for simple text output. In Visual Basic, the *MsgBox* statement is the equivalent workhorse. The MSGBOXES application interactively demonstrates the configurations for the *MsgBox* statement.

MSGBOXES provides an example of using groups of Option Button controls. Three arrays of option buttons allow you to choose parameters for the *MsgBox* statements. Because the application requires more than one group of option buttons, the groups must be separated by placing them in picture boxes or frames. This arrangement allows one option button from each group to be selected simultaneously. If the three arrays of buttons were not separated, only one button among all of them could be selected at one time.

The MSGBOXES application uses picture boxes to contain the three groups. Each option button in a group has a unique index value that identifies it when the attached Click event subprogram is activated. Visual Basic handles the details that ensure the selection of only one option button at a time from each group.

You select one item from each group of parameters to define a message box. Two strings are passed to the *MsgBox* statement: *Title$* and *Message$*. You can enter new strings for these items in the text boxes near the bottom of the MSGBOXES form. Default strings are used if you don't enter a message and title.

The files for the MSGBOXES application are included on the disk packaged with this book. To load the files into the Visual Basic environment, choose the Open Project option from the File menu, and then type *C:\WORKSHOP\MSGBOXES.MAK*. This opens the project and enables you to view and modify the forms and code. The following figures, tables, and code give the details of the application's creation.

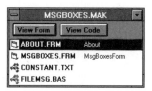

Figure 7-13.
MSGBOXES project list.

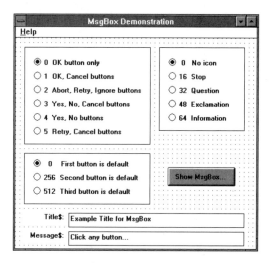

Figure 7-14.
MSGBOXES.FRM during development.

MSGBOXES.FRM Menu Design Window Entries

Caption	Name	Indentation
&Help	menHelpTop	0
&Help on MsgBoxes	menHelpMsgBoxes	1
&About MsgBoxes...	menAboutMsgBoxes	1
-	menSep	1
E&xit	menExit	1

MSGBOXES.FRM Form and Control Properties

Property	Value
Form	
Caption	MsgBox Demonstration
Name	MsgBoxesForm
Picture Box	
Name	Picture1
Option Button	
Caption	0 OK button only
Index	0
Name	Option1
Value	True
Option Button	
Caption	1 OK, Cancel buttons
Index	1
Name	Option1
Option Button	
Caption	2 Abort, Retry, Ignore buttons
Index	2
Name	Option1

(continued)

MSGBOXES.FRM Form and Control Properties *continued*

Property	Value
Option Button	
Caption	3 Yes, No, Cancel buttons
Index	3
Name	Option1
Option Button	
Caption	4 Yes, No buttons
Index	4
Name	Option1
Option Button	
Caption	5 Retry, Cancel buttons
Index	5
Name	Option1
Picture Box	
Name	Picture2
Option Button	
Caption	0 No icon
Index	0
Name	Option2
Value	True
Option Button	
Caption	16 Stop
Index	1
Name	Option2
Option Button	
Caption	32 Question
Index	2
Name	Option2

(continued)

MSGBOXES.FRM Form and Control Properties *continued*

Property	Value
Option Button	
Caption	48 Exclamation
Index	3
Name	Option2
Option Button	
Caption	64 Information
Index	4
Name	Option2
Picture Box	
Name	Picture3
Option Button	
Caption	0 First button is default
Index	0
Name	Option3
Value	True
Option Button	
Caption	256 Second button is default
Index	1
Name	Option3
Option Button	
Caption	512 Third button is default
Index	2
Name	Option3
Command Button	
Caption	Show MsgBox...
Name	Command1
Text Box	
Name	Text1
Text	Example title for MsgBox

(continued)

MSGBOXES.FRM Form and Control Properties *continued*

Property	Value
Text Box	
Name	Text2
Text	Click any button...
Label	
Alignment	1 - Right Justify
Caption	Title$:
Name	Label1
Label	
Alignment	1 - Right Justify
Caption	Message$:
Name	Label2

Source code for MSGBOXES.FRM

```
Dim ButtonType%, IconType%, DefaultButton%

Sub Command1_Click ()
    'Build parameters for MsgBox function
    Index% = ButtonType% + IconType% + DefaultButton%
    Title$ = Text1.Text
    Msg$ = Text2.Text


    'Call MsgBox and display result
    Select Case MsgBox(Msg$, Index%, Title$)
    Case 1
        MsgBox "OK button was clicked"
    Case 2
        MsgBox "Cancel button was clicked"
    Case 3
        MsgBox "Abort button was clicked"
    Case 4
        MsgBox "Retry button was clicked"
    Case 5
        MsgBox "Ignore button was clicked"
    Case 6
        MsgBox "Yes button was clicked"
```

(continued)

MSGBOXES.FRM *continued*

```
        Case 7
            MsgBox "No button was clicked"
        Case Else
            MsgBox "Unknown button was clicked"
        End Select
    End Sub

    Sub Form_Load ()
        'Center form on screen
        Left = (Screen.Width - Width) / 2
        Top = (Screen.Height - Height) / 2
    End Sub

    Sub menAboutMsgBoxes_Click ()
        'Display About dialog box
        About.Label1.Caption = "MSGBOXES"
        About.Show MODAL
    End Sub

    Sub menExit_Click ()
        'All done
        Unload MsgBoxesForm
    End Sub

    Sub menHelpMsgBoxes_Click ()
        'Display some Help text
        FileMsg "MSGBOXES.MSG", 1
    End Sub

    Sub Option1_Click (Index As Integer)
        'Select type of buttons
        ButtonType% = Index
    End Sub

    Sub Option2_Click (Index As Integer)
        'Select type of icon
        IconType% = Index * 16
    End Sub

    Sub Option3_Click (Index As Integer)
        'Select default button
        DefaultButton% = Index * 256
    End Sub
```

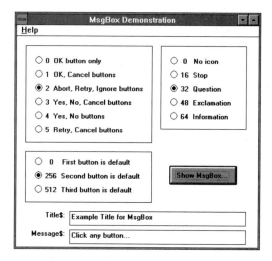

Figure 7-15.
MSGBOXES.FRM in action.

Figure 7-16.
The result of clicking the Show MsgBox button in the window shown in Figure 7-15.

Figure 7-17.
The result of clicking the Ignore button in the message box shown in Figure 7-16.

The INPUTBOX Application

The *InputBox$* function effectively replaces the INPUT function used in previous versions of Basic. Like the *MsgBox* statement (which replaces the PRINT statement), *InputBox$* is powerful and easy to use. You don't need to predefine a form to contain the application's prompt and the user's response because *InputBox$* creates a standard dialog box to interact with the user.

The INPUTBOX application uses the *InputBox$* function to prompt the user for each of the parameters that are used in a call to *InputBox$*. After all the parameters of the function are entered, a call to *InputBox$* displays the resulting dialog box.

This application also presents a simple technique that dramatically changes the appearance of the running application: The form provides a solid-color, full-screen background for the running application. You accomplish this by setting the background color of the form to solid blue, setting the Border Style property to *0 = None*, and setting the MaxButton, MinButton, and ControlBox properties to *False*. The WindowState property is set to *2 - Maximized*, which causes the form to fill the entire screen when it is loaded. When you run the application, the solid-blue background prevents other windows from being a distraction, and it adds a touch of intensity to the application.

The files for the INPUTBOX application are included on the disk packaged with this book. To load the files into the Visual Basic environment, choose the Open Project option from the File menu, and then type *C:\WORKSHOP\INPUTBOX.MAK*. This opens the project and enables you to view and modify the form and code. The following figures, tables, and code give the details of the application's creation.

Figure 7-18.
INPUTBOX project list.

Figure 7-19.
INPUTBOX.FRM during development.

INPUTBOX.FRM Form Properties

Property	Value
Form	
BackColor	&H00FF0000&
BorderStyle	0 - None
ControlBox	False
MaxButton	False
MinButton	False
Name	InputBoxForm
WindowState	2 - Maximized

Source code for INPUTBOX.FRM

```
Sub Form_Load ()
    'Create blank background covering entire screen
    InputBoxForm.Show MODELESS

    'Create newline string
    NL$ = Chr$(13) + Chr$(10)

    'General instructions
    Msg$ = "This program demonstrates the InputBox$" + NL$
    Msg$ = Msg$ + "function. You'll be prompted for each of" + NL$
    Msg$ = Msg$ + "the parameters, and then the dialog box" + NL$
    Msg$ = Msg$ + "you've defined will be displayed." + NL$ + NL$
    Msg$ = Msg$ + "Notice that InputBox$ is called to prompt" + NL$
    Msg$ = Msg$ + "you for each of the parameters." + NL$ + NL$
    Msg$ = Msg$ + "Click OK to continue..."
    MsgBox Msg$

    'Ask user for prompt string
    Prompt$ = "Enter the prompt text."
    Title$ = "InputBox$ Demonstration"
    Defalt$ = "This is the default prompt."
    NewPrompt$ = InputBox$(Prompt$, Title$, Defalt$)

    'Ask user for title string
    Prompt$ = "Enter the title."
    Defalt$ = "This is the default title."
    NewTitle$ = InputBox$(Prompt$, Title$, Defalt$)
```

(continued)

INPUTBOX.FRM *continued*

```
    'Ask user for default input string
    Prompt$ = "Enter the input text."
    Defalt$ = "This is the default input text."
    NewDefalt$ = InputBox$(Prompt$, Title$, Defalt$)

    'Ask user for horizontal position
    Prompt$ = "Enter the X position in" + NL$
    Prompt$ = Prompt$ + "twips, or -1 to center" + NL$
    Prompt$ = Prompt$ + "the box."
    Defalt$ = "-1"
    NewXpos% = Val(InputBox$(Prompt$, Title$, Defalt$))

    'Ask user for vertical position
    If NewXpos% <> -1 Then
        Prompt$ = "Enter the Y position in" + NL$
        Prompt$ = Prompt$ + "twips."
        Defalt$ = "0"
        NewYpos% = Val(InputBox$(Prompt$, Title$, Defalt$))
    End If

    'Inform user we're ready to do it
    Msg$ = "Click OK to see your new dialog box..."
    MsgBox Msg$

    'Do it, centered or at given position
    If NewXpos% = -1 Then
        Result$ = InputBox$(NewPrompt$, NewTitle$, NewDefalt$)
    Else
        Result$ = InputBox$(NewPrompt$, NewTitle$, NewDefalt$,
         NewXpos%, NewYpos%)
    End If

    'Tell user the result
    Msg$ = "Result$ returned by InputBox$..." + NL$ + NL$
    Msg$ = Msg$ + Result$
    MsgBox Msg$

    'Run again if desired
    Msg$ = "Click OK to run this application again."
    N% = MsgBox(Msg$, 1, "InputBox")
    If N% = 1 Then
        Form_Load
    End If

    'Remove background form
    Unload InputBoxForm

End Sub
```

Figure 7-20.
INPUTBOX.FRM in action.

The DRAGDROP Application

The DRAGDROP application interactively demonstrates dragging and dropping operations. Two Image controls, each displaying an icon selected from the many icons shipped with Visual Basic, are set up to be dragged and dropped on the Text control on the right side of the form. The top Image control's DragMode property is set to *1 - Automatic;* the bottom Image control's DragMode property is set to *0 - Manual.* The code required to handle the dragging and dropping of these controls is different in each case, as shown in the program listing that begins on page 171.

The text box's DragOver and DragDrop events cause messages to appear in the text box, letting you see the events as they happen. DragOver events have a parameter that indicates whether the DragOver has just entered the area covered by the control, is continuing to drag across the area, or has just left. The displayed messages show this information as it happens.

The frame is designed to show how a control can indicate that no dropping is allowed on the control. When the top Image control is dragged over the frame, a different icon is temporarily substituted. For the bottom icon, the mouse pointer is temporarily changed to the no-drop pointer.

The files for the DRAGDROP application are included on the disk packaged with this book. To load the files into the Visual Basic environment, choose the Open Project option from the File menu, and then type *C:\WORKSHOP\DRAGDROP.MAK.* This opens the project and enables you to view and modify the forms and code. The following figures, tables, and code give the details of the application's creation.

Figure 7-21.
DRAGDROP project list.

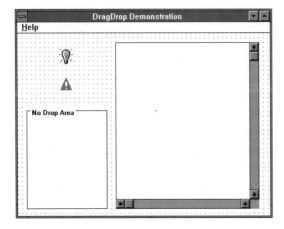

Figure 7-22.
DRAGDROP.FRM during development.

DRAGDROP.FRM Menu Design Window Entries

Caption	Name	Indentation
&Help	menHelp	0
&Help on DragDrop	menHelpDragDrop	1
&About DragDrop...	menAboutDragDrop	1
-	menSep	1
E&xit	menExit	1

DRAGDROP.FRM Form and Control Properties

Property	Value
Form	
Caption	DragDrop Demonstration
Name	DragDrop
Frame	
Caption	No Drop Area
Name	Frame1
Text Box	
MultiLine	True
Name	Text1
ScrollBars	3 - Both
Image	
Name	Image2
Picture	c:\vb\icons\misc\misc02.ico
Image	
DragIcon	c:\vb\icons\misc\lightoff.ico
DragMode	1 - Automatic
Name	Image1
Picture	c:\vb\icons\misc\lighton.ico

Source code for DRAGDROP.FRM

```
Sub Frame1_DragDrop (Source As Control, X As Single, Y As Single)
    'If a DragIcon is in use, we'll change it back
    If Source.DragIcon <> False Then
        Source.DragIcon = Frame1.DragIcon

    'Otherwise, we'll change mouse pointer back to default pointer
    Else
        Source.MousePointer = DEFAULT
    End If
End Sub
```

(continued)

DRAGDROP.FRM *continued*

```
Sub Frame1_DragOver (Source As Control, X As Single, Y As Single,↵
State As Integer)
    'If a DragIcon is in use, we'll change it
    If Source.DragIcon <> False Then
        Select Case State
        Case ENTER
            Frame1.DragIcon = Source.DragIcon
            Source.DragIcon = ↵
             LoadPicture("c:\vb\icons\misc\misc20.ico")
        Case LEAVE
            Source.DragIcon = Frame1.DragIcon
        End Select

        'Otherwise, we'll change mouse pointer
    Else
        Select Case State
        Case ENTER
            'Change to no-drop mouse pointer
            Source.MousePointer = NO_DROP
        Case LEAVE
            'Change to default mouse pointer
            Source.MousePointer = DEFAULT
        End Select
    End If
End Sub

Sub Image2_MouseDown (Button As Integer, Shift As Integer,↵
 X As Single, Y As Single)
    'Manually start dragging operation
    Image2.Drag BEGIN_DRAG
End Sub

Sub Image2_MouseUp (Button As Integer, Shift As Integer,↵
 X As Single, Y As Single)
    'Manually end the dragging, with a drop
    Image2.Drag END_DRAG
End Sub

Sub menAboutDragDrop_Click ()
    'Display About dialog box
    About.Label1.Caption = "DRAGDROP"
    About.Show MODAL
End Sub
```

(continued)

DRAGDROP.FRM *continued*

```
Sub menExit_Click ()
    'All done
    Unload DragDrop
End Sub

Sub menHelpDragDrop_Click ()
    'Display some Help text
    FileMsg "DRAGDROP.MSG", 1
End Sub

Sub Text1_DragDrop (Source As Control, X As Single, Y As Single)
    'Display message in text box
    Tmp$ = "DragDrop    " + Str$(X) + Chr(9) + Str$(Y)
    Text1.Text = Text1.Text + Tmp$ + Chr$(13) + Chr$(10)
End Sub

Sub Text1_DragOver (Source As Control, X As Single, Y As Single, ¬
  State As Integer)
    'If drag just entered, clear messages
    If State = 0 Then Text1.Text = ""

    'Build message
    Tmp$ = "DragOver    "
    Tmp$ = Tmp$ + Str$(X) + Chr$(9)
    Tmp$ = Tmp$ + Str$(Y) + Chr$(9)
    Select Case State
    Case ENTER
        Tmp$ = Tmp$ + "ENTER"
    Case LEAVE
        Tmp$ = Tmp$ + "LEAVE"
    Case OVER
        Tmp$ = Tmp$ + "OVER"
    End Select

    'Display message in text box
    Text1.Text = Text1.Text + Tmp$ + Chr$(13) + Chr$(10)
End Sub
```

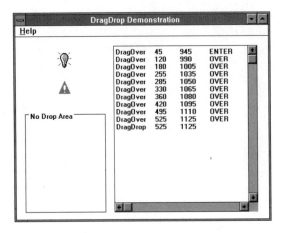

Figure 7-23.
DRAGDROP.FRM in action.

The MENUDEM Application

The MENUDEM application interactively demonstrates many of the menu programming features available in Visual Basic for Windows 3, including the new *PopupMenu* method. This method adds a great deal of flexibility to your menu programming style.

MENUDEM's File menu contains several disabled choices, such as Open, Save, and Save As. It's easy to create these standard menu entries and set the Enabled property of each to *False*. Your application can later enable these choices, or they can serve simply to fill out menus in a standard format and inform the user that these choices are purposefully not available.

Three Check Box controls control properties of the application's Test menu. You can toggle the Checked, Visible, and Enabled properties to see how these settings affect the Test menu choice.

The Test menu also lets you experiment with menu arrays. You select Menu Array Add to grow new menu choices, which are added to the end of the menu, and you select Menu Array Delete to delete the new menu choices one at a time. The code in the associated subprograms shows how these menu array choices are added and deleted.

You can activate the menu selections in three ways: You can select menus directly from the menu bar, you can click on one of the command buttons, or you can activate the Test menu by double-clicking anywhere on the form. When you double-click on the form, the menu pops up at the location of your mouse pointer, which is the default action of the *PopupMenu* method if *xy*-coordinates are not given. You can choose the PopUp command button to see how specifying *xy*-coordinates causes the menu to pop up at any *xy* location relative to the top left corner of the form. In this program, I chose −1000,−1000 (twips) to show how the pop-up menu can even appear outside the form.

However, you can't use the *PopupMenu* method when a pop-up menu is already displayed. To demonstrate this, click on the Popup command button and choose At X,Y Location. The promised pop-up menu doesn't appear.

The menu array technique is a powerful way to modify menus at runtime. Another useful technique is to create extra menu items and simply toggle on and off the Visible properties to show some menus and hide others. To see a simple example of this technique, pay attention to the Test menu when the Visible check box is toggled. Flexible multiple menu schemes can be created by using only this technique.

The files for the MENUDEM application are included on the disk packaged with this book. To load the files into the Visual Basic environment, choose the Open Project option from the File menu, and then type *C:\WORKSHOP\MENUDEM.MAK*. This opens the project and enables you to view and modify the forms and code. The following figures, tables, and code give the details of the application's creation.

Figure 7-24.
MENUDEM project list.

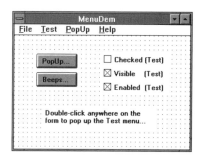

Figure 7-25.
MENUDEM.FRM during development.

MENUDEM.FRM Menu Design Window Entries

Caption	Name	Indentation	Other Information
&File	menFile	0	
&New	menNew	1	Enabled = False
&Open	menOpen	1	Enabled = False
&Save	menSave	1	Enabled = False
Save &As...	menSaveAs	1	Enabled = False
-	menSep1	1	
E&xit	menExit	1	
&Test	menTest	0	
&First Test Item	menFirst	1	Shortcut = Ctrl+F
&Second Test Item	menSecond	1	Shortcut = Ctrl+S
&Cascading Menu	menSub	1	
Cascading Menu Item &1	menSub1	2	
Cascading Menu Item &2	menSub2	2	
-	menSep2	1	
Menu Array &Delete	menAryDel	1	
Menu Array &Add	menAryAdd	1	
-	menSep3	1	
Menu Array 1	menAry	1	Index = 1
&PopUp	menPopUp	0	
Item &1...	menPopUp1	1	
Item &2...	menPopUp2	1	
At &X,Y Location...	menPopUpXY	1	
&Nested	menPopUpNested	1	
Beep &Once	menBeepOnce	2	
Beep &Twice	menBeepTwice	2	
&Help	menHelp	0	
&Help on MenuDem	menHelpMenuDem	1	
&About MenuDem...	menAboutMenuDem	1	

MENUDEM.FRM Form and Control Properties

Property	Value
Form	
Caption	MenuDem
Name	MenuDem
Check Box	
Caption	Enabled (Test)
Name	Check3
Value	1 - Checked
Check Box	
Caption	Visible (Test)
Name	Check2
Value	1 - Checked
Check Box	
Caption	Checked (Test)
Name	Check1
Command Button	
Caption	Beeps...
Name	Command2
Command Button	
Caption	PopUp...
Name	Command1
Label	
Caption	Double-click anywhere on the form to pop up the Test menu...
Name	Label1

Source code for MENUDEM.FRM

```
Dim MenAryCount As Integer

Sub Check1_Click ()
    If Check1.Value = Checked Then
        menFirst.Checked = True
        menSecond.Checked = True
    Else
        menFirst.Checked = False
        menSecond.Checked = False
    End If
End Sub

Sub Check2_Click ()
    If Check2.Value = Checked Then
        menTest.Visible = True
    Else
        menTest.Visible = False
    End If
End Sub

Sub Check3_Click ()
    If Check3.Value = Checked Then
        menTest.Enabled = True
    Else
        menTest.Enabled = False
    End If
End Sub

Sub Command1_Click ()
    PopupMenu menPopUp
End Sub

Sub Command2_Click ()
    PopupMenu menPopUpNested
End Sub

Sub Form_DblClick ()
    PopupMenu menTest
End Sub

Sub Form_Load ()
    'Center form on screen
    Left = (Screen.Width - Width) / 2
    Top = (Screen.Height - Height) / 2
```

(continued)

MENUDEM.FRM *continued*

```
    'Initialize menu array
    MenAryCount = 1
    menAryDel.Enabled = False
End Sub


Sub Label1_DblClick ()
    Form_DblClick
End Sub


Sub menAboutMenuDem_Click ()
    'Display About dialog box
    About.Label1.Caption = "MENUDEM"
    About.Show MODAL
End Sub


Sub menAry_Click (Index As Integer)
    MsgBox "Menu array item" + Str$(Index) + " selected"
End Sub


Sub menAryAdd_Click ()
    MenAryCount = MenAryCount + 1
    Load menAry(MenAryCount)
    menAry(MenAryCount).Caption = "Menu Array" + Str$(MenAryCount)
    menAryDel.Enabled = True
    MsgBox "Menu array item added"
End Sub


Sub menAryDel_Click ()
    If MenAryCount > 1 Then
        Unload menAry(MenAryCount)
        MenAryCount = MenAryCount - 1
    Else
        Beep
    End If

    If MenAryCount = 1 Then
        menAryDel.Enabled = False
    End If

    MsgBox "Menu array item deleted"
End Sub
```

(continued)

MENUDEM.FRM *continued*

```
Sub menBeepOnce_Click ()
    'Beep once
    Beep
End Sub

Sub menBeepTwice_Click ()
    'Beep once
    Beep

    'Wait a half second
    DelayTime = Timer + .5
    Do
    Loop While Timer < DelayTime

    'Beep second time
    Beep
End Sub

Sub menExit_Click ()
    End
End Sub

Sub menFirst_Click ()
    MsgBox "First test item clicked"
End Sub

Sub menHelpMenuDem_Click ()
    FileMsg "MENUDEM.MSG", 1
End Sub

Sub menPopUp1_Click ()
    MsgBox "PopUp 1 selected"
End Sub

Sub menPopUp2_Click ()
    MsgBox "PopUp 2 selected"
End Sub

Sub menPopUpXY_Click ()
    'Prepare user
    NL$ = Chr$(13) + Chr$(10)
    M$ = "The Test menu will now pop up at" + NL$
    M$ = M$ + " -1000,-1000 relative to the form"
    MsgBox M$
```

(continued)

MENUDEM.FRM *continued*

```
        'Pop up at xy-coordinates relative to form
        PopupMenu menTest, -1000, -1000
End Sub

Sub menSecond_Click ()
    MsgBox "Second test item clicked"
End Sub

Sub menSub1_Click ()
    MsgBox "Cascading menu item 1 selected"
End Sub

Sub menSub2_Click ()
    MsgBox "Cascading menu item 2 selected"
End Sub
```

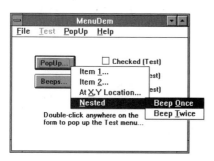

Figure 7-26.
MENUDEM.FRM in action.

## CHAPTER EIGHT

SCREEN SAVERS

This chapter demonstrates two screen saver applications: SSAVER1 and SSDOODLE. Both applications are for Microsoft Windows 3.1, and both are written completely in Visual Basic for Windows 3.

The SSAVER1 Application

SSAVER1 is a generic screen saver application. In theory, a screen saver application can be any application that has been compiled into an executable file that has the extension SCR instead of EXE. This special extension allows Windows' Desktop application (in the Control Panel) to set up the application as a screen saver that runs when no keyboard or mouse activity has been detected for a preset number of minutes.

NOTE: You can create an executable file that has the SCR extension by typing the filename, including the SCR extension, in the File Name text box of the Make EXE File dialog box. If you don't type an extension, Visual Basic adds the default extension EXE.

In practice, however, several implementation details are tricky when you create a screen saver by using Visual Basic. For example, my first screen saver attempt resulted in a program that ran multiple instances of itself after each time-out period, which eventually caused my computer to run out of resources. I solved this problem by using the application property *App.PrevInstance*. This property lets your application know whether any previous instances of itself are already running. If they are, your application can quickly unload to prevent any problems. Look at the Form_Load subprogram of SSAVER1.FRM to see how this is accomplished.

The SSAVER1 application fills the entire screen with random lines of varying thickness and color. At design time, you set several form properties to make the application full screen, with no border details: You set WindowState to *2 - Maximized*, BorderStyle to *0 - None*, and MaxButton, MinButton, and ControlBox to *False*.

Making the mouse pointer disappear is a little trickier. An API function called *ShowCursor* lets applications increment or decrement a special system-global counter that controls the visibility of the mouse pointer. If the count is greater than zero, the pointer is visible; if the count is zero or less, the pointer is hidden. Because the screen saver doesn't know the count when it starts, I added code to record the current count when the application starts and to restore this count just before the application terminates. While the screen saver runs, the count is set to zero to make the mouse pointer disappear. Take a look at the Form_Load and Form_Unload subprograms of SSAVER1.FRM to see how this is done.

The Timer control solves another tricky problem. Visual Basic won't allow an application to unload itself from within its Paint subprogram. If you try to do this, you'll get the error message "Unable to unload within this context." To allow the application to unload at any time, such as when the Form_MouseMove subprogram is activated, while still letting the Paint subprogram efficiently loop and update the graphics, I had to set up a way to inform the Paint subprogram to quit gracefully. If you take a look at the last statement of Form_Paint, you'll see that the timer is enabled. The Unload statement occurs in the Timer1_Timer subprogram, which eliminates the illegal-context problem.

Yet another operational detail must be handled if your screen savers are to exit correctly when they detect mouse movement. A Form_MouseMove event is triggered when the application first loads and when a second instance of the application loads and quickly terminates itself. To prevent the application from being unloaded when it starts up, the first occurrence of the Form_MouseMove event must be ignored; to prevent it from being unloaded when a second instance tries to run, the mouse position must be checked to see if it has really moved. I solved this problem by storing the *xy*-coordinates for the mouse position in static variables and by exiting only when these variables are nonzero and when they change value.

Windows' Desktop dialog box provides a Setup button that you can use while installing screen savers. This button simply runs the screen saver application with the command line parameter /c instead of /s, which is the parameter used when the screen saver is activated normally. A properly written screen saver should recognize the /c parameter; when /c is present, the screen saver should display its setup dialog box instead of running in its usual fashion.

The *Command$* variable lets your Visual Basic screen saver determine which command line parameter was used. The Form_Load subprogram shows how this lets you add a setup dialog box to your screen saver. For SSAVER1, there are no setup options; if a user selects the Setup button, a dialog box generated by the *MsgBox* function informs the user that there aren't any setup options, to prevent any confusion. (The SSDOODLE application, presented later in this chapter, provides an example of how setup information can be added to your screen savers.)

The files for the SSAVER1 application are included on the disk packaged with this book. To load the files into Visual Basic, choose Open Project from the File menu, and then type *C:\WORKSHOP\SSAVER1.MAK*. This opens the project and enables you to view and modify the form and code. The following figures, table, and code give the details of the application's creation.

Figure 8-1.
SSAVER1 project list.

Figure 8-2.
SSAVER1.FRM during development.

SSAVER1.FRM Form and Control Properties

Property	Value
Form	
BackColor	&H00FFFFFF&
BorderStyle	0 - None
ControlBox	False
MaxButton	False
MinButton	False
Name	Form1
WindowState	2 - Maximized

(continued)

SSAVER1.FRM Form and Control Properties *continued*

Property	Value
Timer	
Enabled	False
Interval	1
Name	Timer1

Source code for SSAVER1.FRM

```
Dim QuitFlag As Integer
Dim CursorCount As Integer

Declare Function ShowCursor Lib "User" (ByVal bShow As Integer)→
 As Integer

Sub Form_Click ()
    'Quit if mouse is clicked
    QuitFlag = True
End Sub

Sub Form_KeyDown (KeyCode As Integer, Shift As Integer)
    'Quit if any key is pressed
    QuitFlag = True
End Sub

Sub Form_Load ()
    'Record original mouse-pointer show count
    CursorCount = ShowCursor(False) + 1

    'Hide mouse pointer
    Do While ShowCursor(False) >= -1
    Loop
    Do While ShowCursor(True) < -1
    Loop

    'Don't allow multiple instances of program
    If App.PrevInstance = True Then
        Unload Me
        Exit Sub
    End If
```

(continued)

SSAVER.FRM *continued*

```
    'Process Setup button of Desktop control panel
    If Command$ = "/c" Then

        'Temporarily reshow mouse pointer
        x% = ShowCursor(True)

        'Do any user interaction
        MsgBox "No setup options for this screen saver"

        'Hide mouse pointer
        x% = ShowCursor(False)

        'Don't do any graphics during setup
        Unload Form1
        Exit Sub
    End If
End Sub

Sub Form_MouseMove (Button As Integer, Shift As Integer,
 X As Single, Y As Single)
    Static Xlast, Ylast

    'Get current position
    Xnow = X
    Ynow = Y

    'On first move, simply record position
    If Xlast = 0 And Ylast = 0 Then
        Xlast = Xnow
        Ylast = Ynow
        Exit Sub
    End If

    'Quit only if mouse actually changes position
    If Xnow <> Xlast Or Ynow <> Ylast Then
        QuitFlag = True
    End If
End Sub

Sub Form_Paint ()
    'Graphics initialization
    Scale (0, 0)-(1, 1)
    BackColor = BLACK
```

(continued)

SSAVER.FRM *continued*

```
    'Main processing loop
    Do
        'Occasionally change line color and width
        If Rnd < .01 Then
            ForeColor = QBColor(Int(Rnd * 16))
            DrawWidth = Int(Rnd * 9 + 1)
        End If

        'Draw line
        Line (Rnd, Rnd)-(Rnd, Rnd)

        'Yield execution
        DoEvents

    Loop Until QuitFlag = True

    'Can't quit in this context; let timer do it
    Timer1.Enabled = True
End Sub

Sub Form_Unload (Cancel As Integer)
    'Restore original mouse-pointer show count
    Do While ShowCursor(False) >= CursorCount
    Loop
    Do While ShowCursor(True) < CursorCount
    Loop
End Sub

Sub Timer1_Timer ()
    'Time to quit
    Unload Form1
End Sub
```

Figure 8-3.
SSAVER1.FRM in action.

The SSDOODLE Application

SSDOODLE is a full-featured screen saver application. It expands on the SSAVER1 application by adding setup capabilities and by providing a choice of six screen saver graphics styles.

The PROFILE.BAS module, which is described in Chapter 6, is loaded into this project to allow setup settings to be saved in an initialization file. This means that every time you boot up Windows, the screen saver settings will be in effect. The initialization file, named SSDOODLE.INI, is maintained in the same directory as the SSDOODLE.SCR application file.

Six unique screen savers are provided in this application. You can try them out by accessing the Desktop application in Windows' Control Panel. In the Screen Saver section of the Desktop dialog box, select *SSDoodle*, and click the Setup button. Enter a number in the range 1 through 6, and click OK. Click Test to see the currently selected screen saver. The last selected screen saver number is recorded in SSDOODLE.INI and will be the active mode until it's changed. The following figures, table, and code give the details of the application's creation.

Figure 8-4.
SSDOODLE project list.

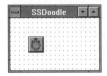

Figure 8-5.
SSDOODLE.FRM during development.

SSDOODLE.FRM Form and Control Properties

Property	Value
Form	
BorderStyle	0 - None
Caption	SSDoodle
ControlBox	False
MaxButton	False
MinButton	False
Name	Doodle
WindowState	2 - Maximized
Timer	
Enabled	False
Interval	1
Name	Timer1

Source code for SSDOODLE.FRM

```
DefInt A-Z

Dim Xai, Yai, Xbi, Ybi As Integer
Dim LineCount As Integer
Dim DoodleType As Integer

Dim Xmax, Ymax As Integer
Dim Inc As Integer

Dim ColorNum() As Integer
Dim Dx1(), Dx2() As Integer
Dim Dy1(), Dy2() As Integer
Dim Xa(), Xb() As Integer
Dim Ya(), Yb() As Integer

Dim CursorCount As Integer
Dim QuitFlag As Integer

Declare Function ShowCursor Lib "User" (ByVal bShow As Integer)→
  As Integer

Sub ColorReset ()
    'Randomize set of colors
    For i = 0 To LineCount
        ColorNum(i) = Int(16 * Rnd)
    Next i

    'Don't let doodles 5 & 6 wash out
    If DoodleType > 4 Then
        ColorNum(0) = Int(15 * Rnd) + 1
    End If
End Sub

Sub DoGraphics ()
    Static j, k, tim#

    'Shuffle line colors every so often
    If Timer > tim# Then
        tim# = Timer + Rnd * 10 + 1
        ColorReset
    End If

    'Process based on count of lines
    For i = 0 To LineCount
```

(continued)

SSDOODLE.FRM *continued*

```
'Doodles above 4 are special
If DoodleType < 5 Then

    'Keep ends of lines in bounds
    If Xa(i) <= 0 Then
        Dx1(i) = Inc * Rnd
    End If

    If Xb(i) <= 0 Then
        Dx2(i) = Inc * Rnd
    End If

    If Ya(i) <= 0 Then
        Dy1(i) = Inc * Rnd
    End If

    If Yb(i) <= 0 Then
        Dy2(i) = Inc * Rnd
    End If

    If Xa(i) >= Xmax Then
        Dx1(i) = -Inc * Rnd
    End If

    If Xb(i) >= Xmax Then
        Dx2(i) = -Inc * Rnd
    End If

    If Ya(i) >= Ymax Then
        Dy1(i) = -Inc * Rnd
    End If

    If Yb(i) >= Ymax Then
        Dy2(i) = -Inc * Rnd
    End If

    'Increment position of line ends
    Xa(i) = Xa(i) + Dx1(i)
    Xb(i) = Xb(i) + Dx2(i)
    Ya(i) = Ya(i) + Dy1(i)
    Yb(i) = Yb(i) + Dy2(i)

    'Each line has a unique color
    ForeColor = QBColor(ColorNum(i))
Else
```

(continued)

SSDOODLE.FRM *continued*

```
        'Doodle 5 & 6 lines are all same color
        ForeColor = QBColor(ColorNum(0))
End If

'Draw lines based on doodle type
Select Case DoodleType
Case 1
        Line (Xa(i), Ya(i))-(Xb(i), Yb(i))
        Line (-Xa(i), -Ya(i))-(-Xb(i), -Yb(i))
        Line (-Xa(i), Ya(i))-(-Xb(i), Yb(i))
        Line (Xa(i), -Ya(i))-(Xb(i), -Yb(i))
Case 2
        Line (Xa(i), Ya(i))-(Xb(i), Yb(i)), , B
        Line (-Xa(i), -Ya(i))-(-Xb(i), -Yb(i)), , B
        Line (-Xa(i), Ya(i))-(-Xb(i), Yb(i)), , B
        Line (Xa(i), -Ya(i))-(Xb(i), -Yb(i)), , B
Case 3
        Circle (Xa(i), Ya(i)), Xb(i)
        Circle (-Xa(i), -Ya(i)), Xb(i)
        Circle (-Xa(i), Ya(i)), Xb(i)
        Circle (Xa(i), -Ya(i)), Xb(i)
Case 4
        Line (Xa(i), Ya(i))-(Xb(i), -Yb(i))
        Line -(-Xa(i), -Ya(i))
        Line -(-Xb(i), Yb(i))
        Line -(Xa(i), Ya(i))

'Doodles above 4 are a little different
Case 5, 6
        If DoodleType = 5 Then
            Line (Xa(i), Ya(i))-(Xb(i), Yb(i)), BackColor
        Else
            Line (Xa(i), Ya(i))-(Xb(i), Yb(i)), BackColor, B
        End If

        If Xai <= -Xmax Then
            Dx1(0) = Inc * Rnd + 1
        End If

        If Xbi <= -Xmax Then
            Dx2(0) = Inc * Rnd + 1
        End If
```

(continued)

SSDOODLE.FRM *continued*

```
                If Yai <= -Ymax Then
                    Dy1(0) = Inc * Rnd + 1
                End If

                If Ybi <= -Ymax Then
                    Dy2(0) = Inc * Rnd + 1
                End If

                If Xai >= Xmax Then
                    Dx1(0) = -Inc * Rnd + 1
                End If

                If Xbi >= Xmax Then
                    Dx2(0) = -Inc * Rnd + 1
                End If

                If Yai >= Ymax Then
                    Dy1(0) = -Inc * Rnd + 1
                End If

                If Ybi >= Ymax Then
                    Dy2(0) = -Inc * Rnd + 1
                End If

                Xai = Xai + Dx1(0)
                Xbi = Xbi + Dx2(0)
                Yai = Yai + Dy1(0)
                Ybi = Ybi + Dy2(0)

                Xa(i) = Xai
                Xb(i) = Xbi
                Ya(i) = Yai
                Yb(i) = Ybi

                If DoodleType = 5 Then
                    Line (Xa(i), Ya(i))-(Xb(i), Yb(i))
                Else
                    Line (Xa(i), Ya(i))-(Xb(i), Yb(i)), , B
                End If
        End Select
    Next i
End Sub
```

(continued)

SSDOODLE.FRM *continued*

```
Sub Form_Click ()
    QuitFlag = True
End Sub

Sub Form_KeyDownPress (KeyCode As Integer, Shift As Integer)
    QuitFlag = True
End Sub

Sub Form_Load ()
    'Record original mouse-pointer show count
    CursorCount = ShowCursor(False) + 1

    'Hide mouse pointer
    Do While ShowCursor(False) >= -1
    Loop
    Do While ShowCursor(True) < -1
    Loop

    'Don't allow multiple instances of program
    If App.PrevInstance = True Then
        Unload Me
        Exit Sub
    End If

    'Process Setup button of Desktop control panel
    If Command$ = "/c" Then

        'Show mouse pointer
        x% = ShowCursor(True)

        'Get current doodle type
        Setup DoodleNumber%

        'Ask user for new doodle type
        Msg$ = "Enter a doodle type from 1 to 6."
        Title$ = "SSDoodle Type"
        DefVal$ = Str$(DoodleNumber%)
        Do
            DoodleNumber% = Val(InputBox$(Msg$, Title$, DefVal$))
        Loop Until DoodleNumber% >= 1 And DoodleNumber% <= 6

        'Save doodle number in INI file
        Setup DoodleNumber%
```

(continued)

SSDOODLE.FRM *continued*

```
            'Hide mouse pointer
            x% = ShowCursor(False)

            'Done with setup; quit for now
            Unload Doodle
            Exit Sub
        End If
End Sub

Sub Form_MouseMove (Button As Integer, Shift As Integer,↴
 X As Single, Y As Single)
    Static Xlast, Ylast

    'Get current position in same variable types
    Xnow = X
    Ynow = Y

    'On first move, simply record position
    If Xlast = 0 And Ylast = 0 Then
        Xlast = Xnow
        Ylast = Ynow
        Exit Sub
    End If

    'Quit only if mouse actually changes position
    If Xnow <> Xlast Or Ynow <> Ylast Then
        QuitFlag = True
    End If
End Sub

Sub Form_Paint ()
    'Do the one-time initializations
    Initialize

    'Main processing loop
    Do
        DoGraphics
        DoEvents
    Loop Until QuitFlag = True

    'Can't quit in this context; let timer do it
    Timer1.Enabled = True
End Sub
```

(continued)

SSDOODLE.FRM *continued*

```
Sub Form_Unload (Cancel As Integer)
    'Restore original mouse-pointer show count
    Do While ShowCursor(False) >= CursorCount
    Loop
    Do While ShowCursor(True) < CursorCount
    Loop
End Sub

Sub Initialize ()
    'A different doodle every time
    Randomize Timer

    'Set graphics parameters
    Inc = 5
    BackColor = BLACK
    Xmax = 300
    Ymax = 300
    Scale (-Xmax, -Ymax)-(Xmax, Ymax)

    'Get current doodle type
    Setup DoodleNumber%

    'Initialize for current doodle type
    Select Case DoodleNumber% - 1
    Case 0
        Caption = "Doodle1"
        LineCount = 5
        DoodleType = 1
    Case 1
        Caption = "Doodle2"
        LineCount = 4
        DoodleType = 2
    Case 2
        Caption = "Doodle3"
        LineCount = 2
        DoodleType = 3
        DrawWidth = 2
    Case 3
        Caption = "Doodle4"
        LineCount = 2
        DoodleType = 4
    Case 4
        Caption = "Doodle5"
        LineCount = 100
        DoodleType = 5
```

(continued)

SSDOODLE.FRM *continued*

```
            Xai = Xmax
            Xbi = Xmax
            Yai = Ymax
            Ybi = Ymax
        Case 5
            Caption = "Doodle6"
            LineCount = 100
            DoodleType = 6
            Xai = Xmax
            Xbi = Xmax
            Yai = Ymax
            Ybi = Ymax
        End Select

        'Do these steps for any doodle type
        SizeArrays
        ColorReset
    End Sub

Sub Setup (DoodleNumber%)
    'Set up parameters for reading and writing profile strings
    lpApplicationName$ = "SSDOODLE"
    lpKeyName$ = "DoodleType"
    lpDefault$ = "1"
    lpReturnedString$ = Space$(81)
    nSize = 81

    'INI file is in application's directory
    lpFileName$ = App.Path + "\SSDOODLE.INI"

    'Read profile string if no DoodleNumber% passed
    If DoodleNumber% = 0 Then
        n% = GetPrivateProfileString%(lpApplicationName$,→
         lpKeyName$, lpDefault$, lpReturnedString$, nSize,→
         lpFileName$)
        lpReturnedString$ = Left$(lpReturnedString$,→
         InStr(lpReturnedString$, Chr$(0)) - 1)
        DoodleNumber% = Val(lpReturnedString$)
        If DoodleNumber% < 1 Or DoodleNumber% > 6 Then
            DoodleNumber% = 1
        End If

    'Otherwise, update INI contents
    Else
        lpReturnedString$ = Str$(DoodleNumber%)
        Result% = WritePrivateProfileString%(lpApplicationName$,→
```

(continued)

SSDOODLE.FRM *continued*

```
          lpKeyName$, lpReturnedString$, lpFileName$)
    End If
End Sub

Sub SizeArrays ()
    'Dynamic array sizing for flexibility
    ReDim ColorNum(LineCount)
    ReDim Xa(LineCount), Xb(LineCount)
    ReDim Ya(LineCount), Yb(LineCount)

    'Doodles above 4 are a little different
    If DoodleType < 5 Then
        ReDim Dx1(LineCount), Dx2(LineCount)
        ReDim Dy1(LineCount), Dy2(LineCount)
    Else
        ReDim Dx1(0), Dx2(0)
        ReDim Dy1(0), Dy2(0)
    End If
End Sub

Sub Timer1_Timer ()
    'Time to quit
    Unload Doodle
End Sub
```

Figure 8-6.
SSDOODLE.FRM in action.

DATES AND TIME

Visual Basic for Windows has a rich set of built-in functions for both date and time computations. The applications in this chapter demonstrate several of these functions. The VBCAL application displays a one-month calendar for any month in the years 1753 through 2077; the TWODATES application uses VBCAL to display the number of days between two dates; and the VBCLOCK application shows how a Timer control can be used to update a clock every second.

The VBCAL Application

The VBCAL form displays a one-month calendar page and lets you select a date. Scroll bars at the bottom of the form enable you to select any year or month that is within the legal range. One day of the month is highlighted, and either double-clicking the day or clicking the OK button returns the date to the calling application.

The main part of the calendar is drawn in a single picture box. Lines divide the box into a 7-by-6 grid, suitable for even the longest month.

Visual Basic provides functions that ease calendar-programming tasks considerably. *DateSerial* and *Now* are built-in functions that return a double-precision number. *DateSerial* returns the date, over a range of years from 100 through 9999, and *Now* returns the computer's date and time. The integer part of the number returned by *Now* determines the exact date, and the fractional part determines the time of day. The built-in functions *Month*, *Day*, *Year*, and *WeekDay* operate on any serial date number to extract information from the number.

VBCAL deals only with years from 1753 through 2078. Calendars for earlier years would be incorrect because of the adoption of the Gregorian calendar in 1752. If you want to look at calendars for years beyond 2078, simply change the Max property of the year scroll bar (HScroll1).

Two global variables in VBCAL return information to the calling application. *DateSelected* is an integer flag that returns *True* or *False* (−1 or 0), depending on the button clicked to exit VBCAL. The OK button sets *DateSelected* to *True*, and Cancel sets it to *False*; these settings let the application know whether the user actually selected a date or simply canceled the dialog box. *DateNum* is a double-precision variable that contains the date selected.

The form VBCALTST.FRM is set as the startup form for the VBCAL application. It repeatedly activates the VBCAL form and displays the selected date until the user clicks the Cancel button or chooses Close from the form's menu.

To add the VBCAL form to one of your applications, add VBCAL.FRM and VBCAL.BAS to the application's project list. VBCAL.BAS contains declarations for the two global variables used to pass information to and from the VBCAL form, as demonstrated in VBCALTST.FRM.

The files for the VBCAL application are included on the disk packaged with this book. To load the files into the Visual Basic environment, choose Open Project from the File menu, and then type *C:\WORKSHOP\VBCAL.MAK*. This opens the project and enables you to view and modify the forms and code. The following figures, tables, and code give the details of the application's creation.

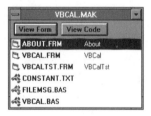

Figure 9-1.
VBCAL project list.

Source code for VBCAL.BAS

```
Global DateNum As Double
Global DateSelected As Integer
```

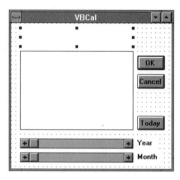

Figure 9-2.
VBCAL.FRM during development.

VBCAL.FRM Form and Control Properties

Property	Value
Form	
BorderStyle	1 - Fixed Single
Caption	VBCal
Name	VBCal
Picture Box	
BorderStyle	0 - None
Name	Pic2
Picture Box	
Height	2055
Left	240
Name	Pic
Top	720
Width	3015
Command Button	
Caption	OK
Default	True
Name	Okay

(continued)

VBCAL.FRM Form and Control Properties *continued*

Property	Value
Command Button	
Caption	Cancel
Cancel	True
Name	Cancel
Command Button	
Caption	Today
Name	Today
Horizontal Scroll Bar	
LargeChange	10
Max	2078
Min	1753
Name	HScroll1
Horizontal Scroll Bar	
LargeChange	3
Max	12
Min	1
Name	HScroll2
Label	
Caption	Year
Name	Label1
Label	
Caption	Month
Name	Label2

Source code for VBCAL.FRM

```
Dim YearNum As Integer
Dim MonthNum As Integer
Dim DayNum As Integer
Dim MarkedDay As Integer
Dim FirstTime As Integer
```

(continued)

VBCAL.FRM *continued*

```
Dim MouseX, MouseY
Dim StartDate

Sub Cancel_Click ()
    'Restore starting date
    DateNum = StartNum

    'Signal that no date was selected
    DateSelected = False

    'All done
    Unload VBCal
End Sub

Sub DrawLines ()
    'Draw lines that separate days
    Pic.Scale (0, 0)-(7, 6)
    Pic.DrawMode = COPY_PEN

    'Draw vertical lines
    For X = 1 To 6
        Pic.Line (X, 0)-(X, 6)
    Next X

    'Draw horizontal lines
    For Y = 1 To 5
        Pic.Line (0, Y)-(7, Y)
    Next Y
End Sub

Sub FillCal ()
    'Get serial date number for 1st of current month
    Serial1 = DateSerial(YearNum, MonthNum, 1)

    'Get serial date number for 1st of next month
    Serial2 = DateSerial(YearNum, MonthNum + 1, 1)

    'Calculate number of days in month
    NumDays = Serial2 - Serial1

    'Skip over blank days at start of month
    DayOffset = Weekday(Serial1) - 1
    For i% = 1 To NumDays
```

(continued)

VBCAL.FRM *continued*

```
        PutNum i% + DayOffset, i%
    Next i%
End Sub

Sub Form_Load ()
    'Default to no date selected
    DateSelected = False

    'Record starting date
    StartDate = DateNum

    'If no starting date, use current date
    If DateNum = 0 Then DateNum = Now

    'Keep track of marked day
    MarkedDay = 0

    'Extract date parts
    YearNum = Year(DateNum)
    MonthNum = Month(DateNum)
    DayNum = Day(DateNum)

    'Note that this is first time through
    FirstTime = True

    'Initialize scroll bars
    HScroll1.Value = YearNum
    HScroll2.Value = MonthNum

    'First time setting scroll bars is done
    FirstTime = False
End Sub

Sub Form_Paint ()
    'Display names of days at top
    WeekDayNames

    'Draw lines that form calendar
    DrawLines

    'Fill calendar with day numbers
    FillCal

    'Update month name
    UpdateTitle
```

(continued)

VBCAL.FRM *continued*

```
    'Mark currently selected day
    MarkDay
End Sub

Sub HScroll1_Change ()
    'Get new year number
    YearNum = HScroll1.Value

    'Redraw calendar and mark the 1st
    If FirstTime = False Then
        DayNum = 1
        Sketch
    End If
End Sub

Sub HScroll2_Change ()
    'Get new month number
    MonthNum = HScroll2.Value

    'Redraw calendar and mark the 1st
    If FirstTime = False Then
        DayNum = 1
        Sketch
    End If
End Sub

Sub MarkDay ()
    'Record day number
    TheDay = DayNum

    'Erase previous mark, and then mark current day
    For i% = 1 To 2

        'Calculate box number for day
        Serial = DateSerial(YearNum, MonthNum, 1)
        DayBox = Weekday(Serial) + DayNum - 1

        'Calculate location of box number
        X% = ((DayBox - 1) Mod 7) + 1
        Y% = ((DayBox - 1) \ 7) + 1

        'Get first corner location of box
        x1 = (X% - 1) * Pic.ScaleWidth / 7
        y1 = (Y% - 1) * Pic.ScaleHeight / 6
```

(continued)

VBCAL.FRM *continued*

```
        'Get second corner location of box
        x2 = x1 + Pic.ScaleWidth / 7
        y2 = y1 + Pic.ScaleHeight / 6

        'XOR box pixels
        Pic.DrawMode = XOR_PEN
        Pic.Line (x1, y1)-(x2, y2), QBColor(15), BF

        'Quit if no previously marked day
        If MarkedDay = 0 Then
            Exit For

        'Prepare to mark currently selected day
        Else
            DayNum = MarkedDay
        End If

    Next i%

    'Reset day number
    DayNum = TheDay

    'Record marked day for next trip through here
    MarkedDay = DayNum
End Sub

Sub Okay_Click ()
    'Build serial date number for selected date
    DateNum = DateSerial(YearNum, MonthNum, DayNum)

    'Signal that date was selected
    DateSelected = True

    'All done
    Unload VBCal
End Sub

Sub Pic_Click ()
    'Get current location of mouse
    X% = Int(MouseX) + 1
    Y% = Int(MouseY) + 1

    'Calculate which day-number box mouse is on
    DayBox% = X% + (Y% - 1) * 7
```

(continued)

VBCAL.FRM *continued*

```
    'Get serial date number for 1st of month
    Serial = DateSerial(YearNum, MonthNum, 1)

    'Get last serial date number for month
    LastDay% = DateSerial(YearNum, MonthNum + 1, 1) - Serial

    'Find day of week for the 1st
    FirstDay% = Weekday(Serial)

    'Determine day number selected
    NewDay = DayBox% - FirstDay% + 1

    'Blank box before the 1st?
    If DayBox% < FirstDay% Then
        Beep
        Exit Sub
    End If

    'Blank box after end of month?
    If DayBox% - FirstDay% + 1 > LastDay% Then
        Beep
        Exit Sub
    End If

    'Passed tests; new day selected
    DayNum = NewDay

    'Re-mark selected day
    MarkDay
End Sub

Sub Pic_DblClick ()
    'Get currently selected date
    DateNum = DateSerial(YearNum, MonthNum, DayNum)

    'Signal that a date was selected
    DateSelected = True

    'All done
    Unload VBCal
End Sub

Sub Pic_MouseMove (Button As Integer, Shift As Integer,⤚
  X As Single, Y As Single)
```

(continued)

VBCAL.FRM *continued*

```
        'Keep track of mouse location when on calendar
        MouseX = X
        MouseY = Y
    End Sub

    Sub PutNum (Square As Integer, Num As Integer)
        'Build string of day-number digits
        n$ = LTrim$(Str$(Num))

        'Calculate location of box
        X% = ((Square - 1) Mod 7) + 1
        Y% = (Square - 1) \ 7 + 1

        'Set print position
        Pic.CurrentX = X% - .5 - Pic.TextWidth(n$) / 2
        Pic.CurrentY = Y% - .5 - Pic.TextHeight(n$) / 2

        'Display day number
        Pic.Print n$
    End Sub

    Sub Sketch ()
        'Clear out previous stuff
        Pic.Cls
        Pic2.Cls
        VBCal.Cls

        'Redraw calendar
        MarkedDay = 0
        Form_Paint
    End Sub

    Sub Today_Click ()
        'Reset selected date to today
        DateNum = Now

        'Redraw calendar
        Pic2.Cls
        Pic.Cls
        Form_Load
        Form_Paint
    End Sub
```

(continued)

VBCAL.FRM *continued*

```
Sub UpdateTitle ()
    'Build long date string for selected month
    WorkDate = DateSerial(YearNum, MonthNum, 1)
    Tmp$ = Format$(WorkDate, "Long Date")

    'Peel off day of week
    Tmp$ = Mid$(Tmp$, InStr(Tmp$, ",") + 2)

    'Discard day number from string
    T1$ = Left$(Tmp$, InStr(Tmp$, " ") - 1)
    Tmp$ = T1$ + Right$(Tmp$, 6)

    'Display month and year at top
    Pic2.CurrentX = 3.5 - Pic2.TextWidth(Tmp$) / 2
    Pic2.CurrentY = 0
    Pic2.Print Tmp$
End Sub

Sub WeekDayNames ()
    'Scale for displaying seven day names
    Pic2.Scale (0, 0)-(7, 1)

    'Display each weekday name
    For i% = 0 To 6

        'Get three-letter abbreviation
        D$ = Format$(CDbl(i% + 1), "ddd")

        'Use two characters if user's font is too wide
        If Pic2.TextWidth("Wed") > 1 Then
            D$ = Left$(D$, 2)
        End If

        'Display each weekday name
        Pic2.CurrentX = i% + .5 - Pic2.TextWidth(D$) / 2
        Pic2.CurrentY = 1 - Pic2.TextHeight(D$)
        Pic2.Print D$

    Next i%
End Sub
```

211

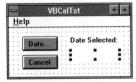

Figure 9-3.
VBCALTST.FRM during development.

VBCALTST.FRM Menu Design Window Entries

Caption	Name	Indentation
&Help	menHelpTop	0
&Help on VBCalTst	menHelpVBCalTst	1
&About VBCalTst...	menAboutVBCalTst	1
-	menSep	1
E&xit	menExit	1

VBCALTST.FRM Form and Control Properties

Property	Value
Form	
Caption	VBCalTst
Name	VBCalTst
Command Button	
Caption	Cancel
Name	Command2
Command Button	
Caption	Date...
Name	Command1
Label	
Alignment	2 - Center
Name	Label2

(continued)

VBCALTST.FRM Form and Control Properties *continued*

Property	Value
Label	
Caption	Date Selected:
Name	Label1

Source code for VBCALTST.FRM

```
Sub Command1_Click ()
    'Make a date with the user
    VBCal.Show MODAL

    'Display selected date
    If DateSelected = True Then
        Label2.Caption = Format$(DateNum, "General Date")
    Else
        Label2.Caption = "(None)"
    End If
End Sub

Sub Command2_Click ()
    'All done
    Unload VBCalTst
End Sub

Sub menAboutVBCalTst_Click ()
    'Show About dialog box
    About.Label1.Caption = "VBCAL"
    About.Show MODAL
End Sub

Sub menExit_Click ()
    'All done
    Unload VBCalTst
End Sub

Sub menHelpVBCalTst_Click ()
    'Display some Help text
    FileMsg "VBCAL.MSG", 1
End Sub
```

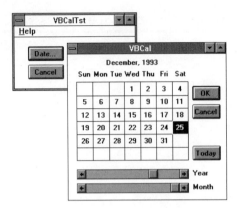

Figure 9-4.
VBCALTST.FRM and VBCAL.FRM in action.

The TWODATES Application

The TWODATES application uses the VBCAL form to select two dates and to calculate and display the number of days between the selected dates.

The VBCAL form returns the serial number of a date in the global variable *DateNum*. To find the number of days between two dates, the TWODATES application simply subtracts one serial date number from the other.

The main purpose of this application is to demonstrate further how you can easily incorporate the VBCAL form into any application so that you can use the VBCAL form to select dates in that application. The MOON application presented in Chapter 5 would also be a good candidate for the inclusion of the VBCAL form. You might recall that MOON uses a call to the *InputBox$* function to prompt for the date and that the format of the entered date has to be exactly correct. VBCAL is a more user-friendly method for entering a date.

The files for the TWODATES application are included on the disk packaged with this book. To load the files into the Visual Basic environment, choose the Open Project option from the File menu, and then type *C:\WORKSHOP\TWODATES.MAK*. This opens the project and enables you to view and modify the forms and code. The following figures, tables, and code give the details of the application's creation.

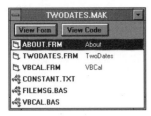

Figure 9-5.
TWODATES project list.

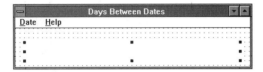

Figure 9-6.
TWODATES.FRM during development.

TWODATES.FRM Menu Design Window Entries

Caption	Name	Indentation
&Date	menDateSelect	0
&First Date...	menFirstDate	1
&Second Date...	menSecondDate	1
-	menSep	1
E&xit	menExit	1
&Help	menHelpTop	0
&Help on TwoDates	menHelpTwoDates	1
&About TwoDates...	menAboutTwoDates	1

TWODATES.FRM Form and Control Properties

Property	Value
Form	
Caption	Days Between Dates
Name	TwoDates

(continued)

TWODATES.FRM Form and Control Properties *continued*

Property	Value
Label	
Alignment	2 - Center
Caption	[none]
Name	Label1

Source code for TWODATES.FRM

```
Dim DateOne
Dim DateTwo


Sub CountDays ()
    'Both dates have been selected
    If DateOne <> 0 And DateTwo <> 0 Then
        a$ = "There are"
        b$ = Str$(Abs(DateTwo - DateOne))
        c$ = " days between "
        d$ = Format$(DateOne, "mm-dd-yyyy")
        e$ = " and "
        f$ = Format$(DateTwo, "mm-dd-yyyy")
        Label1.Caption = a$ + b$ + c$ + d$ + e$ + f$

    'Only one date has been selected
    ElseIf DateOne <> 0 Or DateTwo <> 0 Then
        Label1.Caption = "Now enter the other date"

    'No dates have yet been selected
    Else
        Label1.Caption = "Use the Date menu to enter two dates"
    End If
End Sub


Sub Form_Load ()
    'Initialize label message
    CountDays
End Sub


Sub menAboutTwoDates_Click ()
    'Show About dialog box
    About.Label1.Caption = "TWODATES"
    About.Show MODAL
End Sub
```

(continued)

TWODATES.FRM *continued*

```
Sub menExit_Click ()
    'All done
    Unload TwoDates
End Sub

Sub menFirstDate_Click ()
    'Set starting selection date
    DateNum = DateOne

    'Make a date with the user
    VBCal.Show MODAL

    'Record this date, and display message
    DateOne = DateNum
    CountDays
End Sub

Sub menHelpTwoDates_Click ()
    'Display some Help text
    FileMsg "TWODATES.MSG", 1
End Sub

Sub menSecondDate_Click ()
    'Set starting selection date
    DateNum = DateTwo

    'Make a date with the user
    VBCal.Show MODAL

    'Record this date, and display message
    DateTwo = DateNum
    CountDays
End Sub
```

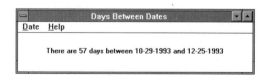

Figure 9-7.
TWODATES.FRM in action.

The VBCLOCK Application

The VBCLOCK application displays an analog clock that has the clock hands in front of a background graphical image. You can resize the form, and you can toggle on and off a digital display of the time that is drawn in the form's top left corner.

You specify the background image in the Picture property of the form, which means that you can have any bitmap, icon, or other image file as the background image. You might want to display your company logo, an advertisement, or your latest artistic efforts from Windows Paintbrush. To change the default image, specify the desired image while you are designing the application in the Visual Basic environment. To temporarily change the background image while VBCLOCK is running, open the Options menu, and then choose File. The image you select is loaded on the fly. The initial default background image is part of the Mandelbrot set, one of the fascinating fractal graphical images that can be generated by several programs that are available for Windows.

The HANDS form presents an interesting technique that lets the user select colors for the clock hands. Each of the three hands can be set to 1 of 16 colors. Rather than use a lot of buttons or lists of color names, HANDS.FRM draws 16 color squares for each hand and responds to mouse clicks on the squares. In effect, this technique demonstrates how you can substitute graphical objects of your own design for buttons.

A Timer control updates the clock hands once each second. Setting the interval property to 1000 milliseconds (1 second) would appear to be the ideal way to kick off the hand-drawing code. However, because of processing delays in the Windows operating system, the actual interval stretches to a little more than a second. As a result, every once in a while the clock stutters, or seems to skip a beat. The solution is to set the timer interval to much shorter than a second—say, to 50 milliseconds—and to make a check for elapsed system time. If the system clock has not yet reached a new second in time, the Timer1_Timer subprogram makes a quick exit. If the system clock has moved to a new second, the subprogram updates the position of the hands. This makes the clock operate much more smoothly.

The VBCLOCK form's AutoRedraw property is set to *True* to provide smooth graphics updates of the hands. All three hands are actually drawn off screen, in a copy of the form's bitmap in memory; when the screen image must be repainted, the memory image is copied onto the form. When AutoRedraw is set to *False,* the hands are redrawn on screen, and the result is not as visually appealing.

The files for the VBCLOCK application are included on the disk packaged with this book. To load the files into the Visual Basic environment, choose the Open Project option from the File menu, and then type *C:\WORKSHOP\VBCLOCK.MAK*. This opens the project and enables you to view and modify the forms and code. The following figures, tables, and code give the details of the application's creation.

Figure 9-8.
VBCLOCK project list.

Source code for VBCLOCK.BAS

```
'Global file for VBCLOCK
Global HourHandColor As Integer
Global MinuteHandColor As Integer
Global SecondHandColor As Integer
```

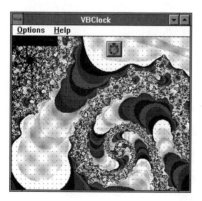

Figure 9-9.
VBCLOCK.FRM during development.

VBCLOCK.FRM Menu Design Window Entries

Caption	Name	Indentation
&Options	menOptionClock	0
&File...	menFileClock	1
&Digital	menDigitalClock	1
&Color...	menColorClock	1
&Set...	menSetClock	1
-	menSep	1
E&xit	menExitClock	1
&Help	menHelpTop	0
&Help on VBClock	menHelpClock	1
&About VBClock...	menAboutClock	1

VBCLOCK.FRM Form and Control Properties

Property	Value
Form	
AutoRedraw	True
Caption	VBClock
Icon	c:\vb\icons\misc\clock01.ico
Name	VBClock
Picture	[any bitmap of your choice]
Picture Box	
BackColor	&H00000000&
FontBold	True
FontName	Courier
FontSize	9.75
ForeColor	&H000000FF&
Name	Digital
Visible	False
Timer	
Interval	50
Name	Timer1

Source code for VBCLOCK.FRM

```
Dim Hnum As Integer
Dim Mnum As Integer
Dim Snum As Integer

Dim Hcolor As Long
Dim Mcolor As Long
Dim Scolor As Long

Dim Hlen As Single
Dim Mlen As Single
Dim Slen As Single

Dim TwoPi As Single
Dim HalfPi As Single

Sub Form_Load ()
    'Set starting hand colors
    HourHandColor = 10
    MinuteHandColor = 14
    SecondHandColor = 12

    'Center clock on screen
    Left = (Screen.Width - Width) / 2
    Top = (Screen.Height - Height) / 2

    'Pixel width of hands
    DrawWidth = 5

    'Length of hands
    Hlen = .8
    Mlen = 1.5
    Slen = 1

    'Useful conversion parameters
    Pi = 4 * Atn(1)
    TwoPi = Pi + Pi
    HalfPi = Pi / 2
End Sub

Sub Form_Resize ()
    'Rescale form when resized
    Scale (-2, -2)-(2, 2)
End Sub
```

(continued)

VBCLOCK.FRM *continued*

```
Sub Form_Unload (Cancel As Integer)
    'Also unload GetFile form
    Unload GetFile
End Sub

Sub menAboutClock_Click ()
    'Show About dialog box
    About.Label1.Caption = "VBCLOCK"
    About.Show MODAL
End Sub

Sub menColorClock_Click ()
    'Show form for selecting hand colors
    Hands.Show MODAL
End Sub

Sub menDigitalClock_Click ()
    'Toggle digital time display
    If menDigitalClock.Checked = True Then
        Digital.Visible = False
        menDigitalClock.Checked = False
    Else
        Digital.Visible = True
        menDigitalClock.Checked = True
    End If
End Sub

Sub menExitClock_Click ()
    'All done
    Unload VBClock
End Sub

Sub menFileClock_Click ()
    'Build newline string
    NL$ = Chr$(13) + Chr$(10)

    'Ask user for image file
    GetFile.Caption = "Select an image file"
    GetFile.FileTypes.AddItem "Pics (*.BMP;*.WMF;*.ICO;*.RLE)"
    GetFile.Show MODAL

    'Was a file selected?
    If GetFile.FullPath.Text = "" Then Exit Sub
```

(continued)

VBCLOCK.FRM *continued*

```
     'Check for valid file type
     Ext$ = UCase$(Right$(GetFile.FullPath.Text, 3))
     If Ext$ = "BMP" Or Ext$ = "ICO" Or Ext$ = "WMF"⌐
      Or Ext$ = "RLE" Then
         Picture = LoadPicture(GetFile.FullPath.Text)
     Else
         Beep
         Msg$ = "Filename must have extension" + NL$
         Msg$ = Msg$ + "of BMP, WMF, ICO, or RLE."
         MsgBox Msg$, 48, "Clock Background Image"
     End If
End Sub

Sub menHelpClock_Click ()
     'Show some Help text
     FileMsg "VBCLOCK.MSG", 1
End Sub

Sub menSetClock_Click ()
     'Ask user for new time
     Prompt$ = "Enter the time, using the format 00:00:00"
     Title$ = "VBClock"
     Defalt$ = Time$
     StartTime$ = Defalt$
     Tim$ = InputBox$(Prompt$, Title$, Defalt$)

     'Check for Cancel or OK with no change
     If Tim$ = "" Or Tim$ = StartTime$ Then
         Exit Sub
     End If

     'Set new time
     On Error GoTo ErrorTrap
     Time$ = Tim$
     Exit Sub

ErrorTrap:
     Msg$ = "The time you entered is invalid... " + Tim$
     MsgBox Msg$, 48, "VBClock"
     Resume Next
End Sub
```

(continued)

VBCLOCK.FRM *continued*

```vb
Sub Timer1_Timer ()
    'Keep track of current second
    Static LastSecond

    'Are we into a new second yet?
    If Second(Now) = LastSecond Then
        Exit Sub
    Else
        LastSecond = Second(Now)
    End If

    'Update time variables
    Hnum = Hour(Now)
    Mnum = Minute(Now)
    Snum = Second(Now)

    'Calculate hand angles
    Hang = TwoPi * (Hnum + Mnum / 60) / 12 - HalfPi
    Mang = TwoPi * (Mnum + Snum / 60) / 60 - HalfPi
    Sang = TwoPi * Snum / 60 - HalfPi

    'Calculate endpoints for each hand
    Hx = Hlen * Cos(Hang)
    Hy = Hlen * Sin(Hang)

    Mx = Mlen * Cos(Mang)
    My = Mlen * Sin(Mang)

    Sx = Slen * Cos(Sang)
    Sy = Slen * Sin(Sang)

    'Draw new hands
    Cls
    Line (0, 0)-(Mx, My), QBColor(MinuteHandColor)
    Line (0, 0)-(Hx, Hy), QBColor(HourHandColor)
    Line (0, 0)-(Sx, Sy), QBColor(SecondHandColor)

    'Update digital display, whether visible or not
    Digital.CurrentX = 0
    Digital.CurrentY = 0
    Digital.Print Time$
End Sub
```

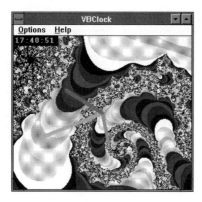

Figure 9-10.
VBCLOCK.FRM in action.

Figure 9-11.
HANDS.FRM during development.

HANDS.FRM Menu Design Window Entries

Caption	Name	Indentation
&Help	menHelpTop	0
&Help on Setting Colors	menHelpColors	1
&About VBClock...	menAboutClock	1

225

HANDS.FRM Form and Control Properties

Property	Value
Form	
Caption	VBClock Hand Colors
Name	Hands
Picture Box	
Name	Picture1
Command Button	
Caption	OK
Default	True
Name	Command1
Picture Box	
Name	Picture2
Command Button	
Cancel	True
Caption	Cancel
Name	Command2
Picture Box	
Name	Picture3
Label	
Alignment	1 - Right Justify
Caption	Hour hand
Name	Label1
Label	
Alignment	1 - Right Justify
Caption	Minute hand
Name	Label2
Label	
Alignment	1 - Right Justify
Caption	Second hand
Name	Label3

Source code for HANDS.FRM

```
Dim HourMouseX As Integer
Dim MinuteMouseX As Integer
Dim SecondMouseX As Integer

Dim HourHand As Integer
Dim MinuteHand As Integer
Dim SecondHand As Integer

Sub Command1_Click ()
    'Reset hand colors
    HourHandColor = HourHand
    MinuteHandColor = MinuteHand
    SecondHandColor = SecondHand

    'Back to clock form
    Unload Hands
End Sub

Sub Command2_Click ()
    'Cancel and don't change hand colors
    Unload Hands
End Sub

Sub Form_Load ()
    'Get current hand colors
    HourHand = HourHandColor
    MinuteHand = MinuteHandColor
    SecondHand = SecondHandColor
End Sub

Sub Form_Paint ()
    'Scale picture boxes
    Picture1.Scale (0, 0)-(16, 1)
    Picture2.Scale (0, 0)-(16, 1)
    Picture3.Scale (0, 0)-(16, 1)

    'Draw the 16 colors in each picture "bar"
    For i = 0 To 15
        'Draw colored boxes
        Picture1.Line (i, 0)-(i + 1, 1), QBColor(i), BF
        Picture2.Line (i, 0)-(i + 1, 1), QBColor(i), BF
        Picture3.Line (i, 0)-(i + 1, 1), QBColor(i), BF
    Next i
```

(continued)

HANDS.FRM *continued*

```
    'Draw check marks for current colors
    Picture1.Line (HourHand + .3, .5)-(HourHand + .5, .7),→
    QBColor(HourHand Xor 15)
    Picture1.Line (HourHand + .5, .7)-(HourHand + .8, .2),→
    QBColor(HourHand Xor 15)

    Picture2.Line (MinuteHand + .3, .5)-(MinuteHand + .5, .7),→
    QBColor(MinuteHand Xor 15)
    Picture2.Line (MinuteHand + .5, .7)-(MinuteHand + .8, .2),→
    QBColor(MinuteHand Xor 15)

    Picture3.Line (SecondHand + .3, .5)-(SecondHand + .5, .7),→
    QBColor(SecondHand Xor 15)
    Picture3.Line (SecondHand + .5, .7)-(SecondHand + .8, .2),→
    QBColor(SecondHand Xor 15)

    'Rescale for easy mouse monitoring
    Picture1.Scale (0, 0)-(1600, 1)
    Picture2.Scale (0, 0)-(1600, 1)
    Picture3.Scale (0, 0)-(1600, 1)
End Sub

Sub menAboutClock_Click ()
    'Show About dialog box
    About.Label1.Caption = "VBClock"
    About.Show MODAL
End Sub

Sub menHelpColors_Click ()
    'Display some Help text
    FileMsg "VBCLOCK.MSG", 2
End Sub

Sub Picture1_Click ()
    'Determine selected hour hand color
    HourHand = Int(HourMouseX / 100)
    Form_Paint
End Sub

Sub Picture1_MouseMove (Button As Integer, Shift As Integer,→
  X As Single, Y As Single)
    'Keep track of mouse location
    HourMouseX = X
End Sub
```

(continued)

HANDS.FRM *continued*

```
Sub Picture2_Click ()
    'Determine selected minute hand color
    MinuteHand = Int(MinuteMouseX / 100)
    Form_Paint
End Sub

Sub Picture2_MouseMove (Button As Integer, Shift As Integer,➝
 X As Single, Y As Single)
    'Keep track of mouse location
    MinuteMouseX = X
End Sub

Sub Picture3_Click ()
    'Determine selected second hand color
    SecondHand = Int(SecondMouseX / 100)
    Form_Paint
End Sub

Sub Picture3_MouseMove (Button As Integer, Shift As Integer,➝
 X As Single, Y As Single)
    'Keep track of mouse location
    SecondMouseX = X
End Sub
```

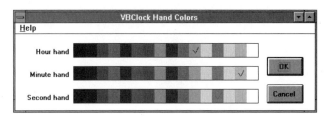

Figure 9-12.
HANDS.FRM in action.

GRAPHICS APPLICATIONS

This chapter demonstrates some of the varied and powerful graphics commands Visual Basic for Windows provides. The COLORBAR application is a useful utility for adjusting the brightness and contrast of your monitor; it demonstrates drawing graphics directly on a form. The PICIRCLE application calculates the numeric value of the constant pi by simulating the throwing of darts at a circle within a square. The FLOOD application demonstrates the use of *FloodFill*, a function available in Windows' GDI (Graphics Device Interface) dynamic link library that fills an irregularly shaped area with color.

The COLORBAR Application

The COLORBAR application fills the form with the primary 16 colors available with the *QBColor* function. Timer1 is enabled whenever the form is resized, and the Timer1_Timer subprogram then draws the 16 color rectangles to exactly fill the form. Timer1_Timer ends by setting the Enabled property of the timer to *False*, which causes the graphics to update only once per resize event.

The timer technique described above isn't the only way to get the graphics on the form. This method was chosen because it provides a convenient way to create an icon of sorts when the form is minimized. Graphics drawn directly on the face of a form show up in the icon area of a minimized form, but getting the graphics to stay there can be tricky. Try running this program and minimizing the form to see how the color rectangles are drawn on the "icon."

If you prefer to cover the whole screen with the color rectangles when adjusting your monitor, you can change the WindowState property of the form from *0 - Normal* to *2 - Maximized*.

The files for the COLORBAR application are included on the disk packaged with this book. To load the files into the Visual Basic environment, choose the Open Project option from the File menu, and then enter the filename

C:\WORKSHOP\COLORBAR.MAK. This opens the project and enables you to view and modify the form and code. The following figures, table, and code give the details of the application's creation.

Figure 10-1.
COLORBAR project list.

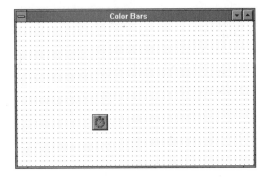

Figure 10-2.
COLORBAR.FRM during development.

COLORBAR.FRM Form and Control Properties

Property	Value
Form	
Caption	Color Bars
Name	ColorBar
Timer	
Enabled	False
Interval	1
Name	Timer1

Source code for COLORBAR.FRM

```
Sub Form_Load ()
    'Center form on screen
    Left = (Screen.Width - Width) / 2
    Top = (Screen.Height - Height) / 2
End Sub

Sub Form_Resize ()
    'Color bars will be drawn soon
    Timer1.Enabled = True
End Sub

Sub Timer1_Timer ()
    'Scale form for convenience
    Scale (0, 0)-(4, 4)

    'Fill in colors
    For x = 0 To 3
        For y = 0 To 3
            Line (x, y)-(x + 1, y + 1), QBColor(x * 4 + y), BF
        Next y
    Next x

    'One-shot drawing of color bars
    Timer1.Enabled = False
End Sub
```

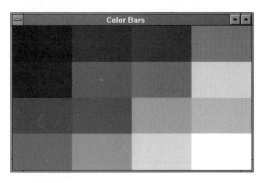

Figure 10-3.
COLORBAR.FRM in action.

The PICIRCLE Application

The PICIRCLE application calculates the numeric value of the constant pi (3.1415926...) by a graphical Monte Carlo method based on random numbers. Simulated darts are thrown at a square target; within the square is a circle that touches the midpoint of each of the square's sides. The ratio of the number of darts that land in the circle to the total number of darts thrown can be used to calculate a rough estimate for pi.

This method of finding pi is extremely slow. However, the application provides a good demonstration of using multiple timers, and it demonstrates several Visual Basic graphics methods, including *PSet* and *Circle*.

This application uses six timers. The various subprograms activated by the timer events run independently of each other in a manner that can be considered a form of multitasking. The Timer1 subprogram throws 200 darts at an interval of 1 millisecond (the smallest interval setting possible). Timer2 updates the displayed estimate for pi every 5 seconds. Timer3 randomly changes the foreground color (the color used by *PSet* to mark where each dart lands) once per minute. Timer4 redraws the circle inside the square once per second. The color of the circle changes randomly to keep it visible as the background becomes saturated with dart "holes." Timer5 and Timer6 were added, as a lark, to cause a bird to fly across the top of the form while everything else is going on. Timer5 starts the bird across the form every 30 seconds, and Timer6 flaps the wings and moves the bird five times per second.

The files for the PICIRCLE application are included on the disk packaged with this book. To load the files into the Visual Basic environment, choose the Open Project option from the File menu, and then enter the filename *C:\WORKSHOP\PICIRCLE.MAK*. This opens the project and enables you to view and modify the forms and code. The following figures, tables, and code give the details of the application's creation.

Figure 10-4.
PICIRCLE project list.

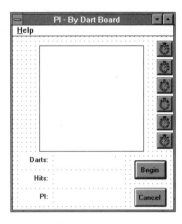

Figure 10-5.
PICIRCLE.FRM during development.

PICIRCLE.FRM Menu Design Window Entries

Caption	Name	Indentation
&Help	menHelpTop	0
&Help on PiCircle	menHelpPiCircle	1
&About PiCircle...	menAboutPiCircle	1

PICIRCLE.FRM Form and Control Properties

Property	Value
Form	
Caption	PI - By Dart Board
Name	PiCircle
Timer	
Enabled	False
Interval	1
Name	Timer1
Picture Box	
Name	Picture1

(continued)

PICIRCLE.FRM Form and Control Properties *continued*

Property	Value
Timer	
Enabled	False
Interval	5000
Name	Timer2
Timer	
Enabled	False
Interval	60000
Name	Timer3
Timer	
Enabled	False
Interval	1000
Name	Timer4
Timer	
Interval	30000
Name	Timer5
Timer	
Interval	200
Name	Timer6
Command Button	
Caption	Begin
Default	True
Name	Command1
Command Button	
Cancel	True
Caption	Cancel
Name	Command2

(continued)

PICIRCLE.FRM Form and Control Properties *continued*

Property	Value
Label	
Alignment	1 - Right Justify
Caption	Darts:
Name	Label4
Label	
Caption	[none]
Name	Label1
Label	
Alignment	1 - Right Justify
Caption	Hits:
Name	Label5
Label	
Caption	[none]
Name	Label2
Label	
Alignment	1 - Right Justify
Caption	PI:
Name	Label6
Label	
Caption	[none]
Name	Label3

Source code for PICIRCLE.FRM

```
Dim Darts As Long
Dim Hits As Long

Dim BirdX As Integer
Dim BirdY As Integer
```

(continued)

PICIRCLE.FRM *continued*

```
Sub Command1_Click ()
    'Different random numbers each time
    Randomize Timer

    'Activate timers
    Timer1.Enabled = True
    Timer2.Enabled = True
    Timer3.Enabled = True
    Timer4.Enabled = True

    'Disable Begin button
    Command1.Enabled = False
End Sub

Sub Command2_Click ()
    'All done
    Unload PiCircle
End Sub

Sub Form_Load ()
    'Center form on screen
    Left = (Screen.Width - Width) / 2
    Top = (Screen.Height - Height) / 2

    'Reset bird
    Timer5_Timer
End Sub

Sub Form_Paint ()
    'Initialize dart board
    Picture1.Scale (0, 0)-(1, 1)
    Picture1.Circle (.5, .5), .5, QBColor(Int(Rnd * 16)), , ,⇥
      Picture1.Height / Picture1.Width
End Sub

Sub menAboutPiCircle_Click ()
    'Display About dialog box
    About.Label1.Caption = "PICIRCLE"
    About.Show MODAL
End Sub

Sub menHelpPiCircle_Click ()
    'Display some Help text
```

(continued)

PICIRCLE.FRM *continued*

```
     FileMsg "PICIRCLE.MSG", 1
End Sub

Sub Timer1_Timer ()
    'Throw 200 darts each time
    For i% = 1 To 200
        Darts = Darts + 1
        x = Rnd
        y = Rnd

        'Draw dart hole
        Picture1.PSet (x, y)

        'Did it hit within circle?
        If x * x + y * y < 1 Then
            Hits = Hits + 1
        End If
    Next i%
End Sub

Sub Timer2_Timer ()
    'Update displayed numbers
    Label1.Caption = Str$(Darts)
    Label2.Caption = Str$(Hits)
    Label3.Caption = Format$(4 * Hits / Darts, " ##.00000000")
End Sub

Sub Timer3_Timer ()
    'Change dart dot color for variety
    Picture1.ForeColor = QBColor(Int(Rnd * 16))
End Sub

Sub Timer4_Timer ()
    'Redraw circle to keep it from fading away
    Picture1.Circle (.5, .5), .5, QBColor(Int(Rnd * 16)), , ,⇥
     Picture1.Height / Picture1.Width
End Sub

Sub Timer5_Timer ()
    'Release bird out to the left somewhere
    BirdX = -1000
    BirdY = 100
End Sub
```

(continued)

PICIRCLE.FRM *continued*

```
Sub Timer6_Timer ()
    'Move bird from left to right
    Const WINGSIZE = 70
    Static Toggle

    'Luke, use the toggle
    If Toggle = 0 Then Toggle = .3

    'Whitewash over previous bird image
    Line (BirdX - WINGSIZE, BirdY - Toggle * WINGSIZE)-→
     (BirdX, BirdY + Toggle * WINGSIZE), QBColor(15)
    Line -(BirdX + WINGSIZE, BirdY - Toggle * WINGSIZE), QBColor(15)

    'Toggle position of bird's wings
    Toggle = -Toggle
    BirdX = BirdX + WINGSIZE * 2

    'Draw new bird image
    Line (BirdX - WINGSIZE, BirdY - Toggle * WINGSIZE)-→
     (BirdX, BirdY + Toggle * WINGSIZE), QBColor(0)
    Line -(BirdX + WINGSIZE, BirdY - Toggle * WINGSIZE), QBColor(0)
End Sub
```

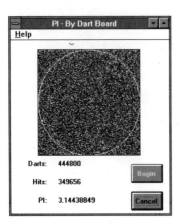

Figure 10-6.
PICIRCLE.FRM in action.

The FLOOD Application

Windows' GDI dynamic link library contains powerful graphics functions that can be called from Visual Basic applications. The FLOOD application demonstrates one of them, *FloodFill*, which fills an irregularly shaped area with a specified color.

If you have the Professional Edition of Visual Basic for Windows 3, you can find the declaration for *FloodFill* in the Windows 3.1 API Help file. Copy the declaration into the general-declarations area of the form for any program in which you want to use the *FloodFill* function.

Use the hDC property for the first parameter of *FloodFill.* The value of this property specifies the device context of the current form so that the GDI function draws in the correct window on the screen.

The *X* and *Y* parameters passed to *FloodFill* define the graphics coordinates where the color filling starts. When calling *FloodFill* from a Visual Basic application, always set the form's ScaleMode property to *3 - Pixel* to coordinate with the function. *FloodFill* interprets the *X* and *Y* values as pixel coordinates regardless of ScaleMode's setting.

This application draws an *n*-sided polygon inside the form (one of the menu options lets you change the number of vertices, or corners, of the polygon), and then the application fills the polygon with a color chosen randomly. The polygon is redrawn twice per second, as set by the Interval property of Timer1. An item in the Options menu lets you toggle between polygons that have sides of equal length (regular polygons) and polygons that have sides of varying lengths (irregular polygons).

The files for the FLOOD application are included on the disk packaged with this book. To load the files into the Visual Basic environment, choose the Open Project option from the File menu, and then enter the filename *C:\WORKSHOP\FLOOD.MAK.* This opens the project and enables you to view and modify the forms and code. The following figures, tables, and code give the details of the application's creation.

Figure 10-7.
FLOOD project list.

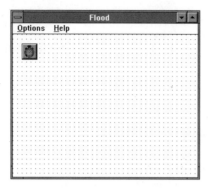

Figure 10-8.
FLOOD.FRM during development.

FLOOD.FRM Menu Design Window Entries

Caption	Name	Indentation
&Options	menOptTop	0
&Number of Vertices...	menVerticesFlood	1
&Regular Polygon	menRegular	1
-	menSep	1
E&xit	menExitFlood	1
&Help	menHelpTop	0
&Help on Flood	menHelpFlood	1
&About Flood...	menAboutFlood	1

FLOOD.FRM Form and Control Properties

Property	Value
Form	
AutoRedraw	True
Caption	Flood
Name	Flood
Timer	
Interval	500
Name	Timer1

Source code for FLOOD.FRM

```
Const PI = 3.141593
Const HALFPI = PI / 2
Const TWOPI = PI * 2
Const SMALLANGLE = HALFPI / 15
Const SIZE = 1.6

Dim Corners As Integer

Declare Function FloodFill Lib "GDI" (ByVal hDC As Integer,→
 ByVal X As Integer, ByVal Y As Integer, ByVal crColor As Long)→
 As Integer

Sub Form_Load ()
    'Default to four-cornered polygon
    Corners = 4
End Sub

Sub menAboutFlood_Click ()
    'Display About dialog box
    About.Label1.Caption = "FLOOD"
    About.Show MODAL
End Sub

Sub menExitFlood_Click ()
    'All done
    Unload Flood
End Sub

Sub menHelpFlood_Click ()
    'Display some Help text
    FileMsg "FLOOD.MSG", 1
End Sub

Sub menRegular_Click ()
    'Toggle regular polygon setting
    menRegular.Checked = Not menRegular.Checked
End Sub

Sub menVerticesFlood_Click ()
    'Let user set number of vertices
    Prompt$ = →
     "Enter the number of vertices (corners) for the polygon"
    Title$ = "Flood"
    Defalt$ = Str$(Corners)
    N$ = InputBox$(Prompt$, Title$, Defalt$)
```

(continued)

FLOOD.FRM *continued*

```
        'Set value entered by user
        Corners = Val(N$)

        'Clip number at reasonable limits
     ·If Corners < 3 Then
            Beep
            Corners = 3
        ElseIf Corners > 50 Then
            Beep
            Corners = 50
        End If
    End Sub

    Sub Timer1_Timer ()
        Static A

        'Initialization
        Cls
        Scale (-SIZE, -SIZE)-(SIZE, SIZE)

        'Rotate polygon slowly
        A = A + SMALLANGLE
        If A > TWOPI Then A = A - TWOPI

        'Set first corner point on polygon
        PSet (Cos(A), Sin(A))

        'Draw edges of polygon
        Delta = TWOPI / Corners
        For i = 1 To Corners - 1
            Angle = A + i * Delta

            'Here's the difference between regular and irregular
            If menRegular.Checked = True Then
                Length = 1
            Else
                Length = Rnd + .5
            End If

            'Draw edge line on polygon
            Line -(Length * Cos(Angle), Length * Sin(Angle))
        Next i
```

(continued)

FLOOD.FRM *continued*

```
    'Connect figure to starting point
    Line -(Cos(A), Sin(A))

    'Generate random fill color
    iRed = Int(Rnd * 256)
    iGreen = Int(Rnd * 256)
    iBlue = Int(Rnd * 256)
    FillColor = RGB(iRed, iGreen, iBlue)
    FillStyle = 0

    'Set scale mode to pixels
    ScaleMode = 3

    'Flood fill starting at center of polygon
    Xcenter% = ScaleWidth / 2
    Ycenter% = ScaleHeight / 2

    'Here's the actual API call
    Res% = FloodFill(hDC, Xcenter%, Ycenter%, 0)
End Sub
```

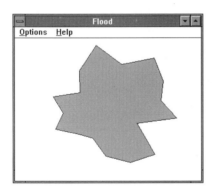

Figure 10-9.
FLOOD.FRM in action.

RANDOM NUMBERS

This chapter presents two applications. The first demonstrates some fast and efficient random-number generation functions, and the second uses these functions to help the user pick lottery numbers.

The RANDOMS Application

The RANDOMS application is a little different from most of the other applications in this book because it demonstrates several functions rather than several forms. At the heart of these routines are two techniques (described in *The Art of Computer Programming, Volume 2: Seminumerical Algorithms, Second Edition* [Addison-Wesley, 1991], by Donald Knuth) that provide for rapid generation of an extremely long sequence of random numbers. One technique generates a long random-number sequence; the other shuffles the order of the numbers.

The RANDOMS.BAS module provides the subprograms and functions for generating six types of random numbers. This module consists of code only (no form) and is intended to be loaded into a project to provide a source of random numbers.

The RandShuffle subprogram seeds the random-number generator to a given sequence. Any string that you pass to this subprogram provides the information to randomize the generator, and every unique string creates a unique sequence. To guarantee a new sequence every time, have your program create the string by using the system date and time. For example, the string *Date$ + Time$* is unique for every second, and *Date$ + Time$ + Str$(Timer)* is unique for every tick of the system clock. (The system clock ticks 18.2 times per second.)

To generate the same sequence every time, pass the same string to RandShuffle. For example, if you pass the string *SEQUENCE 1* to RandShuffle, the generator always creates the same sequence.

The *Rand* function returns a random long integer in the range 0 through 999999999. This function is extremely fast because it does not use multiplication and division operations, only addition and subtraction. The resulting sequence is extremely long because a table of 55 long integers interacts in a cyclic pattern, and a table of 42 long integers further shuffles the results. Each of the other functions calls *Rand*, and each of them modifies the resulting random integer to create the other types of random-number sequences.

RandFrac returns a single-precision number in the range 0 to 1. This function is similar to Visual Basic's *Rnd* function.

RandInteger returns a random integer in the range specified by the parameters *a%* and *b%*, which can be any integers in the range –32768 through 32767.

RandReal returns a value in the range specified by the parameters *x!* and *y!*, which contain single-precision floating-point values. For example, the call *RandReal(0.0, 1.0)* would return the same type of random number that *RandFrac* would return.

RandExponential returns a random number from an exponential distribution that has a given mean.

RandNormal returns a number from a normal distribution, given the mean and standard deviations.

The RANDOMS form demonstrates the random-number generation functions in the RANDOMS.BAS module. The Options menu provides selections for shuffling the random numbers by using either the system clock or a string entered by the user, and it provides a choice of the type of random numbers to be generated and displayed. The generated numbers are displayed on the form for review.

The files for the RANDOMS application are included on the disk packaged with this book. To load the files into the Visual Basic environment, choose the Open Project option from the File menu, and then type *C:\WORKSHOP\RANDOMS.MAK*. This opens the project and enables you to view and modify the forms and code. The following figures, tables, and code give the details of the application's creation.

Figure 11-1.
RANDOMS project list.

248

Source code for RANDOMS.BAS

```
'Array of long integers for generating all random numbers
Dim Shared r&(1 To 100)

Function Rand& ()
    'Get pointers into table
    i% = r&(98)
    j% = r&(99)

    'Subtract the two table values
    t& = r&(i%) - r&(j%)

    'Adjust result if less than zero
    If t& < 0 Then
        t& = t& + 1000000000
    End If

    'Replace table entry with new random number
    r&(i%) = t&

    'Decrement first index, keeping in range 1 through 55
    If i% > 1 Then
        r&(98) = i% - 1
    Else
        r&(98) = 55
    End If

    'Decrement second index, keeping in range 1 through 55
    If j% > 1 Then
        r&(99) = j% - 1
    Else
        r&(99) = 55
    End If

    'Use last random number to index into shuffle table
    i% = r&(100) Mod 42 + 56

    'Grab random number from table as current random number
    r&(100) = r&(i%)

    'Put new calculated random number into table
    r&(i%) = t&

    'Return random number grabbed from table
    Rand& = r&(100)
End Function
```

(continued)

RANDOMS.BAS *continued*

```
Function RandExponential! (mean!)
   RandExponential! = -mean! * Log(RandFrac!())
End Function

Function RandFrac! ()
   RandFrac! = Rand&() / 1000000000#
End Function

Function RandInteger% (a%, b%)
   RandInteger% = a% + (Rand&() Mod (b% - a% + 1))
End Function

Function RandNormal! (mean!, stddev!)
   u1! = RandFrac!()
   u2! = RandFrac!()
   x! = Sqr(-2! * Log(u1!)) * Cos(6.283185 * u2!)
   RandNormal! = mean! + stddev! * x!
End Function

Function RandReal! (x!, y!)
   RandReal! = x! + (y! - x!) * (Rand&() / 1000000000#)
End Function

Sub RandShuffle (key$)
   'Form 97-character string, with key$ as part of it
   Tmp$ = Left$("Abracadabra" + key$ + Space$(86), 97)

   'Use each character to seed table
   For i% = 1 To 97
      r&(i%) = Asc(Mid$(Tmp$, i%, 1)) * 8171717 + i% * 997&
   Next i%

   'Preserve string space
   Tmp$ = ""

   'Initialize pointers into table
   i% = 97
   j% = 12

   'Randomize table to get it warmed up
   For k% = 1 To 997

      'Subtract entries pointed to by i% and j%
      r&(i%) = r&(i%) - r&(j%)
```

(continued)

250

RANDOMS.BAS *continued*

```
        'Adjust result if less than zero
        If r&(i%) < 0 Then
            r&(i%) = r&(i%) + 1000000000
        End If

        'Decrement first index, keeping in range 1 through 97
        If i% > 1 Then
            i% = i% - 1
        Else
            i% = 97
        End If

        'Decrement second index, keeping in range 1 through 97
        If j% > 1 Then
            j% = j% - 1
        Else
            j% = 97
        End If

    Next k%

    'Initialize pointers for use by Rand& function
    r&(98) = 55
    r&(99) = 24

    'Initialize pointer for shuffle table lookup by Rand& function
    r&(100) = 77
End Sub
```

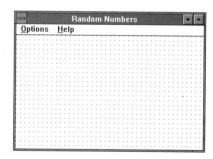

Figure 11-2.
RANDOMS.FRM during development.

RANDOMS.FRM Menu Design Window Entries

Caption	Name	Indentation
&Options	menOptions	0
&Shuffle	menShuffle	1
&Use System Time	menRanTime	2
&Enter a String	menRanString	2
&Generate	menGenerate	1
&Rand	menRand	2
Rand&Integer	menRandInteger	2
Rand&Frac	menRandFrac	2
RandRea&l	menRandReal	2
Rand&Normal	menRandNormal	2
Rand&Exponential	menRandExponential	2
-	menSep	1
E&xit	menExit	1
&Help	menHelp	0
&Help on Randoms	menHelpRandoms	1
&About Randoms...	menAboutRandoms	1

RANDOMS.FRM Form Properties

Property	Value
Form	
AutoRedraw	True
Caption	Random Numbers
Name	Randoms

Source code for RANDOMS.FRM

```
Sub Form_Load ()
    'Ensure that random numbers are shuffled at least once
    RandShuffle Date$ + Time$ + Str$(Timer)
End Sub
```

(continued)

252

RANDOMS.FRM *continued*

```
Sub menAboutRandoms_Click ()
    'Show About dialog box
    About.Label1.Caption = "RANDOMS"
    About.Show MODAL
End Sub

Sub menExit_Click ()
    'All done
    Unload Randoms
End Sub

Sub menHelpRandoms_Click ()
    'Display some Help text
    FileMsg "RANDOMS.MSG", 1
End Sub

Sub menRand_Click ()
    'Display set of random long integers
    Cls
    NL$ = Chr$(13) + Chr$(10)
    Print NL$ + "Random long integers between 0 and 1E9" + NL$ + NL$
    For i% = 1 To 10
        Print Rand(), Rand(), Rand(), Rand()
    Next i%
End Sub

Sub menRandExponential_Click ()
    'Display random numbers from exponential distribution
    Cls
    NL$ = Chr$(13) + Chr$(10)
    Print NL$ + "Random exponentials, Mean = 10" + NL$ + NL$
    For i% = 1 To 10
        For j% = 1 To 4
            Print Format$(RandExponential(10), "###.###"),
        Next j%
        Print
    Next i%
End Sub

Sub menRandFrac_Click ()
    'Display random fractional values
    Cls
    NL$ = Chr$(13) + Chr$(10)
    Print NL$ + "Random fractions between 0.0 and 1.0" + NL$ + NL$
```

(continued)

RANDOMS.FRM *continued*

```
    For i% = 1 To 10
        For j% = 1 To 4
            Print Format$(RandFrac(), "#.#########"),
        Next j%
        Print
    Next i%
End Sub

Sub menRandInteger_Click ()
    'Display set of random integers within range
    Cls
    NL$ = Chr$(13) + Chr$(10)
    Print NL$ + "Random integers between 0 and 100" + NL$ + NL$
    For i% = 1 To 10
        For j% = 1 To 12
            Print Format$(RandInteger(0, 100), "####  ");
        Next j%
        Print
    Next i%
End Sub

Sub menRandNormal_Click ()
    'Display random numbers from normal distribution
    Cls
    NL$ = Chr$(13) + Chr$(10)
    Print NL$ + "Random normals, Mean = 100, StdDev = 5" + NL$ + NL$
    For i% = 1 To 10
        For j% = 1 To 4
            Print Format$(RandNormal(100, 5), "###.###"),
        Next j%
        Print
    Next i%
End Sub

Sub menRandReal_Click ()
    'Display random floating-point numbers within range
    Cls
    NL$ = Chr$(13) + Chr$(10)
    Print NL$ + "Random reals between -1.0 and 1.0" + NL$ + NL$
    For i% = 1 To 10
        For j% = 1 To 4
            Print Format$(RandReal(-1, 1), "#.#########"),
        Next j%
```

(continued)

RANDOMS.FRM *continued*

```
        Print
    Next i%
End Sub

Sub menRanString_Click ()
    'Shuffle random-number generator by using user's string
    NL$ = Chr$(13) + Chr$(10)
    Key$ = InputBox$("Enter a string for randomizing...",
    "Randomizing", "default string")
    If Key$ <> "" Then
        MsgBox "Randomizing string: " + NL$ + Key$

        'Here's where sequence is randomized
        RandShuffle Key$
    End If
End Sub

Sub menRanTime_Click ()
    'Shuffle random-number generator by using clock
    NL$ = Chr$(13) + Chr$(10)

    'Every clock tick generates a unique sequence
    Key$ = Date$ + Space$(1) + Time$ + Str$(Timer)
    MsgBox "Randomizing string: " + NL$ + Key$

    'Here's where sequence is randomized
    RandShuffle Key$
End Sub
```

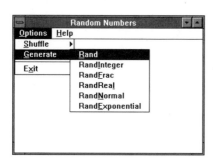

Figure 11-3.
RANDOMS.FRM in action (Options menu).

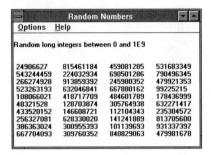

Figure 11-4.

*RANDOMS.FRM in action (*Rand*).*

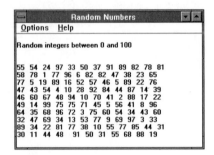

Figure 11-5.

*RANDOMS.FRM in action (*RandInteger*).*

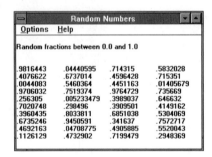

Figure 11-6.

*RANDOMS.FRM in action (*RandFrac*).*

```
┌─────────────────────────────────────────────┐
│ ▬          Random Numbers          ▼ ▲       │
├─────────────────────────────────────────────┤
│  Options   Help                              │
├─────────────────────────────────────────────┤
│ Random reals between -1.0 and 1.0            │
│                                              │
│ .3830784     .6284252    .1629389   .311985  │
│ -.166745     .9872289    .6409554   .2258677 │
│ .2938972     .01588294   .3607037   .8452657 │
│ -.01337605   .9481683    -.869702   .8125528 │
│ -.08830757   .8677064    -.3698518  -.9076849│
│ .7289765     -.9989561   -.775037   -.3772902│
│ .9347664     -.1271459   -.5442608  .8655583 │
│ -.7684357    .7339076    -.4964852  -.9106955│
│ .1950196     .5733653    .6945024   .4698465 │
│ .2629411     .695098     .9388907   -.6688338│
└─────────────────────────────────────────────┘
```

Figure 11-7.
*RANDOMS.FRM in action (*RandReal*).*

```
┌─────────────────────────────────────────────┐
│ ▬          Random Numbers          ▼ ▲       │
├─────────────────────────────────────────────┤
│  Options   Help                              │
├─────────────────────────────────────────────┤
│ Random normals, Mean = 100, StdDev = 5       │
│                                              │
│ 107.644    100.184    91.722    100.325      │
│ 105.056    98.621     99.83     102.736      │
│ 93.09      97.223     100.833   102.517      │
│ 104.296    95.451     101.009   101.783      │
│ 96.537     99.659     93.954    92.859       │
│ 90.583     97.871     100.269   96.392       │
│ 96.804     101.11     100.785   85.717       │
│ 96.529     99.293     99.859    97.56        │
│ 103.591    99.136     105.41    96.263       │
│ 96.738     104.015    98.317    97.368       │
└─────────────────────────────────────────────┘
```

Figure 11-8.
*RANDOMS.FRM in action (*RandNormal*).*

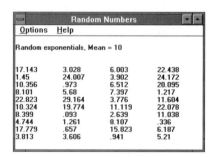

```
┌─────────────────────────────────────────────┐
│ ▬          Random Numbers          ▼ ▲       │
├─────────────────────────────────────────────┤
│  Options   Help                              │
├─────────────────────────────────────────────┤
│ Random exponentials, Mean = 10               │
│                                              │
│ 17.143    3.028     6.003    22.438          │
│ 1.45      24.007    3.902    24.172          │
│ 10.356    .973      6.512    20.095          │
│ 8.101     5.68      7.397    1.217           │
│ 22.823    29.164    3.776    11.604          │
│ 10.324    19.774    11.119   22.078          │
│ 8.399     .093      2.639    11.038          │
│ 4.744     1.261     8.107    .336            │
│ 17.779    .657      15.823   6.187           │
│ 3.813     3.606     .941     5.21            │
└─────────────────────────────────────────────┘
```

Figure 11-9.
*RANDOMS.FRM in action (*RandExponential*).*

The LOTTERY Application

Using the LOTTERY application is a "just-for-fun" way to select lottery numbers. (Of course, if you win, you might be generous enough to forward the author a small but significant percentage of the proceeds!) This program is modeled after the Colorado Lottery, but the program is fairly simple, and any modifications shouldn't be difficult. MAXNUM, for instance, is the highest number printed on the lottery machine's numbered Ping-Pong balls. For the Colorado Lottery, MAXNUM's value is 42. You can change this constant to match your own state's lottery.

The LOTTERY application provides another example of using the RANDOMS.BAS module, which was introduced in the RANDOMS application. The system date and time are used to shuffle the random numbers, which results in a unique sequence of random numbers for every clock tick. The number for a Ping-Pong ball is frozen when you click the Grab Next Ping-Pong Ball button. Each of the six Ping-Pong balls displays a number in the range 1 through 42, without repeating a number that is displayed on another Ping-Pong ball. This simulates the actual selection process fairly well.

For variety, I made this application look a little different from the other applications in this book. The Ping-Pong balls are white against a bright green background, and the numbers are displayed in a large font. This makes the form interesting to look at. It didn't take much to make these dramatic changes—I simply set the BackColor property of the form to *&H0000C000&* (bright green), displayed large-font labels on circular Shape controls, and set the FillColor property of the Shape controls to *&H00FFFFFF&* (white).

The files for the LOTTERY application are included on the disk packaged with this book. To load the files into the Visual Basic environment, choose the Open Project option from the File menu, and then enter the filename *C:\WORKSHOP\LOTTERY.MAK*. This opens the project and enables you to view and modify the forms and code. The following figures, tables, and code give the details of the application's creation.

Figure 11-10.
LOTTERY project list.

258

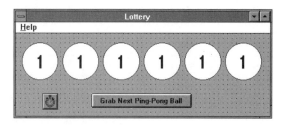

Figure 11-11.
LOTTERY.FRM during development.

LOTTERY.FRM Menu Design Window Entries

Caption	Name	Indentation
&Help	menHelp	0
&Help on Lottery	menHelpLottery	1
&About Lottery...	menAboutLottery	1
-	menSep	1
E&xit	menExit	1

LOTTERY.FRM Form and Control Properties

Property	Value
Form	
BackColor	&H0000C000&
Caption	Lottery
Name	Lottery
Timer	
Interval	100
Name	Timer1
Command Button	
Caption	Grab Next Ping-Pong Ball
Name	Command1

(continued)

LOTTERY.FRM Form and Control Properties *continued*

Property	Value
Label	
Alignment	2 - Center
Caption	1
FontName	MS Sans Serif
FontSize	24
Index	1
Name	Label1
Label	
Alignment	2 - Center
Caption	1
FontName	MS Sans Serif
FontSize	24
Index	2
Name	Label1
Label	
Alignment	2 - Center
Caption	1
FontName	MS Sans Serif
FontSize	24
Index	3
Name	Label1
Label	
Alignment	2 - Center
Caption	1
FontName	MS Sans Serif
FontSize	24
Index	4
Name	Label1

(continued)

LOTTERY.FRM Form and Control Properties *continued*

Property	Value
Label	
Alignment	2 - Center
Caption	1
FontName	MS Sans Serif
FontSize	24
Index	5
Name	Label1
Label	
Alignment	2 - Center
Caption	1
FontName	MS Sans Serif
FontSize	24
Index	6
Name	Label1
Shape	
FillColor	&H00FFFFFF&
FillStyle	0 - Solid
Index	1
Name	Shape1
Shape	3 - Circle
Shape	
FillColor	&H00FFFFFF&
FillStyle	0 - Solid
Index	2
Name	Shape1
Shape	3 - Circle

(continued)

LOTTERY.FRM Form and Control Properties *continued*

Property	Value
Shape	
FillColor	&H00FFFFFF&
FillStyle	0 - Solid
Index	3
Name	Shape1
Shape	3 - Circle
Shape	
FillColor	&H00FFFFFF&
FillStyle	0 - Solid
Index	4
Name	Shape1
Shape	3 - Circle
Shape	
FillColor	&H00FFFFFF&
FillStyle	0 - Solid
Index	5
Name	Shape1
Shape	3 - Circle
Shape	
FillColor	&H00FFFFFF&
FillStyle	0 - Solid
Index	6
Name	Shape1
Shape	3 - Circle

Source code for LOTTERY.FRM

```
Dim Flag(1 To 6)

Const MAXNUM = 42
```

(continued)

LOTTERY.FRM *continued*

```
Sub Command1_Click ()
    'Set command button caption
    Command1.Caption = "Grab Next Ping-Pong Ball"

    'Set grabbed flag for next Ping-Pong ball
    For i = 1 To 6
        If Flag(i) = False Then
            Flag(i) = True

            'Special command button caption
            If i = 6 Then
                Command1.Caption = "Start Over"
            End If

            'Don't need to check further
            Exit Sub
        End If
    Next i

    'If all were grabbed, start over
    For i = 1 To 6
        Flag(i) = False
    Next i
End Sub

Sub Form_Load ()
    'Seed random numbers
    RandShuffle Date$ + Time$ + Str$(Timer)

    'Center form
    Left = (Screen.Width - Width) / 2
    Top = (Screen.Height - Height) / 2
End Sub

Sub menAboutLottery_Click ()
    'Show About dialog box
    About.Label1.Caption = "LOTTERY"
    About.Show MODAL
End Sub

Sub menExit_Click ()
    'All done
    Unload Lottery
End Sub
```

(continued)

LOTTERY.FRM *continued*

```
Sub menHelpLottery_Click ()
    'Display some Help text
    FileMsg "LOTTERY.MSG", 1
End Sub

Sub Timer1_Timer ()
    'Check each Ping-Pong ball
    For i = 1 To 6

        'Flag is True if ball was already grabbed
        If Flag(i) = False Then

            'Generate unique number
            Do

                'Generate any number in range
                n = RandInteger(1, MAXNUM)

                'Previously grabbed?
                OKFlag = True
                For j = 1 To i
                    k = Val(Label1(j).Caption)
                    If j < i And n = k Then
                        OKFlag = False
                        Exit For
                    End If
                Next j

                'Grab only if number is unique
                If OKFlag = True Then
                    Label1(i).Caption = n
                End If
            Loop Until OKFlag = True
        End If
    Next i
End Sub
```

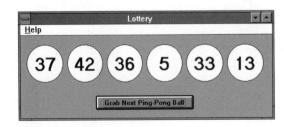

Figure 11-12.
LOTTERY.FRM in action.

UTILITY APPLICATIONS

This chapter presents a variety of utility applications for diverse tasks. FRAC-TION is a calculator designed to solve problems that involve fractions. FILEFACT displays information about a file that a user selects. The GRIDGRAF application displays tables of information, and it demonstrates Visual Basic for Windows' Grid and Graph controls. ICONVIEW lets you browse through directories of icons, and IMAGVIEW lets you scan any directory on any drive to see the icons, bitmaps, and metafiles stored there. The FILECOMP application compares files, and it demonstrates how to create a multiple-document interface (MDI) form. LZ lets you efficiently compress and expand files by using the same technology Microsoft uses for distributing software.

The FRACTION Application

The FRACTION application is a calculator designed to solve problems involving fractions. You can use it to add, subtract, multiply, and divide whole numbers, fractions, and mixed numbers. The application reduces the result to its simplest terms.

The calculator uses a reverse Polish notation (RPN) stack to store the entered values and the intermediate results of calculations. Four text boxes, ordered from bottom to top, form the X, Y, Z, and T registers, where numbers are stored. As you click buttons to enter a number, the value is built up in the X register. Operations (such as addition) work with the values in X and Y, and they store the results back in X. Because all four registers are visible, the stack manipulations are easy to follow.

You use the eight buttons in the top right corner of the form to manipulate the stack. You can move values from any register into X, or you can rotate all four values. The Undo and Last X buttons are handy for backing up a step or recovering a previous value.

As you enter numbers, you can use three special buttons in addition to the 10 digits. The CHS button changes the sign of the entire quantity. The / button inserts a slash character to separate the numerator and denominator of a fraction, and the Spc button inserts a space to separate the whole number part of a value from the fractional part. For example, to enter a value equivalent to 2.75, you would click 2, Spc, 3, /, 4. The X register would show *2 3/4*.

The Reduce key reduces a single quantity in the X register to its simplest terms. For example, 123/456 reduces to 41/152, and 1955/289 reduces to 6 13/17.

The KeyPreview form property, which was introduced in Visual Basic for Windows 2, made it easy to add keyboard capability to this application. The Form_KeyDown and Form_KeyPress subprograms check for the appropriate keypresses and then call the Click subprograms for the corresponding buttons as though the user had clicked the buttons with the mouse.

The files for the FRACTION application are included on the disk packaged with this book. To load the files into the Visual Basic environment, choose the Open Project option from the File menu, and then type *C:\WORKSHOP\FRACTION.MAK*. This opens the project and enables you to view and modify the forms and code. The following figures, tables, and code give the details of the application's creation.

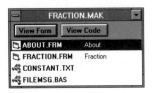

Figure 12-1.
FRACTION project list.

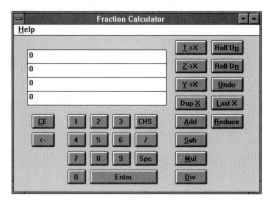

Figure 12-2.
FRACTION.FRM during development.

FRACTION.FRM Menu Design Window Entries

Caption	Name	Indentation
&Help	menHelpTop	0
&Help on Fraction	menHelpFraction	1
&About Fraction...	menAboutFraction	1
-	menSep	1
E&xit	menExit	1

FRACTION.FRM Form and Control Properties

Property	Value
Form	
BackColor	&H00C0FFC0&
Caption	Fraction Calculator
ForeColor	&H00FFFFFF&
KeyPreview	True
Name	Fraction

(continued)

FRACTION.FRM Form and Control Properties *continued*

Property	Value
Text Box	
Index	3
Name	Text1
Text	0
Command Button	
Caption	&T->X
Name	TX
Command Button	
Caption	Roll U&p
Name	RollUp
Text Box	
Index	2
Name	Text1
Text	0
Command Button	
Caption	&Z->X
Name	ZX
Command Button	
Caption	Roll D&n
Name	RollDn
Text Box	
Index	1
Name	Text1
Text	0
Command Button	
Caption	&Y->X
Name	YX

(continued)

FRACTION.FRM Form and Control Properties *continued*

Property	Value
Command Button	
Caption	&Undo
Name	Undo
Text Box	
Index	0
Name	Text1
Text	0
Command Button	
Caption	Dup &X
Name	DupX
Command Button	
Caption	&Last X
Name	LastX
Command Button	
Caption	&CE
Name	ClearEntry
Command Button	
Caption	1
Index	1
Name	Button
Command Button	
Caption	2
Index	2
Name	Button
Command Button	
Caption	3
Index	3
Name	Button

(continued)

FRACTION.FRM Form and Control Properties *continued*

Property	Value
Command Button	
Caption	CHS
Index	10
Name	Button
Command Button	
Caption	&Add
Name	Add
Command Button	
Caption	&Reduce
Name	Reduce
Command Button	
Caption	<-
Name	Backspace
Command Button	
Caption	4
Index	4
Name	Button
Command Button	
Caption	5
Index	5
Name	Button
Command Button	
Caption	6
Index	6
Name	Button

(continued)

FRACTION.FRM Form and Control Properties *continued*

Property	Value
Command Button	
Caption	/
Index	11
Name	Button
Command Button	
Caption	&Sub
Name	Subtract
Command Button	
Caption	7
Index	7
Name	Button
Command Button	
Caption	8
Index	8
Name	Button
Command Button	
Caption	9
Index	9
Name	Button
Command Button	
Caption	Spc
Index	12
Name	Button
Command Button	
Caption	&Mul
Name	Multiply

(continued)

FRACTION.FRM Form and Control Properties *continued*

Property	Value
Command Button	
Caption	0
Index	0
Name	Button
Command Button	
Caption	Enter
Name	Enter
Command Button	
Caption	&Div
Name	Divide

Source code for FRACTION.FRM

```
DefLng A-Z

Dim LiftFlag As Integer
Dim DegFlag As Integer

Dim LastStack(3) As String

Sub Add_Click ()
    Extract (Text1(0).Text), N1, D1
    Extract (Text1(1).Text), N2, D2
    N = N1 * D2 + N2 * D1
    D = D1 * D2
    If D = 0 Then Exit Sub
    SaveStack
    DropStack
    Text1(0).Text = Build$(N, D)
    LiftFlag = True
End Sub

Sub BackSpace_Click ()
    If Len(Text1(0).Text) > 0 Then
        Text1(0).Text = Left$(Text1(0).Text, Len(Text1(0).Text) - 1)
    End If
End Sub
```

(continued)

FRACTION.FRM *continued*

```
Function Build$ (Num, Den)
    'Isolate sign of fraction
    Sign = Sgn(Num) * Sgn(Den)
    Num = Abs(Num)
    Den = Abs(Den)

    'Convert fraction to its simplest terms
    LowestTerms Num, Den

    'Build fraction string
    Whole = Int(Num / Den)
    Num = Num - Whole * Den

    If Whole <> 0 Then
        X$ = LTrim$(Str$(Whole))
        If Num <> 0 Then
            X$ = X$ + " " + Str$(Num) + "/" + LTrim$(Str$(Den))
        End If
    Else
        If Num <> 0 Then
            X$ = LTrim$(Str$(Num)) + "/" + LTrim$(Str$(Den))
        Else
            X$ = "0"
        End If
    End If

    If Sign = -1 Then X$ = "-" + X$

    Build$ = X$
End Function

Sub Button_Click (Index As Integer)
    If LiftFlag = True Then
        LiftStack
        LiftFlag = False
    End If

    X$ = Text1(0).Text

    Select Case Index
    Case 0 To 9
        X$ = X$ + Chr$(48 + Index)
    Case 10
```

(continued)

FRACTION.FRM *continued*

```
        If Left$(X$, 1) = "-" Then
            X$ = Mid$(X$, 2)
        Else
            X$ = "-" + X$
        End If
    Case 11
        If InStr(X$, "/") = 0 Then
            X$ = X$ + "/"
        Else
            Beep
        End If
    Case 12
        If InStr(X$, " ") = 0 And InStr(X$, "/") = 0 Then
            X$ = X$ + " "
        Else
            Beep
        End If
    End Select

    Do While Left$(X$, 1) = " " Or Left$(X$, 1) = "0"
        X$ = Mid$(X$, 2)
    Loop

    Do While Left$(X$, 2) = "-0"
        X$ = "-" + Mid$(X$, 3)
    Loop

    If X$ = "" Then X$ = "0"

    Text1(0).Text = X$
End Sub

Sub ClearEntry_Click ()
    Text1(0).Text = "0"
End Sub

Sub Divide_Click ()
    Extract (Text1(0).Text), N1, D1
    Extract (Text1(1).Text), N2, D2
    N = N2 * D1
    D = N1 * D2
    If D = 0 Then Exit Sub
    SaveStack
    DropStack
```

(continued)

FRACTION.FRM *continued*

```
    Text1(0).Text = Build$(N, D)
    LiftFlag = True
End Sub

Sub DropStack ()
    For i% = 0 To 2
        Text1(i%).Text = Text1(i% + 1).Text
    Next i%
End Sub

Sub DupX_Click ()
    SaveStack
    LiftStack
    Text1(0).Text = Text1(1).Text
End Sub

Sub Enter_Click ()
    SaveStack
    Text1(3).Text = Text1(2).Text
    Text1(2).Text = Text1(1).Text
    Text1(1).Text = Text1(0).Text
    Text1(0).Text = " 0"
    LiftFlag = False
End Sub

Sub Extract (X$, Num, Den)
    X$ = LTrim$(X$)
    If InStr(X$, " ") = 0 Then
        If InStr(X$, "/") Then
            X$ = "0 " + X$
        Else
            X$ = X$ + "/1"
        End If
    ElseIf InStr(X$, "/") = 0 Then
        X$ = X$ + "/0"
    End If

    Spos = InStr(X$, " ")
    Whole = Val(Left$(X$, Spos))
    Num = Val(Mid$(X$, Spos + 1))
    Den = Val(Mid$(X$, InStr(X$, "/") + 1))
```

(continued)

275

FRACTION.FRM *continued*

```
    If Whole < 0 Then
        Num = -Num
    End If

    Num = Num + Whole * Den

    If Den = 0 Then
        MsgBox "Undefined fraction; denominator = 0", 48, "Fraction"
    End If
End Sub

Sub Form_KeyDown (KeyCode As Integer, Shift As Integer)
    If KeyCode = 32 Then
        X$ = Text1(0).Text
        If InStr(X$, " ") = 0 And InStr(X$, "/") = 0 Then
            X$ = X$ + " "
        Else
            Beep
        End If
        Text1(0).Text = X$
        KeyCode = 0
    End If
End Sub

Sub Form_KeyPress (KeyAscii As Integer)
    Select Case LCase$(Chr$(KeyAscii))
    Case "t"
        TX_Click
    Case "z"
        ZX_Click
    Case "y"
        YX_Click
    Case "x"
        DupX_Click
    Case "p"
        RollUp_Click
    Case "n"
        RollDn_Click
    Case "u"
        Undo_Click
    Case "l"
        LastX_Click
    Case "r"
```

(continued)

276

FRACTION.FRM *continued*

```
            Reduce_Click
        Case "a"
            Add_Click
        Case "s"
            Subtract_Click
        Case "m"
            Multiply_Click
        Case "d"
            Divide_Click
        Case "c"
            ClearEntry_Click
        Case Chr$(8)
            Backspace_Click
        Case "0" To "9"
            Button_Click KeyAscii - 48
        Case "-"
            Button_Click 10
        Case "/"
            Button_Click 11
    End Select
    Enter.SetFocus
End Sub

Sub Form_Load ()
    'Initialization
    LiftFlag = False
    SaveStack

    'Center form
    Left = (Screen.Width - Width) / 2
    Top = (Screen.Height - Height) / 2

    'Set focus to Enter button
    Show
    Enter.SetFocus
End Sub

Sub LastX_Click ()
    LiftStack
    Text1(0).Text = LastStack(0)
End Sub
```

(continued)

FRACTION.FRM *continued*

```
Sub LiftStack ()
    For i% = 3 To 1 Step -1
        Text1(i%).Text = Text1(i% - 1).Text
    Next i%
    Text1(0).Text = "0"
End Sub


Sub LowestTerms (Num, Den)
    s = Num
    t = Den
    Do
        u = Int(s / t) * t
        u = s - u
        s = t
        t = u
    Loop While u > 0
    Num = Num / s
    Den = Den / s
End Sub


Sub menAboutFraction_Click ()
    About.Label1.Caption = "FRACTION"
    About.Show MODAL
End Sub


Sub menExit_Click ()
    Unload Fraction
End Sub


Sub menHelpFraction_Click ()
    'Show three pages of Help information
    For i% = 1 To 3
        FileMsg "FRACTION.MSG", i%
    Next i%
End Sub


Sub Multiply_Click ()
    Extract (Text1(0).Text), N1, D1
    Extract (Text1(1).Text), N2, D2
    N = N1 * N2
    D = D1 * D2
    If D = 0 Then Exit Sub
    SaveStack
    DropStack
```

(continued)

FRACTION.FRM *continued*

```
    Text1(0).Text = Build$(N, D)
    LiftFlag = True
End Sub

Sub Reduce_Click ()
    Extract (Text1(0).Text), N, D
    If D = 0 Then Exit Sub
    SaveStack
    Text1(0).Text = Build$(N, D)
    LiftFlag = True
End Sub

Sub RestoreStack ()
    For i% = 0 To 3
        Text1(i%).Text = LastStack(i%)
    Next i%
End Sub

Sub RollDn_Click ()
    SaveStack
    DropStack
    Text1(3).Text = LastStack(0)
End Sub

Sub RollUp_Click ()
    SaveStack
    LiftStack
    Text1(0).Text = LastStack(3)
End Sub

Sub SaveStack ()
    For i% = 0 To 3
        LastStack(i%) = Text1(i%).Text
    Next i%
End Sub

Sub Subtract_Click ()
    Extract (Text1(0).Text), N1, D1
    Extract (Text1(1).Text), N2, D2
    N = N2 * D1 - N1 * D2
    D = D1 * D2
    If D = 0 Then Exit Sub
    SaveStack
    DropStack
    Text1(0).Text = Build$(N, D)
    LiftFlag = True
End Sub
```

(continued)

FRACTION.FRM *continued*

```
Sub Text1_KeyPress (Index As Integer, KeyAscii As Integer)
    KeyAscii = 0
End Sub

Sub TX_Click ()
    SaveStack
    Tmp$ = Text1(3).Text
    Text1(3).Text = Text1(2).Text
    Text1(2).Text = Text1(1).Text
    Text1(1).Text = Text1(0).Text
    Text1(0).Text = Tmp$
End Sub

Sub Undo_Click ()
    RestoreStack
End Sub

Sub YX_Click ()
    SaveStack
    Tmp$ = Text1(1).Text
    Text1(1).Text = Text1(0).Text
    Text1(0).Text = Tmp$
End Sub

Sub ZX_Click ()
    SaveStack
    Tmp$ = Text1(2).Text
    Text1(2).Text = Text1(1).Text
    Text1(1).Text = Text1(0).Text
    Text1(0).Text = Tmp$
End Sub
```

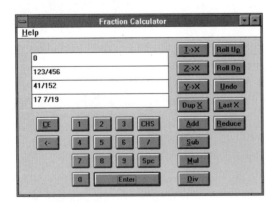

Figure 12-3.
FRACTION.FRM in action.

The FILEFACT Application

The FILEFACT application displays information about a file that the user selects. The ASCII Count button displays a table that lists how many occurrences there are of each character in the file; the Word Count button gives the number of words in the file; the Checksum button displays a checksum (a calculated value that can be used to test whether the file has been copied correctly); the Length button gives the number of bytes in the file; and the Cancel button unloads the form.

When you click the Length button, the file opens in random-access mode (any mode would work for this purpose), and the *LOF* function returns the length of the file. No data is read from the file, and the file is closed immediately after the length is determined.

To get the word count, the application opens the file for sequential input and reads in one line at a time by using the *Line Input* statement. The application parses each string from the file to get a count of the words in the string, and it displays the total word count when it reaches the end of the file.

The checksum and character-count routines access the file in a similar manner. The file is opened in binary mode, and large chunks of bytes from the file are read by using the *Get* statement. The checksum computation processes 1 byte at a time from the string buffers, and the count of bytes is also tallied 1 byte at a time. Notice that the checksum subprogram, Checksm_Click, uses a *GoSub* statement. This statement lets you build subroutines local to a subprogram or function, which can prevent the duplication of code.

The form FILFACT2.FRM is used to display the table of character counts. The table is built up as a single string that's displayed in a scrollable text box sized to fill the form. This technique is also used in the EDITBOX application in Chapter 6 and in other applications in this book. For the column headings above the text box, I've added a picture box with its Align property set to *1 - Align Top*, which causes the picture box to stretch exactly across the top of the form and align snugly against the top edge.

The files for the FILEFACT application are included on the disk packaged with this book. To load the files into the Visual Basic environment, choose the Open Project option from the File menu, and then enter the filename *C:\WORKSHOP\FILEFACT.MAK*. This opens the project and enables you to view and modify the forms and code. The following figures, tables, and code give the details of the application's creation.

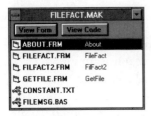

Figure 12-4.
FILEFACT project list.

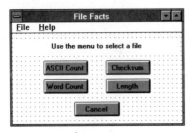

Figure 12-5.
FILEFACT.FRM during development.

FILEFACT.FRM Menu Design Window Entries

Caption	Name	Indentation
&File	menFileTop	0
&Select a File...	menSelectFile	1
-	menSep	1
E&xit	menExitFileFact	1
&Help	menHelpTop	0
&Help on FileFact	menHelpFileFact	1
&About FileFact...	menAboutFileFact	1

FILEFACT.FRM Form and Control Properties

Property	Value
Form	
Caption	File Facts
MaxButton	False
Name	FileFact
Command Button	
Caption	ASCII Count
Name	ASCIICnt
Command Button	
Caption	Checksum
Name	Checksm
Command Button	
Caption	Word Count
Name	WordCnt
Command Button	
Caption	Length
Name	Length
Command Button	
Caption	Cancel
Name	Cancel
Label	
Alignment	2 - Center
Caption	Use the menu to select a file
Name	Label1

Source code for FILEFACT.FRM

```
Dim Cnt&(0 To 255)

Sub ASCIICnt_Click ()
    'Ensure that a file was selected
    If GetFile.FullPath.Text = "" Then
        Beep
        NoFile
        Exit Sub
    End If

    'Change mouse pointer to hourglass
    MousePointer = 11

    'Open file in binary mode
    Open GetFile.FullPath.Text For Binary As #1

    'Determine size of file for reading chunks
    ChunkSize% = 32000
    N1& = LOF(1)
    N2% = N1& \ ChunkSize%
    N3% = N1& Mod ChunkSize%

    'Read in and process each big chunk
    Chunk$ = Space$(ChunkSize%)
    For i% = 1 To N2%
        Get #1, , Chunk$
        ByteCount Chunk$
    Next i%

    'Read smaller leftover chunk
    Chunk$ = Space$(N3%)
    Get #1, , Chunk$
    ByteCount Chunk$

    'Close file
    Close #1

    'Build string to display ASCII count
    NL$ = Chr$(13) + Chr$(10)
    TB$ = Chr$(9)
```

(continued)

FILEFACT.FRM *continued*

```
      For i% = 0 To 255
          If Cnt&(i%) Then
              StringShow$ = StringShow$ + Str$(i%) + TB$ + →
              Hex$(i%) + TB$ + Str$(Cnt&(i%)) + NL$
          End If
      Next i%

      'Display string in other form's Text Box control
      FilFact2.Text1.Text = StringShow$

      'Change mouse pointer back to default
      MousePointer = 0

      'Display results
      FilFact2.Show MODAL
  End Sub

  Sub ByteCount (Chunk$)
      'Total bytes in string
      For i% = 1 To Len(Chunk$)
          j% = Asc(Mid$(Chunk$, i%, 1))
          Cnt&(j%) = Cnt&(j%) + 1
      Next i%
  End Sub

  Sub Cancel_Click ()
      'All done
      Unload FileFact
  End Sub

  Sub Checksm_Click ()
      'Set size of file pieces to process
      Const Chunk = 10000

      'Ensure that a file was selected
      If GetFile.FullPath.Text = "" Then
          Beep
          NoFile
          Exit Sub
      End If
```

(continued)

FILEFACT.FRM *continued*

```
    'Change mouse pointer to hourglass
    MousePointer = 11

    'Open file in binary mode
    Open GetFile.FullPath.Text For Binary As #1

    'Process all bytes of file
    LenFil = LOF(1)
    A$ = Space$(Chunk)
    Do While LenFil > Chunk
        Get #1, , A$

        'Call local subroutine
        GoSub ProcessString
        LenFil = LenFil - Chunk
    Loop

    'Process last chunk of file
    A$ = Space$(LenFil)
    Get #1, , A$
    GoSub ProcessString

    'Close file
    Close #1

    'Change mouse pointer back to default
    MousePointer = 0

    'Display resulting checksum
    Msg$ = "File checksum is" + Str$(CheckSum)
    MsgBox Msg$, 64, "File Facts"

    'Don't fall into local subroutine
    Exit Sub

ProcessString:

    'Modify checksum for each file byte
    For i = 1 To Len(A$)
        Byte = Asc(Mid$(A$, i, 1))
        CheckSum = ((CheckSum Xor Byte) + i) Mod 100000
    Next i
```

(continued)

FILEFACT.FRM *continued*

```
        'Return from local subroutine
        Return
    End Sub

    Sub Form_Unload (Cancel As Integer)
        'Unload GetFile form
        Unload GetFile
    End Sub

    Sub Length_Click ()
        'Ensure that a file was selected
        If GetFile.FullPath.Text = "" Then
            Beep
            NoFile
            Exit Sub
        End If

        'Change mouse pointer to hourglass
        MousePointer = 11

        'Open file in random-access mode and get length
        Open GetFile.FullPath.Text For Random As #1
        FilLen& = LOF(1)

        'Close file
        Close #1

        'Change mouse pointer back to default
        MousePointer = 0

        'Display length of file
        Msg$ = "Length of the file is" + Str$(FilLen&) + " bytes."
        MsgBox Msg$, 64, "File Facts"
    End Sub

    Sub menAboutFileFact_Click ()
        'Display About dialog box
        About.Label1.Caption = "FILEFACT"
        About.Show MODAL
    End Sub
```

(continued)

FILEFACT.FRM *continued*

```
Sub menExitFileFact_Click ()
    'All done
    Unload FileFact
End Sub

Sub menHelpFileFact_Click ()
    'Display some Help text
    FileMsg "FILEFACT.MSG", 1
End Sub

Sub menSelectFile_Click ()
    'Use GetFile form to get filename from user
    GetFile.Caption = "Select file for FileFact"
    GetFile.Show MODAL

    'Show selected filename
    Label1.Caption = GetFile.FullPath.Text
End Sub

Sub NoFile ()
    'Notify user that no file has been selected
    Msg$ = "You must select a file first."
    MsgBox Msg$, 48, "File Facts"
End Sub

Sub WordCnt_Click ()
    'Ensure that a file was selected
    If GetFile.FullPath.Text = "" Then
        Beep
        NoFile
        Exit Sub
    End If

    'Change mouse pointer to hourglass
    MousePointer = 11

    'Open file in sequential input mode
    Open GetFile.FullPath.Text For Input As #1

    'Define space, tab, and comma as word separators
    Sep$ = " " + Chr$(9) + ","

    'Read in and process each line
    Do
```

(continued)

FILEFACT.FRM *continued*

```
        Line Input #1, A$
        TotalCount& = TotalCount& + WordCount(A$, Sep$)
    Loop Until EOF(1)

    'Close file
    Close #1

    'Change mouse pointer back to default
    MousePointer = 0

    'Display word count
    Msg$ = "Number of words is" + Str$(TotalCount&)
    MsgBox Msg$, 64, "File Facts"
End Sub

Function WordCount (A$, Sep$)
    'Initialize some variables
    Number = 0
    Flag% = 0
    LenStr% = Len(A$)

    'Proceed if both parameters have valid contents
    If LenStr% > 0 And Sep$ <> "" Then

        'Process each character in string
        For i% = 1 To LenStr%

            'Count each separator character...
            If InStr(Sep$, Mid$(A$, i%, 1)) Then

                '...but only one count per grouping
                If Flag% Then
                    Flag% = 0
                    Number = Number + 1
                End If

            'Reset flag if not in separator group
            Else
                Flag% = 1
            End If
        Next i%
    End If

    'Return number of words counted
    WordCount = Number + Flag%
End Function
```

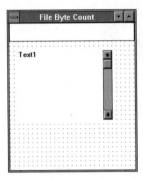

Figure 12-6.
FILFACT2.FRM during development.

FILFACT2.FRM Form and Control Properties

Property	Value
Form	
BorderStyle	3 - Fixed Double
Caption	File Byte Count
MaxButton	False
MinButton	False
Name	FilFact2
ScaleMode	4 - Character
Picture Box	
Align	1 - Align Top
Height	2
Name	Picture1
Text Box	
BorderStyle	0 - None
MultiLine	True
Name	Text1
ScrollBars	2 - Vertical
Text	Text1

Source code for FILFACT2.FRM

```
Sub Form_Load ()
    'Size text box to fill form
    P = Picture1.Height
    W = ScaleWidth
    H = ScaleHeight - P
    Text1.Move 0, P, W, H
End Sub

Sub Form_Paint ()
    'Display caption near top of form
    Picture1.Cls
    Picture1.Print GetFile.FullPath.Text
    Picture1.Print "Dec        Hex        Count"
End Sub
```

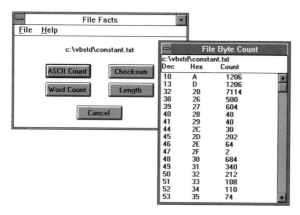

Figure 12-7.
FILEFACT.FRM and FILFACT2.FRM in action.

The GRIDGRAF Application

The GRIDGRAF application demonstrates two controls that were introduced in Visual Basic for Windows 2: the Grid control and the Graph control. (The Graph control is available only in the Professional Editions of Visual Basic for Windows 2 and 3.)

The Grid control provides a convenient way to display information in rows and columns, much like a spreadsheet application. Not only numbers but also strings and bit-mapped images can be displayed in each cell of a Grid control. In this application, data is read from a file named GRIDGRAF.DAT and placed in a grid set up with two columns and as many rows as there are data items in the file. The first column is a text label, and the second column is a numeric amount. For our example, the labels are various fruits, and the amounts are quantities of the indicated fruit. The Form_Load subprogram contains the code that loads the data into the grid.

After the data is loaded into the grid, the Graph control uses the data to generate a graph. At first the GraphStyle property is set to *0 - Default* and the GraphType property is set to *2 - 3D Pie*, but the application allows you to experiment with many other combinations of GraphStyle and GraphType settings. Below the graph are two command buttons that let you cycle through the various settings for these two properties. (A few of the settings are skipped because the data used in this example won't work for all graph types.)

Three buttons to the left of the graph let you copy the graph to the Clipboard, send it to a file, or send it to a printer. Each of these tasks is accomplished simply by setting a number in the graph's DrawMode property. Sending the graph to a printer this way results in a higher-resolution printout than is usually the case when you copy a screen capture to the Paintbrush application or use a similar technique.

You can edit GRIDGRAF.DAT, but be sure to keep the same two-column format for the data contents unless you plan to make a considerable number of modifications to the application. If more than nine fruits are listed in the file, scroll bars appear on the grid. This allows the grid to handle many more rows than would fit comfortably on the form.

The files for the GRIDGRAF application are included on the disk packaged with this book. To load the files into the Visual Basic environment, choose the Open Project option from the File menu, and then enter the filename *C:\WORKSHOP\GRIDGRAF.MAK*. This opens the project and enables you to view and modify the forms and code. The following figures, tables, and code give the details of the application's creation.

Figure 12-8.
GRIDGRAF project list.

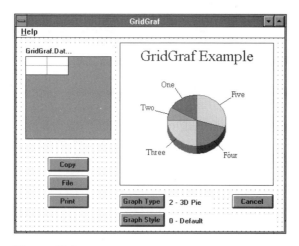

Figure 12-9.
GRIDGRAF.FRM during development.

GRIDGRAF.FRM Menu Design Window Entries

Caption	Name	Indentation
&Help	menHelp	0
&Help on GridGraf	menHelpGridGraf	1
&About GridGraf...	menAboutGridGraf	1
-	menSep	1
E&xit	menExit	1

GRIDGRAF.FRM Form and Control Properties

Property	Value
Form	
Caption	GridGraf
Name	GridGraf
Command Button	
Caption	Copy
Name	cmdCopy

(continued)

293

GRIDGRAF.FRM Form and Control Properties *continued*

Property	Value
Command Button	
Caption	File
Name	cmdFile
Command Button	
Caption	Print
Name	cmdPrint
Command Button	
Caption	Graph Style
Name	cmdStyle
Command Button	
Caption	Graph Type
Name	cmdType
Command Button	
Caption	Cancel
Name	cmdCancel
Graph	
GraphTitle	GridGraf Example
GraphType	2 - 3D Pie
GridStyle	1 - Horizontal
Name	Graph1
NumSets	2
RandomData	0 - Off
Grid	
FixedCols	0
FixedRows	0
Name	Grid1

(continued)

GRIDGRAF.FRM Form and Control Properties *continued*

Property	Value
Label	
Caption	0 - Default
Name	lblStyle
Label	
Caption	2 - 3D Pie
Name	lblType
Label	
Caption	GridGraf.Dat...
Name	Label1

Source code for GRIDGRAF.FRM

```
Sub cmdCancel_Click ()
    'All done
    Unload GridGraf
End Sub

Sub cmdCopy_Click ()
    'Copy graph to Clipboard
    Graph1.DrawMode = 4
    MsgBox "Graph is now copied to Clipboard"
End Sub

Sub cmdFile_Click ()
    'Make graph a bitmap
    Graph1.DrawMode = 3   '(for metafiles, delete this line)

    'Send graph to file
    Graph1.ImageFile = "GRIDGRAF"
    Graph1.DrawMode = 6
    MsgBox "Graph written to GRIDGRAF.BMP (or GRIDGRAF.WMF)"
```

(continued)

GRIDGRAF.FRM *continued*

```
    'Make graph a metafile
    Graph1.DrawMode = 2
End Sub

Sub cmdPrint_Click ()
    'Send graph to printer
    Graph1.DrawMode = 5
End Sub

Sub cmdStyle_Click ()
    'Increment style based on type
    Select Case Graph1.GraphType
    Case 1 To 4, 6, 7, 10
        Graph1.GraphStyle = (Graph1.GraphStyle + 1) Mod 8
    Case 8
        Graph1.GraphStyle = (Graph1.GraphStyle + 1) Mod 3
    Case 9
        Graph1.GraphStyle = 0
    End Select

    'Update type and style descriptions
    UpdateLabels
End Sub

Sub cmdType_Click ()
    'Increment type of graph, skipping Gantt and HLC
    Do
        Graph1.GraphType = (Graph1.GraphType Mod 11) + 1
    Loop While Graph1.GraphType = 5 Or Graph1.GraphType = 11

    'Set default graph style
    Graph1.GraphStyle = 0

    'Update type and style descriptions
    UpdateLabels
End Sub

Sub Form_Load ()
    'Size cells across Grid control
    Grid1.ColWidth(0) = Grid1.Width \ 2
    Grid1.ColWidth(1) = Grid1.Width \ 2 - 30
```

(continued)

GRIDGRAF.FRM *continued*

```
'Load data from GRIDGRAF.DAT
Open "GRIDGRAF.DAT" For Input As #1
Do Until EOF(1)

    'Read data from file
    Input #1, Lbl$, Amount

    'Add data to grid
    Grid1.AddItem Lbl$ + Chr$(9) + Str$(Amount), GridCount

    'Increment count
    GridCount = GridCount + 1

    'Turn on scroll bars if needed
    If GridCount = 10 Then Grid1.ScrollBars = 2

    'Add new rows based on file size
    Grid1.Rows = GridCount
Loop
Close #1

'Build graph data from grid data
Graph1.NumSets = 1
Graph1.NumPoints = Grid1.Rows
Graph1.AutoInc = 1

'Loop through and get label strings
Graph1.ThisSet = 1
Graph1.ThisPoint = 1
For r = 0 To Grid1.Rows - 1

    'Get label string
    Grid1.Row = r
    Grid1.Col = 0
    Lbl$ = Grid1.Text

    'Add label string to graph
    Graph1.LabelText = Lbl$
Next r

'Loop through and get amounts
Graph1.ThisSet = 1
Graph1.ThisPoint = 1
For r = 0 To Grid1.Rows - 1
```

(continued)

GRIDGRAF.FRM *continued*

```
        'Get amount
        Grid1.Row = r
        Grid1.Col = 1
        Amount = Val(Grid1.Text)

        'Add amount to graph
        Graph1.GraphData = Amount
    Next r

    'Add title to graph
    Graph1.GraphTitle = "GridGraf Example"

End Sub

Sub menAboutGridGraf_Click ()
    'Display About dialog box
    About.Label1.Caption = "GRIDGRAF"
    About.Show MODAL
End Sub

Sub menExit_Click ()
    'All done
    Unload GridGraf
End Sub

Sub menHelpGridGraf_Click ()
    'Display some Help text
    FileMsg "GRIDGRAF.MSG", 1
End Sub

Sub UpdateLabels ()
    'Update graph type description
    Select Case Graph1.GraphType
    Case 1
        lblType.Caption = "1 - 2D Pie"
    Case 2
        lblType.Caption = "2 - 3D Pie"
    Case 3
        lblType.Caption = "3 - 2D Bar"
    Case 4
        lblType.Caption = "4 - 3D Bar"
    Case 6
        lblType.Caption = "6 - Line"
```

(continued)

GRIDGRAF.FRM *continued*

```
Case 7
    lblType.Caption = "7 - Log/Lin"
Case 8
    lblType.Caption = "8 - Area"
Case 9
    lblType.Caption = "9 - Scatter"
Case 10
    lblType.Caption = "10 - Polar"
End Select

'Update graph style description
Select Case Graph1.GraphType
Case 1, 2
    Select Case Graph1.GraphStyle
    Case 0
        lblStyle.Caption = "0 - Default"
    Case 1
        lblStyle.Caption = "1 - No label lines"
    Case 2
        lblStyle.Caption = "2 - Colored labels"
    Case 3
        lblStyle.Caption = "3 - Colored labels, no lines"
    Case 4
        lblStyle.Caption = "4 - % labels"
    Case 5
        lblStyle.Caption = "5 - % labels, no lines"
    Case 6
        lblStyle.Caption = "6 - % colored labels"
    Case 7
        lblStyle.Caption = "7 - % colored labels, no lines"
    End Select
Case 3, 4
    Select Case Graph1.GraphStyle
    Case 0
        lblStyle.Caption = "0 - Default"
    Case 1
        lblStyle.Caption = "1 - Horizontal"
    Case 2
        lblStyle.Caption = "2 - Stacked"
    Case 3
        lblStyle.Caption = "3 - Horizontal stacked"
    Case 4
        lblStyle.Caption = "4 - Stacked %"
    Case 5
```

(continued)

GRIDGRAF.FRM *continued*

```
                lblStyle.Caption = "5 - Horizontal stacked %"
        Case 6
                lblStyle.Caption = "6 - Z-clustered"
        Case 7
                lblStyle.Caption = "7 - Horizontal Z-clustered"
        End Select
    Case 6, 7, 10
        Select Case Graph1.GraphStyle
        Case 0
                lblStyle.Caption = "0 - Default"
        Case 1
                lblStyle.Caption = "1 - Symbols"
        Case 2
                lblStyle.Caption = "2 - Sticks"
        Case 3
                lblStyle.Caption = "3 - Sticks and symbols"
        Case 4
                lblStyle.Caption = "4 - Lines"
        Case 5
                lblStyle.Caption = "5 - Lines and symbols"
        Case 6
                lblStyle.Caption = "6 - Lines and sticks"
        Case 7
                lblStyle.Caption = "7 - Lines, sticks, and symbols"
        End Select
    Case 8
        Select Case Graph1.GraphStyle
        Case 0
                lblStyle.Caption = "0 - Default"
        Case 1
                lblStyle.Caption = "1 - Absolute"
        Case 2
                lblStyle.Caption = "2 - Percentage"
        End Select
    Case 9
        lblStyle.Caption = "0 - Default"
    End Select

    'Force graph to redraw
    Graph1.DrawMode = 2
End Sub
```

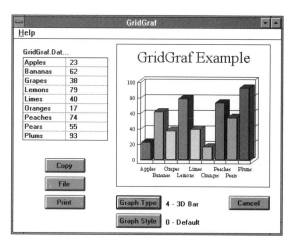

Figure 12-10.
GRIDGRAF.FRM in action.

The ICONVIEW Application

Visual Basic for Windows is shipped with several subdirectories of icons and an excellent sample application named ICONWRKS that lets you edit icon files or create icons of your own. You can load icons into Image or Picture Box controls, or you can attach icons to a form for display when the form is minimized. Icons add a nice touch to Visual Basic applications.

The ICONVIEW application demonstrates how icons can be loaded into Image controls at runtime. It also lets you easily browse through the icon directories when you're looking for an icon to fit a specific application.

To use this application, you use the Directory List Box control to select a directory that contains icons. An array of nine Image controls lets the application simultaneously display up to nine icons from the selected directory. You click the >> button to advance to the next set of nine icons in the directory, and you click the << button to view the previous set of icons. The filename of the center icon is displayed at the top of the form. You can click any of the nine displayed icons to shift that icon to the center Image control. This application lets you quickly scan a directory of icons and makes it easy to determine any icon's filename.

The files for the ICONVIEW application are included on the disk packaged with this book. To load the files into the Visual Basic environment, choose the Open Project option from the File menu, and then type

C:\WORKSHOP\ICONVIEW.MAK. This opens the project and enables you to view and modify the forms and code. The following figures, tables, and code give the details of the application's creation.

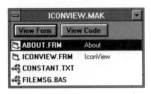

Figure 12-11.
ICONVIEW project list.

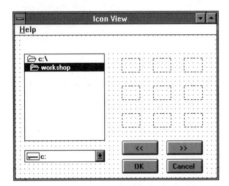

Figure 12-12.
ICONVIEW.FRM during development.

ICONVIEW.FRM Menu Design Window Entries

Caption	Name	Indentation
&Help	menHelpTop	0
&Help on IconView	menHelpIconView	1
&About IconView...	menAboutIconView	1
-	menSep	1
E&xit	menExit	1

ICONVIEW.FRM Form and Control Properties

Property	Value
Form	
BorderStyle	3 - Fixed Double
Caption	Icon View
Icon	c:\vb\icons\misc\eye.ico
Name	IconView
Drive List Box	
Name	Drive1
Command Button	
Caption	OK
Name	cmdOK
Directory List Box	
Name	Dir1
Command Button	
Caption	>>
Name	ScanForward
Command Button	
Caption	<<
Name	ScanBack
Command Button	
Caption	Cancel
Name	cmdExit
Image	
Index	8
Name	Image1
Image	
Index	7
Name	Image1

(continued)

ICONVIEW.FRM Form and Control Properties *continued*

Property	Value
Image	
Index	6
Name	Image1
Image	
Index	5
Name	Image1
Image	
Index	4
Name	Image1
Image	
Index	3
Name	Image1
Image	
Index	2
Name	Image1
Image	
Index	1
Name	Image1
Image	
Index	0
Name	Image1
Label	
Height	255
Name	Label1
Width	5055

Source code for ICONVIEW.FRM

```
Dim IconList() As String
Dim IconIndex As Integer
Dim IconCount As Integer

Sub cmdExit_Click ()
    'Force exit via menu Exit option
    menExit_Click
End Sub

Sub cmdOK_Click ()
    'OK button works like Dir double click
    Dir1.Path = Dir1.List(Dir1.ListIndex)
    Dir1_Change
End Sub

Sub Dir1_Change ()
    'Grab current directory path from list
    Directory = Dir1.List(-1)

    'If not root directory, add backslash to path
    If Right$(Directory, 1) <> "\" Then
        Directory = Directory + "\"
    End If

    'If directory contains no icons...
    If Dir$(Directory + "*.ico") = "" Then
        IconCount = 0
        ReDim IconList(0)

        '... empty images,...
        For i = 0 To 8
            Image1(i).Picture = LoadPicture()
        Next i

        '... replace displayed icon filename,...
        Label1.Caption = "Select icon directory..."

        '... and quit subprogram
        Exit Sub
    End If
```

(continued)

ICONVIEW.FRM *continued*

```
    'Get filename of first icon in directory
    IconCount = 1
    ReDim IconList(IconCount)
    IconList(IconCount) = ⟶
     LCase$(Directory + Dir$(Directory + "*.ICO"))

    'Find rest of icons in directory
    Do
        NextIcon$ = Dir$
        If NextIcon$ = "" Then Exit Do
        IconCount = IconCount + 1
        ReDim Preserve IconList(IconCount)
        IconList(IconCount) = LCase$(Directory + NextIcon$)
    Loop

    'Show first icon in directory
    IconIndex = 1
    ShowIcons
End Sub

Sub Drive1_Change ()
    'Drive selected
    Dir1.Path = Drive1.Drive
End Sub

Sub Form_Load ()
    'Center form
    Left = (Screen.Width - Width) / 2
    Top = (Screen.Height - Height) / 2

    'Force check of starting directory for icons
    Dir1_Change
End Sub

Sub Image1_Click (Index As Integer)
    'Set index to show clicked icon in center
    IconIndex = IconIndex + Index - 4

    'Keep index in valid range
    If IconIndex < 1 Then IconIndex = 1
    If IconIndex > IconCount Then IconIndex = IconCount
```

(continued)

ICONVIEW.FRM *continued*

```
        'Display set of up to nine icons
        ShowIcons
End Sub


Sub menAboutIconView_Click ()
        'Display About dialog box
        About.Label1.Caption = "ICONVIEW"
        About.Show MODAL
End Sub


Sub menExit_Click ()
        'All done
        Unload IconView
End Sub


Sub menHelpIconView_Click ()
        'Display some Help text
        FileMsg "ICONVIEW.MSG", 1
End Sub


Sub ScanBack_Click ()
        'Decrement icon list index
        IconIndex = IconIndex - 9

        'Don't go too far
        If IconIndex < 1 Then IconIndex = 1

        'Display icons
        ShowIcons
End Sub


Sub ScanForward_Click ()
        'Increment icon list index
        IconIndex = IconIndex + 9

        'Don't go too far
        If IconIndex > IconCount Then IconIndex = IconCount

        'Display icons
        ShowIcons
End Sub
```

(continued)

ICONVIEW.FRM *continued*

```
Sub ShowIcons ()
    'Show nine icons, centered at IconIndex
    For i = -4 To 4
        j = IconIndex + i
        k = i + 4
        If j > 0 And j <= IconCount Then
            Image1(k) = LoadPicture(IconList(j))
        Else
            Image1(k) = LoadPicture()
        End If
    Next i

    'Display filename of center icon
    If IconCount > 0 Then
        Label1.Caption = IconList(IconIndex)
    End If
End Sub
```

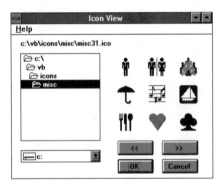

Figure 12-13.
ICONVIEW.FRM in action.

The IMAGVIEW Application

The IMAGVIEW application displays bitmap, metafile, or icon image files from any directory on any drive. An Image control displays the image, and a Check Box control lets you toggle the Image control's Stretch property. When Stretch is set to *True*, the image is stretched or shrunk to fit the size of the Image control.

To use this program, you click one of the three option buttons in the bottom left part of the form to select the type of image files to be viewed: bitmap files (BMP), metafiles (WMF), or icons (ICO). Then you use the Directory List Box control to select a directory that contains the given type of images. If any of the specified type of image files are in the selected directory, the first of these files is displayed. You can click the >> button to advance to the next image in the directory, and you can click the << button to view the previous image. The filename of the displayed image is shown at the top of the form.

The files for the IMAGVIEW application are included on the disk packaged with this book. To load the files into the Visual Basic environment, choose the Open Project option from the File menu, and then enter the filename *C:\WORKSHOP\IMAGVIEW.MAK*. This opens the project and enables you to view and modify the forms and code. The following figures, tables, and code give the details of the application's creation.

Figure 12-14.
IMAGVIEW project list.

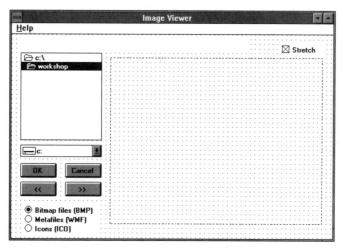

Figure 12-15.
IMAGVIEW.FRM during development.

IMAGVIEW.FRM Menu Design Window Entries

Caption	Name	Indentation
&Help	menHelpTop	0
&Help on ImagView	menHelpImagView	1
&About ImagView...	menAboutImagView	1
-	menSep	1
E&xit	menExit	1

IMAGVIEW.FRM Form and Control Properties

Property	Value
Form	
Caption	Image Viewer
Icon	c:\vb\icons\misc\eye.ico
Name	ImageView
Drive List Box	
Name	Drive1
Check Box	
Caption	Stretch
Name	Check1
Value	1 - Checked
Option Button	
Caption	Icons (ICO)
Name	Option3
Option Button	
Caption	Metafiles (WMF)
Name	Option2

(continued)

IMAGVIEW.FRM Form and Control Properties *continued*

Property	Value
Option Button	
Caption	Bitmap files (BMP)
Name	Option1
Value	True
Command Button	
Caption	OK
Name	cmdOK
Directory List Box	
Name	Dir1
Command Button	
Caption	>>
Name	ScanForward
Command Button	
Caption	<<
Name	ScanBack
Command Button	
Caption	Cancel
Name	cmdExit
Image	
Name	Image1
Stretch	True
Label	
Height	255
Name	Label1
Width	6015

Source code for IMAGVIEW.FRM

```
Dim ImageList() As String
Dim Extension As String
Dim ImageIndex As Integer
Dim ImageCount As Integer
Dim Image1Width As Integer
Dim Image1Height As Integer

Sub Check1_Click ()
    If Check1.Value = CHECKED Then
        Image1.Stretch = True
    Else
        Image1.Stretch = False
    End If
    Image1.Width = Image1Width
    Image1.Height = Image1Height
End Sub

Sub cmdExit_Click ()
    'Force exit via menu Exit option
    menExit_Click
End Sub

Sub cmdOK_Click ()
    'OK button works like Dir double click
    Dir1.Path = Dir1.List(Dir1.ListIndex)
    Dir1_Change
End Sub

Sub Dir1_Change ()
    'Grab current directory path from list
    Directory = Dir1.List(-1)

    'If not root directory, add backslash to path
    If Right$(Directory, 1) <> "\" Then
        Directory = Directory + "\"
    End If

    'If directory contains no images...
    If Dir$(Directory + Extension) = "" Then
        ImageCount = 0
        ReDim ImageList(0)
```

(continued)

IMAGEVIEW.FRM *continued*

```
        '... delete current image,...
        Image1.Picture = LoadPicture()

        '... replace displayed image filename,...
        Label1.Caption = "Select image directory..."

        '... and quit subprogram
        Exit Sub
    End If

    'Get filename of first image in directory
    ImageCount = 1
    ReDim ImageList(ImageCount)
    ImageList(ImageCount) = LCase$(Directory + Dir$(Directory + ↴
     Extension))

    'Find rest of images in directory
    Do
        NextImage$ = Dir$
        If NextImage$ = "" Then Exit Do
        ImageCount = ImageCount + 1
        ReDim Preserve ImageList(ImageCount)
        ImageList(ImageCount) = LCase$(Directory + NextImage$)
    Loop

    'Show first image in directory
    ImageIndex = 1
    ShowImage
End Sub

Sub Drive1_Change ()
    'Drive selected
    Dir1.Path = Drive1.Drive
End Sub

Sub Form_Load ()
    'Center form
    Left = (Screen.Width - Width) / 2
    Top = (Screen.Height - Height) / 2

    'Initialize for BMP files
    Extension = "*.BMP"
```

(continued)

IMAGEVIEW.FRM *continued*

```
    'Initialize Image control for stretch
    Image1.Stretch = True

    'Record original image size
    Image1Width = Image1.Width
    Image1Height = Image1.Height

    'Force check of starting directory for images
    Dir1_Change
End Sub

Sub menAboutImagView_Click ()
    'Display About dialog box
    About.Label1.Caption = "IMAGVIEW"
    About.Show MODAL
End Sub

Sub menExit_Click ()
    'All done
    Unload ImageView
End Sub

Sub menHelpImagView_Click ()
    'Display some Help text
    FileMsg "IMAGVIEW.MSG", 1
End Sub

Sub Option1_Click ()
    'Show bitmap files
    Extension = "*.BMP"
    Dir1_Change
End Sub

Sub Option2_Click ()
    'Show metafiles
    Extension = "*.WMF"
    Dir1_Change
End Sub
```

(continued)

IMAGEVIEW.FRM *continued*

```
Sub Option3_Click ()
    'Show icon files
    Extension = "*.ICO"
    Dir1_Change
End Sub


Sub ScanBack_Click ()
    'Decrement image list index
    If ImageIndex > 1 Then
        ImageIndex = ImageIndex - 1

        'Display image
        ShowImage
    End If
End Sub


Sub ScanForward_Click ()
    'Increment image list index
    If ImageIndex < ImageCount Then
        ImageIndex = ImageIndex + 1

        'Display image
        ShowImage
    End If
End Sub


Sub ShowImage ()
    'Show image
    Image1.Picture = LoadPicture(ImageList(ImageIndex))

    'Display filename of image
    If ImageCount > 0 Then
        Label1.Caption = ImageList(ImageIndex)
    End If
End Sub
```

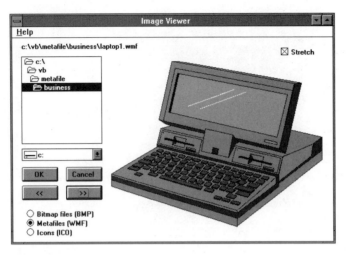

Figure 12-16.
IMAGVIEW.FRM in action.

The FILECOMP Application

The FILECOMP application provides an example of a multiple-document interface (MDI) form. By tiling the child forms side by side or vertically, you can quickly compare the contents of files that have been loaded into the child forms.

To create an MDI form such as FILECOMP.FRM, you select New MDI Form from the File menu. You create a child form by setting the MDIChild property of a form to *True.*

The FILECOMP project loads one child form, named CHILDFRM.FRM, into the development environment. However, when the application runs, multiple instances of CHILDFRM are activated, one for each file you open for comparison. The menOpen_Click subprogram in FILECOMP.FRM and the Form_Load routine in CHILDFRM.FRM show how multiple instances can be activated in this way.

When any child form has the focus, its menu replaces the parent form's menu. The FILECOMP form's menu contains only those commands necessary to open a file in a child form, to end the application, and to see some Help information. After you open a CHILDFRM form, its menu goes into action. This menu duplicates many of the choices on the FILECOMP form's menu, and it adds choices for manipulating windows. Creating this interplay of parent and child menus is a little tricky at first, but the scheme is flexible and powerful.

The options on a CHILDFRM form's Window menu allow you to rearrange the child forms in standard ways: You can cascade them, tile them horizontally, and tile them vertically. The Arrange Icons option lets you arrange the minimized child form icons. Useful constants are defined in CONSTANT.TXT for each type of Window command.

The files for the FILECOMP application are included on the disk packaged with this book. To load the files into the Visual Basic environment, choose the Open Project option from the File menu, and then type *C:\WORKSHOP\FILECOMP.MAK*. This opens the project and enables you to view and modify the forms and code. The following figures, tables, and code give the details of the application's creation.

Figure 12-17.
FILECOMP project list.

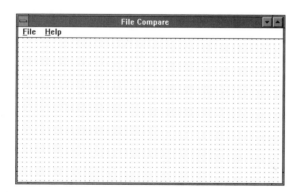

Figure 12-18.
FILECOMP.FRM during development.

317

FILECOMP.FRM Menu Design Window Entries

Caption	Name	Indentation
&File	menFile	0
&Open	menOpen	1
-	menSep	1
E&xit	menExit	1
&Help	menHelp	0
&Help on FileComp	menHelpFileComp	1
&About FileComp...	menAboutFileComp	1

FILECOMP.FRM Form Properties

Property	Value
MDI Form	
Caption	File Compare
Name	MDIForm1
WindowState	2 - Maximized

Source code for FILECOMP.FRM

```
Sub MDIForm_Load ()
    'Show parent form
    Show

    'Load first file
    menOpen_Click
End Sub

Sub MDIForm_Unload (Cancel As Integer)
    'Unload any child forms still loaded
    For i = Forms.Count - 1 To 0 Step -1
        Unload Forms(i)
    Next i
End Sub

Sub menAboutFileComp_Click ()
```

(continued)

FILECOMP.FRM *continued*

```
    'Show About dialog box
    About.Label1.Caption = "FILECOMP"
    About.Show MODAL
End Sub

Sub menExit_Click ()
    'All done
    Unload MDIForm1
End Sub

Sub menHelpFileComp_Click ()
    'Display some Help text
    FileMsg "FILECOMP.MSG", 1
End Sub

Sub menOpen_Click ()
    'Start first child form
    Dim NewForm As New ChildFrm
    NewForm.Show

    'If no filename entered, unload form
    If NewForm.Caption = "" Then
        Unload NewForm
    End If
End Sub
```

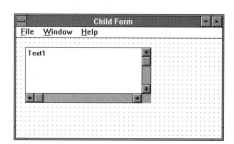

Figure 12-19.
CHILDFRM.FRM during development.

CHILDFRM.FRM Menu Design Window Entries

Caption	Name	Indentation
&File	menFile	0
&Open	menOpen	1
&Close	menClose	1
-	menSep1	1
E&xit	menExit	1
&Window	menWindow	0
&Cascade	menCascade	1
Tile &Horizontally	menTileHorizontally	1
Tile &Vertically	menTileVertically	1
-	menSep2	1
Arrange &Icons	menArrangeIcons	1
&Help	menHelp	0
&Help on FileComp	menHelpFileComp	1
&About FileComp...	menAboutFileComp	1

CHILDFRM.FRM Form and Control Properties

Property	Value
Form	
Caption	Child Form
MDIChild	True
Name	ChildFrm
Text Box	
MultiLine	True
Name	Text1
ScrollBars	3 - Both

Source code for CHILDFRM.FRM

```
Sub Form_Load ()
    'Get filename from user
    GetFile.Caption = "File Open"
    GetFile.Show MODAL
    Caption = GetFile.FullPath.Text

    'Load file's contents
    NL$ = Chr$(13) + Chr$(10)
    If Caption <> "" Then
        Open Caption For Input As #1
        Do Until EOF(1) Or Len(T$) > 32000
            Line Input #1, T$
            A$ = A$ + T$ + NL$
        Loop
        Close #1
        Text1.Text = A$
    End If
End Sub

Sub Form_Resize ()
    'Keep size of text box same as size of form
    Text1.Move 0, 0, ScaleWidth, ScaleHeight
End Sub

Sub menAboutFileComp_Click ()
    'Show About dialog box
    About.Label1.Caption = "FILECOMP"
    About.Show MODAL
End Sub

Sub menArrangeIcons_Click ()
    MDIForm1.Arrange ARRANGE_ICONS
End Sub

Sub menCascade_Click ()
    MDIForm1.Arrange CASCADE
End Sub

Sub menClose_Click ()
    'Unload current child form
    Unload MDIForm1.ActiveForm
End Sub
```

(continued)

CHILDFRM.FRM *continued*

```
Sub menExit_Click ()
    'All done
    Unload MDIForm1
End Sub

Sub menHelpFileComp_Click ()
    'Display some Help text
    FileMsg "FILECOMP.MSG", 1
End Sub

Sub menOpen_Click ()
    'Create new copy of child form
    Dim NewForm As New ChildFrm

    'If no filename entered, unload child form
    If NewForm.Caption = "" Then Unload NewForm
End Sub

Sub menTileHorizontally_Click ()
    MDIForm1.Arrange TILE_HORIZONTAL
End Sub

Sub menTileVertically_Click ()
    MDIForm1.Arrange TILE_VERTICAL
End Sub
```

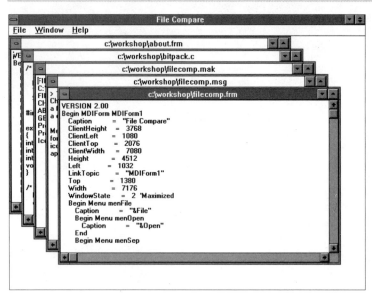

Figure 12-20.

FILECOMP.FRM in action.

(continued)

FIGURE 12-20. *continued*

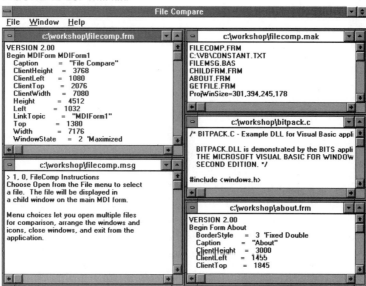

The LZ Application

The LZ application uses calls to Windows' Lempel-Ziv decompression API to expand files. If you have the Professional Edition of Visual Basic for Windows 3, this application also lets you compress files by running the COMPRESS.EXE program provided in the Setup Kit.

This application calls six related functions in the file LZEXPAND.DLL, which is one of the normal suite of dynamic link libraries (DLLs) provided with Windows. Most of these functions have names that start with *LZ*, so you can find online documentation for these functions by searching under *LZ* in the Windows 3.1 SDK online Help.

Functions for compressing files are not included in Windows' standard DLLs (I wish they were), so we have to use the external MS-DOS application COMPRESS.EXE to perform compatible Lempel-Ziv compression on files. Fortunately, the Setup Kit provides this utility to help you set up installation routines for your applications. The *Shell* command makes it easy to run this utility, so you almost feel that it's part of the LZ application.

A data structure is passed as a parameter to some of the API functions the LZ application calls. This structure must be declared in a module rather than in a form, so all the global declarations and this Type structure declaration are grouped in a separate module named LZ.BAS.

To use the LZ application, you select a source directory by using the controls on the left side of the form, and then you select a destination directory by using the controls on the right. When you click the Compress button or the Expand button, all files in the selected source directory are compressed or expanded as they are copied to the destination directory. A large arrow, created from three Line controls, is drawn on the center of the form to remind you of the direction in which the compression or expansion takes place. The ForeColor property of the text boxes is set to gray, which reinforces the fact that individual files are not selected, but rather entire directories are selected. The grayed filenames let you review the contents of the directory.

A built-in feature of the expansion functions in LZEXPAND.DLL is that if you try to expand a file that is not compressed, the file is copied anyway, without modification. This feature adds a degree of safety because if you're not sure whether the files in a directory are compressed, it won't hurt to try expanding them.

The files for this application are included on the disk packaged with this book. To load the files into the Visual Basic environment, choose Open Project from the File menu, and then type *C:\WORKSHOP\LZ.MAK*. This opens the project and enables you to view and modify the forms and code. The following figures, tables, and code give the details of the application's creation.

Figure 12-21.
LZ project list.

Source code for LZ.BAS

```
Type OFSTRUCT
    cBytes As String * 1
    fFixedDisk As String * 1
    nErrCode As Integer
    reserved As String * 4
    szPathName As String * 128
End Type

Declare Function LZStart Lib "LZexpand.dll" () As Integer
Declare Function GetExpandedName Lib "LZexpand.dll" (ByVal→
    lpszSource As String, ByVal lpszBuffer As String) As Integer
Declare Function LZOpenFile Lib "LZexpand.dll" (ByVal lpszFile As→
    String, lpOf As OFSTRUCT, ByVal style As Integer) As Integer
Declare Function CopyLZFile Lib "LZexpand.dll" (ByVal hfSource As→
    Integer, ByVal hfDest As Integer) As Long
Declare Sub LZClose Lib "LZexpand.dll" (ByVal hfFile As Integer)
Declare Sub LZDone Lib "LZexpand.dll" ()
```

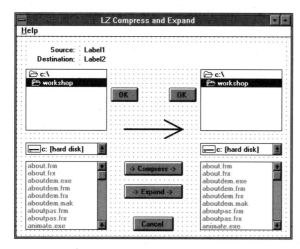

Figure 12-22.
LZ.FRM during development.

LZ.FRM Menu Design Window Entries

Caption	Name	Indentation
&Help	menHelp	0
&Help on LZ	menHelpLZ	1
&About LZ...	menAboutLZ	1
-	menSep	1
E&xit	menExit	1

LZ.FRM Form and Control Properties

Property	Value
Form	
Caption	LZ Compress and Expand
Name	LZ
Command Button	
Caption	OK
Name	cmdOK2
Command Button	
Caption	OK
Name	cmdOK1
File List Box	
ForeColor	&H00C0C0C0&
Name	File2
Drive List Box	
Name	Drive2
Directory List Box	
Name	Dir2
Command Button	
Caption	Cancel
Name	cmdCancel

(continued)

LZ.FRM Form and Control Properties *continued*

Property	Value
CommandButton	
Caption	-> Expand ->
Name	cmdExpand
File List Box	
ForeColor	&H00C0C0C0&
Name	File1
Directory List Box	
Name	Dir1
Drive List Box	
Name	Drive1
Command Button	
Caption	-> Compress ->
Name	cmdCompress
Line	
BorderWidth	2
Name	Line3
X1	3960
X2	4440
Y1	2640
Y2	2400
Line	
BorderWidth	2
Name	Line2
X1	3960
X2	4440
Y1	2160
Y2	2400

(continued)

LZ.FRM Form and Control Properties *continued*

Property	Value
Line	
BorderWidth	3
Name	Line1
X1	2880
X2	4440
Y1	2400
Y2	2400
Label	
Alignment	1 - Right Justify
Caption	Destination:
Name	Label4
Label	
Alignment	1 - Right Justify
Caption	Source:
Name	Label3
Label	
Caption	Label2
Name	Label2
Label	
Caption	Label1
Name	Label1

Source code for LZ.FRM

```
Sub cmdCancel_Click ()
    'All done
    Unload LZ
End Sub

Sub cmdCompress_Click ()
    'Shell to MS-DOS and use COMPRESS.EXE utility
    Cmd$ = "COMPRESS -r " + Dir1.Path + "\*.* " + Dir2.Path
    x% = Shell(Cmd$)
End Sub

Sub cmdExpand_Click ()
    'Constants for LZOpenFile function
    Const OF_READ = 0
    Const OF_CREATE = &H1000

    'Structures for opened files
    Dim lpOfSrc As OFSTRUCT
    Dim lpOfDst As OFSTRUCT

    'First step in Lempel-Ziv calls
    x% = LZStart()

    'Process each file in current directory
    For i% = 0 To File1.ListCount - 1

        'Build full path to source file
        FilSrc$ = Dir1.Path + "\" + File1.List(i%)

        'Get original, uncompressed filename
        FilBuf$ = String$(128, 0)
        x% = GetExpandedName(FilSrc$, FilBuf$)

        'Build new destination filename
        Do
            n% = InStr(FilBuf$, "\")
            If n% = 0 Then Exit Do
            FilBuf$ = Mid$(FilBuf$, n% + 1)
        Loop
        FilDst$ = Dir2.Path + "\" + FilBuf$

        'Open source and destination files
        hfSrc% = LZOpenFile(FilSrc$, lpOfSrc, OF_READ)
        hfDst% = LZOpenFile(FilDst$, lpOfDst, OF_CREATE)
```

(continued)

LZ.FRM *continued*

```
            'Do the copy by using built-in expansion
            Rtn& = CopyLZFile(hfSrc%, hfDst%)

            'Close both files
            LZClose hfSrc%
            LZClose hfDst%
    Next i%

    'Last step in Lempel-Ziv calls
    LZDone

    'Update destination file list box
    File2.Refresh
End Sub

Sub cmdOK1_Click ()
    'Force update of directory list box
    Dir1.Path = Dir1.List(Dir1.ListIndex)
End Sub

Sub cmdOK2_Click ()
    'Force update of directory list box
    Dir2.Path = Dir2.List(Dir2.ListIndex)

    'Update destination file list box
    File2.Refresh
End Sub

Sub Dir1_Change ()
    'User selected directory
    File1.Path = Dir1.Path
    Label1.Caption = Dir1.Path
End Sub

Sub Dir2_Change ()
    'User selected directory
    File2.Path = Dir2.Path
    Label2.Caption = Dir2.Path
End Sub

Sub Drive1_Change ()
    'User selected drive
    Dir1.Path = Drive1.Drive
End Sub
```

(continued)

LZ.FRM *continued*

```
Sub Drive2_Change ()
    'User selected drive
    Dir2.Path = Drive2.Drive
End Sub

Sub Form_Load ()
    'Display source and destination paths
    Label1.Caption = Dir1.Path
    Label2.Caption = Dir2.Path
End Sub

Sub menAboutLZ_Click ()
    'Show About dialog box
    About.Label1.Caption = "LZ"
    About.Show MODAL
End Sub

Sub menExit_Click ()
    'All done
    Unload LZ
End Sub

Sub menHelpLZ_Click ()
    'Display some Help text
    FileMsg "LZ.MSG", 1
End Sub
```

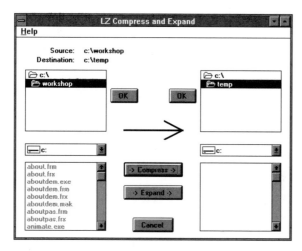

Figure 12-23.
LZ.FRM in action.

## PART III

ADVANCED PROGRAMMING CONCEPTS

DYNAMIC DATA EXCHANGE (DDE)

Setting up Dynamic Data Exchange (DDE) links might at first appear to be a complicated and confusing task. However, the way Visual Basic for Windows handles DDE makes it easy to pass data to or take data from any application for Windows that also supports DDE. The three applications presented in this chapter provide simple working examples to help clarify the process. After you've examined these applications, you'll find it much easier to add DDE to your own Visual Basic for Windows applications.

The VBSOURCE Application

The first DDE application presented in this chapter is named **VBSOURCE**. This is a relatively simple application that requires only a Timer control and a Label control. Once every 1000 milliseconds (1 second), code in the Timer1_Timer subprogram reads the system clock and updates the label with the current date and time.

An application that supplies data to another application through a DDE link is called a *source*, and an application that requests and receives this data is called a *destination*. The VBSOURCE application is set up as a source that can provide a date-and-time string to any destination applications that request it.

To make an application a source, you must properly set two properties of its source form: You set LinkMode to *1 - Source*, and you enter a meaningful name for the LinkTopic property. (In VBSOURCE, LinkTopic is set to *DateTime*.) That's all there is to it! Destination applications can then request the contents of any text boxes, labels, or picture boxes on the source form.

VBSOURCE can run by itself; it will display the current date and time until it's stopped. However, the real magic happens when you build the next application, VBDEST, and establish a DDE link between the two applications.

To create the DDE link from VBDEST, you'll need to run VBSOURCE as a separate application outside the Visual Basic environment. You can run the VBSOURCE.EXE file that is included on the disk packaged with this book, or you can use Visual Basic for Windows to create your own executable file.

To load the VBSOURCE application's files into Visual Basic for Windows, choose the Open Project option from the File menu, and then type *C:\WORKSHOP\VBSOURCE.MAK*. This opens the project and enables you to view and modify the forms and code. The following figures, tables, and code give the details of the application's creation.

Figure 13-1.
VBSOURCE project list.

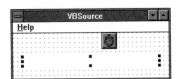

Figure 13-2.
VBSOURCE.FRM during development.

VBSOURCE.FRM Menu Design Window Entries

Caption	Name	Indentation
&Help	menHelpTop	0
&Help on VBSource	menHelpVBSource	1
&About VBSource...	menAboutVBSource	1
-	menSep	1
E&xit	menExit	1

VBSOURCE.FRM Form and Control Properties

Property	Value
Form	
Caption	VBSource
LinkMode	1 - Source
LinkTopic	DateTime
Name	VBSource
Timer	
Interval	1000
Name	Timer1
Label	
Alignment	2 - Center
Caption	[none]
Name	Label1

Source code for VBSOURCE.FRM

```
Sub menAboutVBSource_Click ()
    'Display About dialog box
    About.Label1.Caption = "VBSOURCE"
    About.Show MODAL
End Sub

Sub menExit_Click ()
    'All done
    Unload VBSource
End Sub

Sub menHelpVBSource_Click ()
    'Display some Help text
    FileMsg "VBSOURCE.MSG", 1
End Sub

Sub Timer1_Timer ()
    'Display current date and time in label
    Label1.Caption = Format$(Now, "mmmm d, yyyy  h:mm:ss AM/PM")
End Sub
```

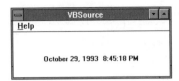

Figure 13-3.
VBSOURCE.FRM in action.

The VBDEST Application

The VBDEST application establishes a DDE link to VBSOURCE, requesting that the data in VBSOURCE's Label control be copied to a text box in VBDEST whenever that data changes.

To establish a DDE link from a Visual Basic destination application during design time, the source application must be running while the destination application is built. Use the Run command in either File Manager or Program Manager to start VBSOURCE.EXE. After VBSOURCE is running, minimize File Manager or Program Manager, and move VBSOURCE out of the way on the screen so that you can work on the VBDEST form. The date and time will change continuously in the VBSOURCE window while you create VBDEST.

VBDEST is a simple application. It contains a single text box in which data received across the DDE link is displayed. As previously mentioned, in source applications you change two link-related properties of the source form: LinkMode and LinkTopic. In destination applications you change three link-related properties of the receiving control: LinkTopic, LinkItem, and LinkMode. In this case, the Text1 control receives data, so you set its three link-related properties.

LinkTopic is set to *VBSOURCE|DateTime*. This string comprises two parts, which are separated by a vertical bar character. The first part, *VBSOURCE*, is the name of the source application. The second part, *DateTime*, is the value of the source form's LinkTopic property. This can be any convenient (and preferably meaningful) name that describes the group of items to be requested from the source form.

LinkItem is set to *Label1*. LinkItem is the name of the text box, label, or picture box on the source form from which data will be accessed. The Label1 control on VBSOURCE contains the continually updated date and time. The LinkItem property can be set to any text box, label, or picture box on the indicated source form, and your program can even switch items while the application is running.

LinkMode is set to *1 - Automatic.* When you complete this setting, the VBDEST text box displays the same date and time information that's displayed in VBSOURCE. The DDE link works even while you edit and work on the VBDEST form. Setting LinkMode to *2 - Manual* is another viable option; this causes data to transfer across the established link only when the VBDEST application explicitly requests it by using the *LinkRequest* method. The automatic link is used for the examples in this book.

VBDEST has only a small amount of program code. Every time the DDE link changes the data in the text box, the Text1_Changed subprogram is activated, so this subprogram is a good place to add any code that is to act on the new data. For this example, the data is merely displayed for review.

To properly establish the DDE link between VBSOURCE and VBDEST, always run VBSOURCE before you run VBDEST. Otherwise VBDEST tries—and fails—to establish the DDE link, and a message to that effect pops up. This is true whether VBDEST is compiled and run as an executable program or whether it's simply opened for editing in Visual Basic for Windows.

The files for the VBDEST application are included on the disk packaged with this book. To load the files into the Visual Basic environment, choose the Open Project option from the File menu, and then enter the filename *C:\WORKSHOP\VBDEST.MAK.* This opens the project and enables you to view and modify the forms and code. The following figures, tables, and code give the details of the application's creation.

Figure 13-4.
VBDEST project list.

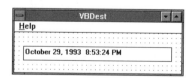

Figure 13-5.
VBDEST.FRM during development.

VBDEST.FRM Menu Design Window Entries

Caption	Name	Indentation
&Help	menHelpTop	0
&Help on VBDest	menHelpVBDest	1
&About VBDest...	menAboutVBDest	1
-	menSep	1
E&xit	menExit	1

VBDEST.FRM Form and Control Properties

Property	Value
Form	
Caption	VBDest
Name	VBDest
Text Box	
LinkItem	Label1
LinkMode	1 - Automatic
LinkTopic	VBSOURCE|DateTime
Name	Text1

Source code for VBDEST.FRM

```
Sub menAboutVBDest_Click ()
    'Show About dialog box
    About.Label1.Caption = "VBDEST"
    About.Show MODAL
End Sub

Sub menExit_Click ()
    'All done
    Unload VBDest
End Sub

Sub menHelpVBDest_Click ()
    'Display some Help text
    FileMsg "VBDEST.MSG", 1
End Sub
```

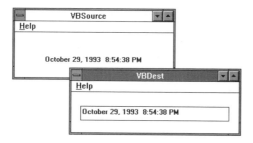

Figure 13-6.
VBSOURCE.FRM and VBDEST.FRM in action.

Dynamic Data Exchange with Word for Windows

DDE links can be set up between Visual Basic applications and other applications for Windows. The VBSOURCE application can be used, without any changes, to demonstrate how a Microsoft Word for Windows document can easily access data from a running Visual Basic for Windows application.

Start VBSOURCE, and move it off to one corner of the screen so that it won't get in the way while Word is running. Start Word, and open a test document for editing. Move the text cursor to any location in the document where it is convenient to insert the date-and-time string. From Word's Insert menu, choose the Field command. At the bottom of the dialog box is a text field labeled Field Code. Delete any characters that might be in the text field, enter *ddeauto VBSOURCE DateTime Label1,* and click OK. The date-and-time string appears in the document and begins updating once each second, as shown in Figure 13-7.

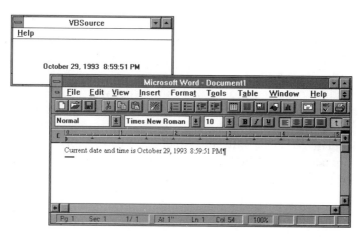

Figure 13-7.
Word document and VBSOURCE.FRM in action.

341

DDE links can be set up throughout a Word document. Names, dates, and other data can instantly appear throughout a document as they are entered or created in a Visual Basic for Windows application.

The WORDSMIN Application

The WORDSMIN application demonstrates how a Visual Basic for Windows application can use a DDE link to access data entered in a Microsoft Word for Windows document. (You can use WORDSMIN with any application that supports DDE, but a word processing application is best for this example.) As text is typed into a Word document, the text is transferred to a hidden text box on the WORDSMIN form. The change in the text box contents activates the subprogram Text1_Change, which calculates an average words-per-minute rate for the entered text and displays the number of characters, number of seconds, and rate in Label controls.

The WORDSMIN form contains a text box and six labels. Because the text coming from the DDE link doesn't need to be displayed, the text box is small and its Visible property is set to *False.*

The WORDSMIN application's Paste Link command enables the user to set up a DDE link between the WORDSMIN application and any document. The PasteLink_Click subprogram copies information from the Clipboard and uses it to set the link-related properties of the form's text box.

To use this application, run both WORDSMIN and Word (which can be started in either order), and size and move them so that they're both visible. In Word, select any text (such as the space in a new document), and choose the Edit Copy command to copy the text and the link information to the Clipboard. Then move to the WORDSMIN application, and choose the Edit Paste Link command. The link is now up and running; when you type in the Word document where the text was selected, the WORDSMIN application lets you know your average words per minute. The calculation for the typing speed is somewhat crude, but the main purpose of this example is to show how the DDE link can be used to access and process data outside the Word application.

The files for the WORDSMIN application are included on the disk packaged with this book. To load the files into Visual Basic, select Open Project from the File menu, and type *C:\WORKSHOP\WORDSMIN.MAK.* This opens the project and enables you to view and modify the forms and code. The following figures, tables, and code give the details of the application's creation.

Figure 13-8.
WORDSMIN project list.

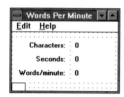

Figure 13-9.
WORDSMIN.FRM during development.

WORDSMIN.FRM Menu Design Window Entries

Caption	Name	Indentation
&Edit	menEditTop	0
Paste &Link	menPasteLink	1
-	menSep	1
E&xit	menExitWordsMin	1
&Help	menHelpTop	0
&Help on WordsMin	menHelpWordsMin	1
&About WordsMin...	menAboutWordsMin	1

WORDSMIN.FRM Form and Control Properties

Property	Value
Form	
Caption	Words Per Minute
Name	WordsMinForm

(continued)

WORDSMIN.FRM Form and Control Properties *continued*

Property	Value
Text Box	
MultiLine	True
Name	Text1
Visible	False
Label	
Alignment	1 - Right Justify
Caption	Characters:
Name	Label4
Label	
Caption	0
Name	Label1
Label	
Alignment	1 - Right Justify
Caption	Seconds:
Name	Label5
Label	
Caption	0
Name	Label2
Label	
Alignment	1 - Right Justify
Caption	Words/minute:
Name	Label6
Label	
Caption	0
Name	Label3

Source code for WORDSMIN.FRM

```
Sub menAboutWordsMin_Click ()
    'Show About dialog box
    About.Label1.Caption = "WORDSMIN"
    About.Show MODAL
End Sub

Sub menExitWordsMin_Click ()
    'All done
    Unload WordsMinForm
End Sub

Sub menHelpWordsMin_Click ()
    'Display some Help text
    FileMsg "WORDSMIN.MSG", 1
End Sub

Sub menPasteLink_Click ()
    'Create newline string
    NL$ = Chr$(13) + Chr$(10)

    'Access link information in Clipboard
    Link$ = Clipboard.GetText(CF_LINK)

    'Was link information there?
    If Link$ = "" Then
        Beep
        Msg$ =⌐
         "You must first open a Word for Windows document," + NL$
        Msg$ = Msg$ + "select some text, and choose Edit Copy." +⌐
         NL$ + NL$
        Msg$ = Msg$ + "Try again..."
        MsgBox Msg$, 48, "Words Per Minute (Paste Link)"

    'Use link information string to complete DDE
    Else

        'Extract topic and item from string
        Topic$ = Left$(Link$, InStr(Link$, "!") - 1)
        Item$ = Mid$(Link$, InStr(Link$, "!") + 1)
```

(continued)

345

WORDSMIN.FRM *continued*

```
        'Set Text1 link parameters
        Text1.LinkTopic = Topic$
        Text1.LinkItem = Item$
        Text1.LinkMode = LINK_AUTOMATIC
    End If
End Sub

Sub Text1_Change ()
    Static T0

    'Access text from Word document
    A$ = Text1.Text

    'Start timing when typing starts
    If T0 = 0 And A$ <> "" Then
        T0 = Timer
        Exit Sub
    End If

    'Get current time
    T1 = Timer

    'Calculate words per minute
    Wmin% = (Len(A$) / 5#) / ((T1 - T0) / 60#)

    'Display character count
    Label1.Caption = Str$(Len(A$))

    'Display elapsed time
    Label2.Caption = Str$(Int(T1 - T0))

    'Display words per minute
    Label3.Caption = Str$(Wmin%)
End Sub
```

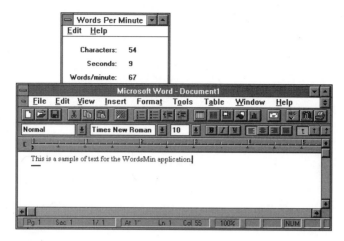

Figure 13-10.
WORDSMIN.FRM in action.

OBJECT LINKING AND EMBEDDING (OLE)

Visual Basic's OLE control makes it easy to link or embed data from other applications for Windows into your Visual Basic applications. This chapter presents an application called OLEDEMO that demonstrates the OLE control.

The OLEDEMO Application

The OLEDEMO application provides a demonstration of Object Linking and Embedding (OLE) using the OLE control. Two OLE controls let you activate Windows' Sound Recorder and Paintbrush applications. You will be able to use Sound Recorder only if your system has a sound driver.

OLE Automation is also available in Visual Basic for Windows 3, but as of the time this book was going to press no standard applications for Windows provided objects and methods that were compatible with OLE 2. By the time you read this, a lot of industry-standard OLE-compatible applications might be available. OLE Automation lets Visual Basic effectively serve as a systemwide macro language for programming applications external to their native environments or programming languages. The online Help facility for Visual Basic 3 provides a good explanation of OLE Automation.

When the OLEDEMO application loads, the Sound Recorder and Paintbrush applications are linked by setting the Class properties of each OLE control. While you're in Visual Basic, you can see a list of the classes available on your system by selecting an OLE control, clicking on Class in the Properties window, and clicking on the ellipsis to display a list of classes. Feel free to experiment with the classes provided by applications on your system.

The SourceDoc property determines the data file for the linked or embedded program to use. In this example, the TADA.WAV sound-clip file is loaded into Sound Recorder, and the SHEEP.BMP bitmap file is loaded into Paintbrush. After these applications are activated, you are free to use their menus to load other data files, but these two files will always load first by default.

The Action property is set last, to create the link to the external application. The constant OLE_CREATE_LINK is defined in the file CONSTANT.TXT, which is provided with Visual Basic for Windows. If you change the setting of the Action property to OLE_CREATE_EMBED, the data and application functionality will be embedded within OLEDEMO rather than only linked to it. Sometimes this affects the behavior of the embedded application, depending on its design. For example, the Sound Recorder application will simply play the TADA.WAV file without popping up its standard dialog box.

OLEDEMO provides a relatively simple example of the use of OLE in your applications—just enough to get you started and to provide a sense of OLE's powerful capabilities. As I hinted earlier, OLE Automation is an exciting and important feature that will be blossoming in the very near future; you'll be hearing a lot about that as time goes on.

The files for the OLEDEMO application are included on the disk packaged with this book. To load the files into the Visual Basic environment, choose the Open Project option from the File menu, and then enter the filename *C:\WORKSHOP\OLEDEMO.MAK*. This opens the project and enables you to view and modify the forms and code. The following figures, tables, and code give the details of the application's creation.

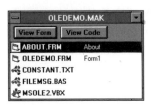

Figure 14-1.
OLEDEMO project list.

Figure 14-2.
OLEDEMO.FRM during development.

OLEDEMO.FRM Menu Design Window Entries

Caption	Name	Indentation
&Help	menHelp	0
&Help on OLEDemo	menHelpOLEDemo	1
&About OLEDemo...	menAboutOLEDemo	1
-	menSep	1
E&xit	menExit	1

OLEDEMO.FRM Form and Control Properties

Property	Value
Form	
Caption	OLE Demo
Name	Form1
Command Button	
Cancel	True
Caption	Cancel
Default	True
Name	cmdCancel
OLE	
BorderStyle	0 - None
DisplayType	1 - Icon
Name	OLE1

(continued)

OLEDEMO.FRM Form and Control Properties *continued*

Property	Value
OLE	
BorderStyle	0 - None
DisplayType	1 - Icon
Name	OLE2

Source code for OLEDEMO.FRM

```
Sub cmdCancel_Click ()
    End
End Sub

Sub Form_Load ()
    'Center form
    Left = (Screen.Width - Width) / 2
    Top = (Screen.Height - Height) / 2

    'Wire for sound the first OLE control
    OLE1.Class = "SoundRec"
    OLE1.SourceDoc = "tada.wav"
    OLE1.Action = OLE_CREATE_LINK

    'Prepare to be sheepish
    OLE2.Class = "PBrush"
    OLE2.SourceDoc = "sheep.bmp"
    OLE2.Action = OLE_CREATE_LINK
End Sub

Sub menAboutOLEDemo_Click ()
    'Display About dialog box
    About.Label1.Caption = "OLEDEMO"
    About.Show MODAL
End Sub

Sub menExit_Click ()
    End
End Sub

Sub menHelpOLEDemo_Click ()
    'Display some Help text
    FileMsg "OLEDEMO.MSG", 1
End Sub
```

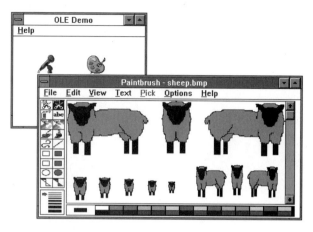

Figure 14-3.
OLEDEMO.FRM in action.

## CHAPTER FIFTEEN

DATA ACCESS

One of the hottest new features of Visual Basic 3 is its ability to work with a variety of standard databases. You can easily create, view, maintain, and update databases by using the new Data control and a rich new set of database objects and functions. Much of this functionality is compatible with Microsoft Access because the Access database engine has been incorporated into Visual Basic 3.

Visual Basic 3's new Data control simplifies database programming to the point that you might not have to write any code at all! The Data control is extremely easy to use; you can access databases simply by setting a few properties of the Data control and any controls that are bound to the Data control. The AREACODE application presented in this chapter demonstrates this by using two Data controls to provide easy access to a single database of nationwide area codes. Before we jump into the AREACODE application, however, let's look at some of the major features that the Standard and Professional Editions of Visual Basic 3 provide for database programming.

The Data Control

Often you'll need only the Data control to create complete, full-featured database applications. All you have to do is set a few properties of the Data control, and you can easily bind controls to it and use them to access the database contents. You set the DatabaseName property to the database filename, and you set the RecordSource property to a table or query name in the database. The Data control has a few other useful properties (ReadOnly, for instance), but the RecordSource and DatabaseName properties are the two most important. At runtime, the Data control provides an interface similar to that of a scroll bar. The user uses this interface to move through the database records. All bound controls update to show the current database record. You can also set the current record in an application's code and hide the Data control from the user.

Bound Controls

Several of the standard controls have the new properties DataSource and DataField, which you can use to bind these controls to a Data control. You set the DataSource property to the name of a Data control, and you set the DataField property to the name of a field in the table or query referenced by the Data control. Let's say that these properties are set for a Text Box control. At runtime, the Text property of the Text Box control displays the contents of the field in the record currently accessed by the Data control. Controls that can be bound to a Data control include the Picture Box, Text Box, Label, Check Box, and Image controls.

Database Objects

Another approach to creating Visual Basic database applications is provided by a new set of objects that you can declare and manipulate like other variables. The *Dim* statement creates objects of types such as *Database, TableDef, Field, Index, DynaSet,* and *SnapShot.* Each of these objects contains several properties and methods you can use to provide access to your databases. Using program code to access databases provides flexibility and power, but it precludes the use of bound controls. The Professional Edition of Visual Basic 3 provides a few more of these objects and functions than the Standard Edition does; the extra objects and functions are useful for especially complex or demanding database programming tasks.

Databases

Your database can be stored on your hard disk, on a shared network server, or on an Open Database Connectivity (ODBC) connection. The database can be in the form of a single MDB file (the type of file created by Microsoft Access); a directory containing database, data, index, and support files; or a registered ODBC data source name. You can use Visual Basic, Access, FoxPro, Paradox, dBASE, or any other compatible database manager to create the database.

The AREACODE application provides a working demonstration of a database created by using Visual Basic. AREACODE is a starting point for exploring Visual Basic database application development; for more information and programming examples, see the extensive documentation on this subject in your Visual Basic 3 package. Visual Basic's online Help facility also provides a lot of guidance and information.

The AREACODE Application

The AREACODE form uses two Data controls to access the same database in different ways. The first Data control, in the top half of the form, accesses a table of area codes in the database file ACODE.MDB, which was created by using Microsoft Access. Let's take a look at the top half of the form first; then we'll look at the Data2 control in the bottom half.

Several Text Box controls display the fields from the area code records that the Data1 control accesses. No coding is required to access simple databases in this way. You simply add a Data control to your form, set its DatabaseName property to the name of the database file, and set its RecordSource property to the name of a table or query. Then you set the DataSource and DataField properties of the Text Box or Label controls in which the database contents are to be displayed. At runtime, you simply click the Data control to scroll through the records.

Although you can access the ACODE database by clicking the Data1 control, I've added some code to demonstrate another way to manipulate the database records. The txtAreaCode text box lets the user type in a three-digit area code. After the user enters three digits, a bookmark is set to record the current record (so that the current record can be redisplayed if the search fails), and several RecordSet properties of Data1 are set to cause code in the txtAreaCode_Change subprogram to immediately begin searching for a matching area code in the database. The Data control is powerful and easy to use, even without any coding at all, yet RecordSet and other properties are powerful features for advanced database programming applications.

The second Data control, Data2, is located in the bottom half of the form. This control accesses the same records in ACODE.MDB as Data1 does; however, Data2's RecordSource property is set to ByState, a query I created by using Access that sorts the records in ascending order according to the two-letter state abbreviations. This query is stored in the database file. The Data2 control lets you cycle through the same set of records one at a time according to state abbreviation instead of area code. You can have multiple Data controls access the same database file simultaneously to provide different views of the same data.

The files for the AREACODE application are included on the disk packaged with this book. To load the files into the Visual Basic environment, choose Open Project from the File menu, and type *C:\WORKSHOP\AREACODE.MAK*. This opens the project and enables you to view and modify the form and code. The following figures, tables, and code give the details of the application's creation.

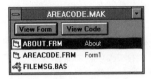

Figure 15-1.
AREACODE project list.

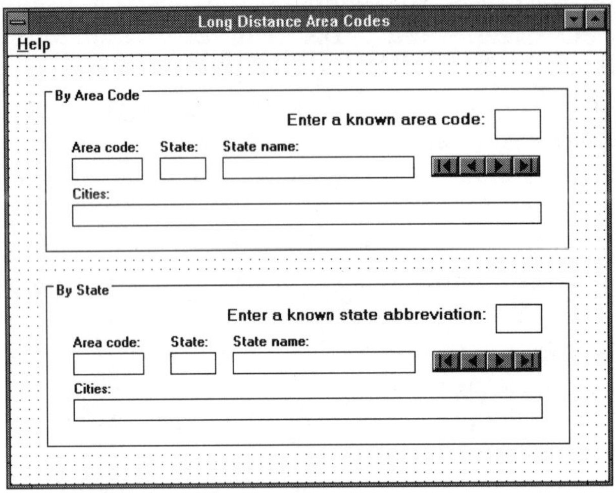

Figure 15-2.
AREACODE.FRM during development.

AREACODE.FRM Menu Design Window Entries

Caption	Name	Indentation
&Help	menHelp	0
&Help on AreaCode	menHelpAreaCode	1
&About AreaCode...	menAboutAreaCode	1
-	menSep	1
E&xit	menExit	1

AREACODE.FRM Form and Control Properties

Property	Value
Form	
BorderStyle	3 - Fixed Double
Caption	Long Distance Area Codes
MaxButton	False
Name	Form1
Data	
DatabaseName	c:\workshop\acode.mdb
Name	Data1
RecordSource	ACODE
Frame	
Caption	By State
Name	Frame2
Text Box	
DataField	StateName
DataSource	Data2
Name	Text8
TabStop	False
Text Box	
Alignment	2 - Center
FontSize	9.75
Name	txtState
Data	
DatabaseName	c:\workshop\acode.mdb
Name	Data2
RecordSource	Bystate

(continued)

AREACODE.FRM Form and Control Properties *continued*

Property	Value
Text Box	
DataField	Cities
DataSource	Data2
Name	Text6
TabStop	False
Text Box	
DataField	State
DataSource	Data2
Name	Text5
TabStop	False
Text Box	
DataField	Areacode
DataSource	Data2
Name	Text4
TabStop	False
Label	
Caption	State name:
Name	Label10
Label	
Alignment	1 - Right Justify
Caption	Enter a known state abbreviation:
FontSize	9.75
Name	Label8
Label	
Caption	Cities:
Name	Label6
Label	
Caption	State:
Name	Label5

(continued)

AREACODE.FRM Form and Control Properties *continued*

Property	Value
Label	
Caption	Area code:
Name	Label4
Frame	
Caption	By Area Code
Name	Frame1
Text Box	
DataField	StateName
DataSource	Data1
Name	Text7
TabStop	False
Text Box	
Alignment	2 - Center
FontSize	9.75
Name	txtAreaCode
Text Box	
DataField	Cities
DataSource	Data1
Name	Text3
TabStop	False
Text Box	
DataField	State
DataSource	Data1
Name	Text2
TabStop	False
Text Box	
DataField	Areacode
DataSource	Data1
Name	Text1
TabStop	False

(continued)

AREACODE.FRM Form and Control Properties *continued*

Property	Value
Label	
Caption	State name:
Name	Label9
Label	
Alignment	1 - Right Justify
Caption	Enter a known area code:
FontSize	9.75
Name	Label7
Label	
Caption	Cities:
Name	Label3
Label	
Caption	State:
Name	Label2
Label	
Caption	Area code:
Name	Label1

Source code for AREACODE.FRM

```
Sub Form_Load ()
    'Center form
    Left = (Screen.Width - Width) / 2
    Top = (Screen.Height - Height) / 2
End Sub

Sub menAboutAreaCode_Click ()
    'Show About dialog box
    About.Label1.Caption = "AREACODE"
    About.Show MODAL
End Sub
```

(continued)

AREACODE.FRM *continued*

```
Sub menExit_Click ()
    End
End Sub

Sub menHelpAreaCode_Click ()
    'Display some Help text
    FileMsg "AREACODE.MSG", 1
End Sub

Sub txtAreaCode_Change ()
    'Wait for user to enter all three digits
    If Len(txtAreaCode.Text) = 3 Then

        'Record current record
        Bookmark = Data1.RecordSet.Bookmark

        'Search for first matching area code
        Criteria$ = "Areacode = " + txtAreaCode.Text
        Data1.RecordSet.FindFirst Criteria$

        'Was area code not found?
        If Data1.RecordSet.NoMatch Then
            Beep
            Data1.RecordSet.Bookmark = Bookmark
        End If
    End If
End Sub

Sub txtAreaCode_KeyPress (KeyAscii As Integer)
    If Len(txtAreaCode.Text) = 3 Then
        txtAreaCode.Text = ""
    End If
End Sub

Sub txtState_Change ()
    'Wait for user to enter two-letter abbreviation
    If Len(txtState.Text) = 2 Then

        'Record current record
        Bookmark = Data2.RecordSet.Bookmark

        'Search for first matching state
        Criteria$ = "State = '" + txtState.Text + "'"
        Data2.RecordSet.FindFirst Criteria$
```

(continued)

AREACODE.FRM *continued*

```
        'Was state not found?
        If Data2.RecordSet.NoMatch Then
            Beep
            Data2.RecordSet.Bookmark = Bookmark
        End If
    End If
End Sub

Sub txtState_KeyPress (KeyAscii As Integer)
    KeyAscii = Asc(UCase$(Chr$(KeyAscii)))
    If Len(txtState.Text) = 2 Then
        txtState.Text = ""
    End If
End Sub
```

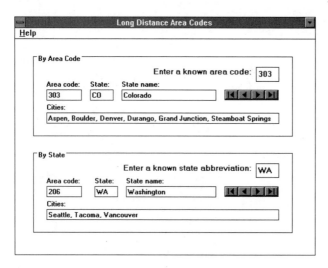

Figure 15-3.
AREACODE.FRM in action.

CALLING WINDOWS API FUNCTIONS

An exciting and powerful feature of Visual Basic for Windows is its capability of easily calling Windows application programming interface (API) functions. When Windows is running, several hundred API functions are available to applications. These functions are contained in dynamic link libraries (DLLs) provided—and used—by Windows. The three main DLLs are KERNEL.DLL, GDI.DLL, and USER.DLL; these DLLs are usually found in the directory C:\WINDOWS\SYSTEM. This chapter provides a sampling of the many API functions available to you.

Although the best way to understand these functions and how they work together is to purchase the Microsoft Windows Software Development Kit (SDK). However, the Professional Edition of Visual Basic for Windows 3 includes several online Help files that can provide an excellent resource for understanding and using these functions. The Windows 3.1 SDK Help file provides declarations for all standard Windows API functions and constants in C syntax, and the Windows 3.1 API Help file provides declarations for all standard Windows API functions and constants in Visual Basic syntax.

Feel free to experiment with these functions; it's fairly easy to guess the purpose and operation of many of them. Be forewarned, however: Any mistake in the use of these functions can make Windows operate unpredictably. Save your work often, and be prepared to reboot your system if necessary.

This chapter presents applications that use a few API functions, simply to give you a feel for how to go about calling these functions from your own applications. When you have the time, scan through the Help files to see what kinds of Windows API functions are available to your Visual Basic applications.

The FLASHWIN Application

The FLASHWIN application calls *FlashWindow,* a function that is located in USER.DLL. This function momentarily toggles the appearance of the window's border and title bar. *FlashWindow* can be useful, for example, to get the user to notice an important window that requires immediate attention. If you minimize the FLASHWIN application while its window is flashing, the application's icon will flash.

The *FlashWindow* declaration in the Windows 3.1 API Help file was copied to the general-declarations area of the FLASHWIN form. In general, you should copy the declarations directly from this Help file rather than trying to type the declarations yourself. This reduces the chance that a typographic error will creep into your declaration and cause you grief when you try to run the application. Also, some of the declarations are quite long, and copying the text can save time.

To flash the window, a Timer control is set up to call *FlashWindow* twice a second. If the bInvert parameter is not zero, *FlashWindow* toggles the window's title bar and border from active to inactive or vice versa; if the bInvert parameter is zero, *FlashWindow* sets the window's title bar and border to the original state. The Form_Load and Form_Click subprograms control the value of bInvert, causing the window to flash, or not flash, each time *FlashWindow* is called.

The files for the FLASHWIN application are included on the disk packaged with this book. To load the files into the Visual Basic environment, choose the Open Project option from the File menu, and then type *C:\WORKSHOP\FLASHWIN.MAK.* This opens the project and enables you to view and modify the forms and code. The following figures, tables, and code give the details of the application's creation.

Figure 16-1.
FLASHWIN project list.

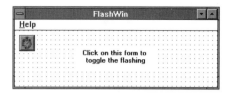

Figure 16-2.
FLASHWIN.FRM during development.

FLASHWIN.FRM Menu Design Window Entries

Caption	Name	Indentation
&Help	menHelpTop	0
&Help on FlashWin	menHelpFlashWin	1
&About FlashWin...	menAboutFlashWin	1
-	menSep	1
E&xit	menExit	1

FLASHWIN.FRM Form and Control Properties

Property	Value
Form	
Caption	FlashWin
Icon	c:\vb\icons\misc\lighton.ico
Name	FlashWin
Timer	
Interval	500
Name	Timer1
Label	
Alignment	2 - Center
Caption	Click on this form to toggle the flashing
Name	Label1

Source code for FLASHWIN.FRM

```
Dim bInvert As Integer

Declare Function FlashWindow Lib "User" (ByVal hWnd As Integer,→
 ByVal bInvert As Integer) As Integer

Sub Form_Click ()
    'Toggle bInvert parameter
    bInvert = Not bInvert
End Sub

Sub Form_Load ()
    'Set bInvert to True to start
    bInvert = True
End Sub

Sub Label1_Click ()
    'Send this click to form
    Form_Click
End Sub

Sub menAboutFlashWin_Click ()
    'Display About dialog box
    About.Label1.Caption = "FLASHWIN"
    About.Show MODAL
End Sub

Sub menExit_Click ()
    'All done
    Unload FlashWin
End Sub

Sub menHelpFlashWin_Click ()
    'Display some Help text
    FileMsg "FLASHWIN.MSG", 1
End Sub

Sub Timer1_Timer ()
    'Call API function
    x% = FlashWindow(hWnd, bInvert)
End Sub
```

Figure 16-3.
FLASHWIN.FRM in action, with the title bar and border toggled active.

Figure 16-4,
FLASHWIN.FRM in action, with the title bar and border toggled inactive.

The SYSINFO Application

The Windows API functions provide information that is not directly accessible from Visual Basic. The SYSINFO application demonstrates several functions that return system information such as the version of Windows, the available memory, and whether a math coprocessor is present.

The declarations and constants were copied directly from the Windows 3.1 API Help file. Some of the functions return one piece of information, and others return an integer value in which each bit provides a piece of the sought-after information. Not all information returned by these functions is displayed on the form—only a sampling of some of the more important data to show how it's done.

The files for the SYSINFO application are included on the disk packaged with this book. To load the files into the Visual Basic environment, choose the Open Project option from the File menu, and then type *C:\WORKSHOP\SYSINFO.MAK*. This opens the project and enables you to view and modify the forms and code. The following figures, tables, and code give the details of the application's creation.

Figure 16-5.
SYSINFO project list.

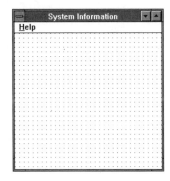

Figure 16-6.
SYSINFO.FRM during development.

SYSINFO.FRM Menu Design Window Entries

Caption	Name	Indentation
&Help	menHelpTop	0
&Help on SysInfo	menHelpSysInfo	1
&About SysInfo...	menAboutSysInfo	1
-	menSep	1
E&xit	menExit	1

SYSINFO.FRM Form Properties

Property	Value
Form	
Caption	System Information
Name	SysInfo

Source code for SYSINFO.FRM

```
'Declarations for SYSINFO

'Version of Windows
Declare Function GetVersion Lib "Kernel" () As Long

'Available memory
Declare Function GetFreeSpace Lib "Kernel" (ByVal wFlags As→
  Integer) As Long

'Hardware information
Declare Function GetWinFlags Lib "Kernel" () As Long
Const WF_PMODE = &H1
Const WF_CPU286 = &H2
Const WF_CPU386 = &H4
Const WF_CPU486 = &H8
Const WF_STANDARD = &H10
Const WF_WIN286 = &H10
Const WF_ENHANCED = &H20
Const WF_WIN386 = &H20
Const WF_CPU086 = &H40
Const WF_CPU186 = &H80
Const WF_LARGEFRAME = &H100
Const WF_SMALLFRAME = &H200
Const WF_80x87 = &H400

'Milliseconds since system started
Declare Function GetCurrentTime Lib "User" () As Long

'Mouse double-click time
Declare Function GetDoubleClickTime Lib "User" () As Integer

'System metrics
Declare Function GetSystemMetrics Lib "User" (ByVal nIndex As→
  Integer) As Integer
Const SM_CXSCREEN = 0
Const SM_CYSCREEN = 1
Const SM_CXVSCROLL = 2
Const SM_CYHSCROLL = 3
Const SM_CYCAPTION = 4
Const SM_CXBORDER = 5
Const SM_CYBORDER = 6
Const SM_CXDLGFRAME = 7
Const SM_CYDLGFRAME = 8
Const SM_CYVTHUMB = 9
```

(continued)

SYSINFO.FRM *continued*

```
Const SM_CXHTHUMB = 10
Const SM_CXICON = 11
Const SM_CYICON = 12
Const SM_CXCURSOR = 13
Const SM_CYCURSOR = 14
Const SM_CYMENU = 15
Const SM_CXFULLSCREEN = 16
Const SM_CYFULLSCREEN = 17
Const SM_CYKANJIWINDOW = 18
Const SM_MOUSEPRESENT = 19
Const SM_CYVSCROLL = 20
Const SM_CXHSCROLL = 21
Const SM_DEBUG = 22
Const SM_SWAPBUTTON = 23
Const SM_RESERVED1 = 24
Const SM_RESERVED2 = 25
Const SM_RESERVED3 = 26
Const SM_RESERVED4 = 27
Const SM_CXMIN = 28
Const SM_CYMIN = 29
Const SM_CXSIZE = 30
Const SM_CYSIZE = 31
Const SM_CXFRAME = 32
Const SM_CYFRAME = 33
Const SM_CXMINTRACK = 34
Const SM_CYMINTRACK = 35
Const SM_CMETRICS = 36


Sub Form_Click ()
    'Force update of displayed information
    Form_Resize
End Sub


Sub Form_Resize ()
    'Display system information
    Cls

    'Version of Windows and MS-DOS (API call)
    V& = GetVersion()
    Print "MS-DOS version:",
    Print Format$((V& \ &H1000000) And &HFF, " ##"); ".";
    Print Format$((V& \ &H10000) And &HFF, "0")
    Print "Windows version:",
    Print Format$(V& And &HFF, " ##"); ".";
    Print Format$((V& \ &H100) And &HFF, "0")
```

(continued)

SYSINFO.FRM *continued*

```
    'Memory (API call)
    Mem& = GetFreeSpace(0)
    Print "Memory bytes free:", Mem&

    'Hardware information (API call)
    WinFlags& = GetWinFlags()
    Print "80x87 coprocessor:", YesNo(WinFlags& And WF_80x87)
    Print "CPU is 8086: ", YesNo(WinFlags& And WF_CPU086)
    Print "CPU is 80186:", YesNo(WinFlags& And WF_CPU186)
    Print "CPU is 80286:", YesNo(WinFlags& And WF_CPU286)
    Print "CPU is 80386:", YesNo(WinFlags& And WF_CPU386)
    Print "CPU is 80486:", YesNo(WinFlags& And WF_CPU486)
    Print "386 enhanced mode:", YesNo(WinFlags& And WF_ENHANCED)
    Print "EMS large frame:", YesNo(WinFlags& And WF_LARGEFRAME)
    Print "EMS small frame:", YesNo(WinFlags& And WF_SMALLFRAME)
    Print "Protected mode:", YesNo(WinFlags& And WF_PMODE)
    Print "Standard mode:", YesNo(WinFlags& And WF_STANDARD)

    'Time since Windows started (API call)
    Print "System milliseconds:", GetCurrentTime()

    'Mouse information (API call)
    Print "Mouse available:",→
     YesNo(GetSystemMetrics(SM_MOUSEPRESENT))
    Print "Buttons swapped:", YesNo(GetSystemMetrics(SM_SWAPBUTTON))
    Print "Double-click msec:", GetDoubleClickTime()
End Sub

Sub menAboutSysInfo_Click ()
    'Display About dialog box
    About.Label1.Caption = "SYSINFO"
    About.Show MODAL
End Sub

Sub menExit_Click ()
    'All done
    Unload SysInfo
End Sub

Sub menHelpSysInfo_Click ()
    'Display some Help text
    FileMsg "SYSINFO.MSG", 1
End Sub
```

(continued)

SYSINFO.FRM *continued*

```
Function YesNo (n&) As String
    'Converts value to Yes or No string
    If n& Then
        YesNo = " Yes"
    Else
        YesNo = " No"
    End If
End Function
```

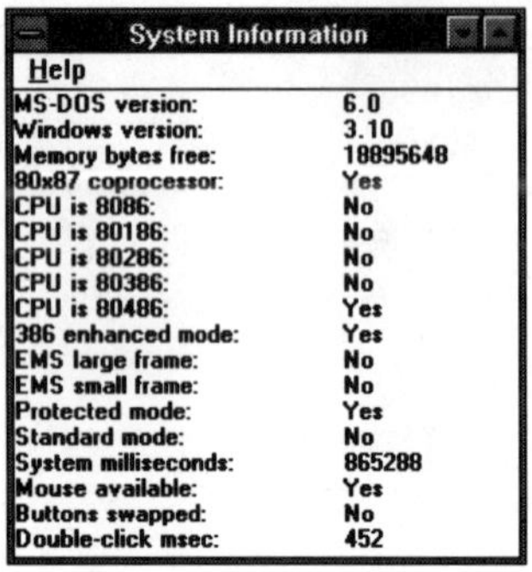

System Information		
Help		
MS-DOS version:	6.0	
Windows version:	3.10	
Memory bytes free:	18895648	
80x87 coprocessor:	Yes	
CPU is 8086:	No	
CPU is 80186:	No	
CPU is 80286:	No	
CPU is 80386:	No	
CPU is 80486:	Yes	
386 enhanced mode:	Yes	
EMS large frame:	No	
EMS small frame:	No	
Protected mode:	Yes	
Standard mode:	No	
System milliseconds:	865288	
Mouse available:	Yes	
Buttons swapped:	No	
Double-click msec:	452	

Figure 16-7.
SYSINFO.FRM in action.

The GRAFSAMP Application

The GRAFSAMP application shows how you can call the *DrawFocusRect* API function to create the transparent focus rectangle commonly used to select a region of a graphics image. It also shows how you can use the *RoundRect* function to draw rectangles that have rounded corners.

The *DrawFocusRect* function draws the dashed focus rectangle by using the XOR (exclusive OR) draw mode, which means that simply drawing the focus rectangle again in the same location erases the first focus rectangle and restores its original pixels. You've probably seen this function in action when selecting a rectangular region in Windows Paintbrush.

The application's Picture Box control monitors mouse events to determine when and where to draw the focus rectangle. You create a focus rectangle by clicking and dragging with the mouse. When you release the mouse button, the focus rectangle is erased, and a rounded rectangle is drawn by using the *RoundRect* function.

Scroll bars let you select the percentage of rounding (0 percent creates rectangles that have square corners, and 100 percent creates ellipses) and the thickness, in pixels, of the rectangle's lines. As a final touch, the Erase button enables you to erase the picture box when it gets cluttered with rectangles.

The *DrawFocusRect* and *RoundRect* functions are handy for paint programs. In particular, the *DrawFocusRect* function is useful whenever a rectangular region of graphics is to be selected by the user.

The files for **GRAFSAMP** are included on the disk packaged with this book. To load the files into the Visual Basic environment, choose the Open Project option from the File menu, and then enter the filename *C:\WORKSHOP\GRAFSAMP.MAK.* This opens the project and enables you to view and modify the forms and code. The following figures, tables, and code give the details of the application's creation.

Figure 16-8.
GRAFSAMP project list.

Source code for GRAFSAMP.BAS

```
'Global declarations for GRAFSAMP

Type RECT
    left As Integer
    top As Integer
    right As Integer
    bottom As Integer
End Type

Declare Function RoundRect Lib "GDI" (ByVal hDC As Integer,⌐
    ByVal X1 As Integer, ByVal Y1 As Integer, ByVal X2 As Integer,⌐
    ByVal Y2 As Integer, ByVal X3 As Integer, ByVal Y3 As Integer)⌐
    As Integer
Declare Sub DrawFocusRect Lib "User" (ByVal hDC As Integer,⌐
    lpRect As RECT)
```

Figure 16-9.
GRAFSAMP.FRM during development.

GRAFSAMP.FRM Menu Design Window Entries

Caption	Name	Indentation
&Help	menHelpTop	0
&Help on GrafSamp	menHelpGrafSamp	1
&About GrafSamp...	menAboutGrafSamp	1
-	menSep	1
E&xit	menExit	1

GRAFSAMP.FRM Form and Control Properties

Property	Value
Form	
Caption	GrafSamp
Name	GrafSamp
Command Button	
Caption	Erase
Name	Command1
Picture Box	
Name	Picture1

(continued)

GRAFSAMP.FRM Form and Control Properties *continued*

Property	Value
Horizontal Scroll Bar	
LargeChange	10
Max	100
Name	HScroll1
Horizontal Scroll Bar	
Max	20
Min	1
Name	HScroll2
Value	1
Label	
Caption	Percent Rounding
Name	Label1
Label	
Alignment	2 - Center
Caption	0%
Name	Label2
Label	
Caption	Pixel Thickness
Name	Label3
Label	
Alignment	2 - Center
Caption	1
Name	Label4

Source code for GRAFSAMP.FRM

```
Dim FocusRec As RECT

Dim X1 As Integer, Y1 As Integer
Dim X2 As Integer, Y2 As Integer
Dim X3 As Integer, Y3 As Integer
```

(continued)

GRAFSAMP.FRM *continued*

```
Sub Command1_Click ()
    'Erase drawing area
    Picture1.Cls
End Sub

Sub Form_Load ()
    'Set pixel scale mode
    Picture1.ScaleMode = 3
End Sub

Sub HScroll1_Change ()
    'Display percentage of rounding
    Label2.Caption = Str$(HScroll1.Value) + "%"
End Sub

Sub HScroll2_Change ()
    'Display line thickness
    Label4.Caption = Str$(HScroll2.Value)
End Sub

Sub menAboutGrafSamp_Click ()
    'Show About dialog box
    About.Label1.Caption = "GRAFSAMP"
    About.Show MODAL
End Sub

Sub menExit_Click ()
    'All done
    Unload GrafSamp
End Sub

Sub menHelpGrafSamp_Click ()
    'Display some Help text
    FileMsg "GRAFSAMP.MSG", 1
End Sub

Sub Picture1_MouseDown (Button As Integer, Shift As Integer,⟶
 X As Single, Y As Single)
    'Be sure it's the left button
    If (Button And 1) = 0 Then Exit Sub

    'Set starting corner of box
    X1 = X
    Y1 = Y
End Sub
```

(continued)

GRAFSAMP.FRM *continued*

```
Sub Picture1_MouseMove (Button As Integer, Shift As Integer, ⬎
X As Single, Y As Single)
    'Be sure left button is depressed
    If (Button And 1) = 0 Then Exit Sub

    'Erase focus rectangle if it exists
    If X2 Or Y2 Then
        DrawFocusRect Picture1.hDC, FocusRec
    End If

    'Update coordinates
    X2 = X
    Y2 = Y

    'Update rectangle
    FocusRec.left = X1
    FocusRec.top = Y1
    FocusRec.right = X2
    FocusRec.bottom = Y2

    'Adjust rectangle
    If Y2 < Y1 Then Swap FocusRec.top, FocusRec.bottom

    'Draw focus rectangle
    DrawFocusRect Picture1.hDC, FocusRec
End Sub

Sub Picture1_MouseUp (Button As Integer, Shift As Integer, ⬎
X As Single, Y As Single)
    'Be sure it's the left button
    If (Button And 1) = 0 Then Exit Sub

    'Erase focus rectangle if it exists
    If FocusRec.right Or FocusRec.bottom Then
        DrawFocusRect Picture1.hDC, FocusRec
    End If

    'Set line thickness
    Picture1.DrawWidth = HScroll2.Value

    'Put coordinates in correct order
    If X2 < X1 Then Swap X1, X2
    If Y2 < Y1 Then Swap Y1, Y2
```

(continued)

GRAFSAMP.FRM *continued*

```
    'Set up rounding parameters
    X3 = (X2 - X1) * HScroll1.Value / 100
    Y3 = (Y2 - Y1) * HScroll1.Value / 100

    'Draw rounded rectangle
    Ret% = RoundRect(Picture1.hDC, X1, Y1, X2, Y2, X3, Y3)

    'Zero the rectangle coordinates
    X1 = 0
    Y1 = 0
    X2 = 0
    Y2 = 0
End Sub

Sub Swap (X As Integer, Y As Integer)
    'Swap contents of two integer variables
    Tmp% = X
    X = Y
    Y = Tmp%
End Sub
```

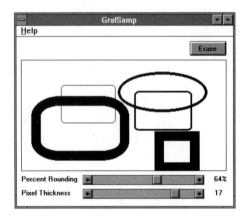

Figure 16-10.
GRAFSAMP.FRM in action.

CREATING YOUR OWN DYNAMIC LINK LIBRARY (DLL)

This chapter presents a powerful programming technique: creating your own dynamic link library (DLL). It is especially useful to you if you're a C programmer who is considering using a combination of Visual Basic and C to create Windows-based applications. Visual Basic provides a superior interface-development environment, and C provides the ultimate in performance for complex coding tasks. This chapter includes a simple working example of a DLL written in C; this DLL contains functions that can be called from Visual Basic.

An excellent source of detailed information on creating DLLs (and on all C programming for Windows) is *Programming Windows 3.1* by Charles Petzold (Microsoft Press, 1992). I created the DLL presented in this chapter after I had studied Petzold's book and the documentation in the Microsoft Windows Software Development Kit. To thoroughly understand the art of writing DLLs, you should read these references; however, the following DLL example can provide a working template to get you started.

If you don't have a C compiler, you needn't worry. The disk included with this book contains both the C source-code files for the DLL and the DLL itself. You can use the DLL to run the Visual Basic application BITS that is presented later in this chapter.

C Language Source File

The following C language source file, which you can create by using a text editor of your choice, creates four functions. The *HiByte* function returns the most significant byte (the left 8 bits) of a signed integer, and the *LoByte* function returns the least significant byte (the right 8 bits) of a signed integer. The

PackInt function combines two integer values, in the range 0 through 255, to form a signed integer value. The *RevStr* function reverses the order of the characters in a string; it was added to this DLL to show how strings are processed in a DLL function. *LibMain* is a special function that must be present in any DLL you create. It provides an entry point for Windows when the DLL is loaded.

Source code for BITPACK.C

```
/* BITPACK.C - Example DLL for Visual Basic applications.

   BITPACK.DLL is demonstrated by the BITS application in
   MICROSOFT VISUAL BASIC WORKSHOP. */

#include <windows.h>

extern "C"
{
int FAR PASCAL _export HiByte( unsigned sInteger );
int FAR PASCAL _export LoByte( int sInteger );
int FAR PASCAL _export PackInt( int sHiInteger, int sLoInteger );
void FAR PASCAL _export RevStr( LPSTR lpString );
}


/* This function is the library entry point.
   It should be present in any DLL you create
   for Visual Basic applications. */

int FAR PASCAL LibMain( HANDLE hInstance, WORD wDataSeg,
                        WORD wHeapSize, LPSTR lpszCmdLine )
{
   if ( wHeapSize > 0 )
      UnlockData( 0 );
   return( 1 );
}


/* Extracts an integer's most significant byte. */

int FAR PASCAL _export HiByte( unsigned sInteger )
{
   return( sInteger >> 8 );
}


/* Extracts an integer's least significant byte. */
```

(continued)

BITPACK.C *continued*

```
int FAR PASCAL _export LoByte( int sInteger )
{
    return( sInteger & 0xFF );
}

/* Combines two bytes into an integer. */

int FAR PASCAL _export PackInt( int sHiInteger, int sLoInteger )
{
    return(( sHiInteger << 8 ) | ( sLoInteger & 0xFF ));
}

/* Reverses a string. */

void FAR PASCAL _export RevStr( LPSTR lpString )
{
    int i, j;
    char chTemp;

    i = 0;
    j = lstrlen( lpString ) - 1;

    while ( i < j )
        {
        chTemp = lpString[i];
        lpString[i++] = lpString[j];
        lpString[j--] = chTemp;
        }
}
```

To properly compile and link the BITPACK dynamic link library, you must create a corresponding module-definition (DEF) file and make (MAK) file. The EXPORTS section, which is sometimes seen in DEF files in old projects, is no longer required. Instead, the lines containing the *_export* modifier in BITPACK.C inform the compiler of functions that can be called from Visual Basic.

Source code for BITPACK.DEF

```
; BITPACK.DEF
; module-definition file

LIBRARY         BITPACK
```

(continued)

BITPACK.DEF *continued*

```
DESCRIPTION     'DLL example for Microsoft Visual Basic Workshop'
EXETYPE         WINDOWS
CODE            PRELOAD MOVEABLE DISCARDABLE
DATA            PRELOAD MOVEABLE SINGLE
HEAPSIZE        1024
```

The BITPACK.MAK file gives the C compiler, linker, and resource editor instructions for creating the DLL.

Source code for BITPACK.MAK

```
# BITPACK.MAK

bitpack.dll : bitpack.obj bitpack.def
    $(DLLLINK) bitpack, bitpack.dll, NUL, $(DLLLIB), bitpack
    rc -t bitpack.dll

bitpack.obj : bitpack.c
    $(DLLCC) bitpack.c
```

The BITPACK.BAT file sets up environment variables for definitions used in BITPACK.MAK. It then runs NMAKE to build the DLL modules from all the files.

Source code for BITPACK.BAT

```
REM - Set up environment and run C/C++ 7 NMAKE

SET DLLCC=cl -c -ASw -G2sw -Ow -W3 -Zp -Tp
SET DLLLINK=link /nod libentry
SET DLLLIB=sdllcew oldnames libw
SET DLLRC=rc -r
NMAKE bitpack.mak
```

With BITPACK.C, BITPACK.DEF, BITPACK.MAK, and BITPACK.BAT ready to go, you can now run the compiler to create BITPACK.DLL. Enter the following command at the MS-DOS prompt:

```
BITPACK
```

You might have to modify BITPACK.BAT and BITPACK.MAK, depending on your compiler. The example presented here was compiled and linked by using Microsoft C/C++ 7. Check the documentation for your C compiler for more information.

When you run a program that calls a DLL function, Windows loads the DLL into memory. Windows can access the DLL only if the DLL is contained in a directory that appears in your path or if the DLL is contained in the same directory as the program that calls it. Generally, DLL files should be stored in the Windows system directory (C:\WINDOWS\SYSTEM). If you're working in the Visual Basic environment and you don't want to put the DLL in the Windows system directory, you should place it in the directory that contains Visual Basic. Be sure to copy BITPACK.DLL to the proper directory before you run BITS, the Visual Basic application that demonstrates the functions in the DLL.

The BITS Application

The BITS application demonstrates how easy it is to call functions contained in a DLL you've created. BITS calls the four functions in BITPACK.DLL, and it displays the results on the BITS form.

Two scroll bars on the form let you select two separate byte values in the range 0 through 255. Whenever the scroll bar values change, the BITPACK functions *HiByte*, *LoByte*, and *PackInt* are called to immediately update the byte values and the integer value they create. You can change all displayed values to hexadecimal notation by choosing the Hexadecimal command from the Options menu.

You can type any string in the text box below the scroll bars. The string will be reversed and displayed in the bottom text box as fast as the characters are entered, demonstrating the *RevStr* function in BITPACK.DLL.

The files for the BITS application are included on the disk packaged with this book. To load the files into the Visual Basic environment, choose Open Project from the File menu, and then type *C:\WORKSHOP\BITS.MAK*. This opens the project and enables you to view and modify the forms and code. The following figures, tables, and code give the details of the application's creation.

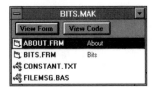

Figure 17-1.
BITS project list.

Figure 17-2.
BITS.FRM during development.

BITS.FRM Menu Design Window Entries

Caption	Name	Indentation
&Options	menOptTop	0
&Decimal	menDecimal	1
&Hexadecimal	menHexadecimal	1
-	menSep	1
E&xit	menExitBits	1
&Help	menHelpTop	0
&Help on Bits	menHelpBits	1
&About Bits...	menAboutBits	1

BITS.FRM Form and Control Properties

Property	Value
Form	
AutoRedraw	True
Caption	BITPACK.DLL Demonstration
Name	Bits
Horizontal Scroll Bar	
LargeChange	10
Max	255
Name	HScroll1

(continued)

BITS.FRM Form and Control Properties *continued*

Property	Value
Horizontal Scroll Bar	
LargeChange	10
Max	255
Name	HScroll2
Text Box	
Name	Text1
Text Box	
Name	Text2
Label	
Caption	Hi byte
Name	Label1
Label	
Caption	0
Name	Label3
Label	
Caption	Lo byte
Name	Label2
Label	
Caption	0
Name	Label4
Label	
Alignment	1 - Right Justify
Caption	PackInt:
Name	Label5
Label	
Caption	0
Name	Label8

(continued)

BITS.FRM Form and Control Properties *continued*

Property	Value
Label	
Alignment	1 - Right Justify
Caption	HiByte:
Name	Label6
Label	
Caption	0
Name	Label9
Label	
Alignment	1 - Right Justify
Caption	LoByte:
Name	Label7
Label	
Caption	0
Name	Label10
Label	
Caption	Enter a string...
Name	Label11
Label	
Caption	Reversed string...
Name	Label12

Source code for BITS.FRM

```
'Declarations for BITS

Declare Function HiByte Lib "BITPACK.DLL"
 (ByVal Number As Integer) As Integer
Declare Function LoByte Lib "BITPACK.DLL"
 (ByVal Number As Integer) As Integer
Declare Function PackInt Lib "BITPACK.DLL"
 (ByVal HiByte As Integer, ByVal LoByte As Integer) As Integer
```

(continued)

BITS.FRM *continued*

```
Declare Sub RevStr Lib "BITPACK.DLL" (ByVal lpString As String)

Sub HScroll1_Change ()
    'Get scroll bar values
    Hi = HScroll1.Value
    Lo = HScroll2.Value

    'Pack the two bytes into an integer
    Packed = PackInt(Hi, Lo)

    'Display numbers in decimal
    If menDecimal.Checked = True Then
        Label3.Caption = Hi
        Label4.Caption = Lo
        Label8.Caption = Packed
        Label9.Caption = HiByte(Packed)
        Label10.Caption = LoByte(Packed)

    'Display numbers in hexadecimal
    Else
        Label3.Caption = Hex$(Hi)
        Label4.Caption = Hex$(Lo)
        Label8.Caption = Hex$(Packed)
        Label9.Caption = Hex$(HiByte(Packed))
        Label10.Caption = Hex$(LoByte(Packed))
    End If
End Sub

Sub HScroll1_Scroll ()
    HScroll1_Change
End Sub

Sub HScroll2_Change ()
    HScroll1_Change
End Sub

Sub HScroll2_Scroll ()
    HScroll1_Change
End Sub

Sub menAboutBits_Click ()
    'Show About dialog box
    About.Label1.Caption = "BITS"
    About.Show MODAL
End Sub
```

(continued)

389

BITS.FRM *continued*

```
Sub menDecimal_Click ()
    'Set decimal display mode
    menDecimal.Checked = True
    menHexadecimal.Checked = False

    'Force update of display
    HScroll1_Change
End Sub

Sub menExitBits_Click ()
    'All done
    Unload Bits
End Sub

Sub menHelpBits_Click ()
    'Display some Help text
    FileMsg "BITS.MSG", 1
End Sub

Sub menHexadecimal_Click ()
    'Set hexadecimal display mode
    menDecimal.Checked = False
    menHexadecimal.Checked = True

    'Force display to update
    HScroll1_Change
End Sub

Sub Text1_Change ()
    'Reverse text as each character is typed
    A$ = Text1.Text
    RevStr A$
    Text2.Text = A$
End Sub

Sub Text2_Change ()
    'Reverse text if user enters in Text2
    A$ = Text2.Text
    RevStr A$
    Text1.Text = A$
End Sub
```

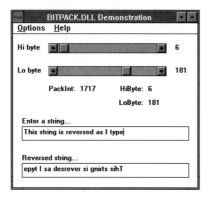

Figure 17-3.
BITS.FRM in action.

CREATING A CUSTOM CONTROL

This chapter presents an example custom control named VBINI that is designed to provide easy access to initialization strings in INI files. A Visual Basic application called INIDEMO demonstrates VBINI.

The VBINI Custom Control

The VBINI.VBX custom control makes it easy to read and write initialization strings stored in INI files. Initialization strings are used to record operational settings, such as window sizes, window locations, and users' color choices. The VBini control is invisible at runtime, like the Timer control, and it provides four easy-to-use properties for defining where and what to record in the INI files.

The VBINI.VBX control can be implemented in several ways. I chose to use the standard *Refresh* method to trigger the reading or writing of the string data. The control's String property is checked, and if a string of characters is found, the string is written to the indicated file. If no characters are in the String property, the indicated file is read in an attempt to find the string. The FileName, Section, and Entry properties determine the location of the filed string data.

To create custom controls, you need a C compiler and a good source of information about techniques for programming applications for Windows. Microsoft C/C++ 7, the Microsoft Windows Software Development Kit (SDK), and the Professional Edition of Visual Basic for Windows 3 are the tools I used for the example presented here, and I recommend them. If you are using Microsoft C version 6, QuickC, or Borland's C compiler, you might need to make some minor changes to the source-code files. The Professional Edition of Visual Basic for Windows 3 provides a wealth of information and several example custom controls. I found it to be a valuable source of information and examples.

It's beyond the scope of this book to go into all the details of programming custom controls. You should refer to the documentation provided with your development software for in-depth information. The VBini custom control presented in this chapter is designed to introduce you to programming custom controls and to let you get a feel for what's involved. The VBini custom control itself is also a handy tool to add to your bag of tricks, even if you don't dive right in and start creating your own custom controls.

Several files are required for the C compiler, resource compiler, and linker to build the VBINI.VBX file. After the VBX file is built, however, it is all that needs to be loaded into the Visual Basic development environment to use the new control. All the required files are described in the next few sections. To build the VBINI.VBX custom control module, you place all these files in one directory and type *NMAKE* at the MS-DOS prompt. (Both the source files and the finished VBX file are included on the disk packaged with this book.)

The MAKEFILE File

The NMAKE utility acts on the MAKEFILE file to control the entire process of building the custom control. If a file in the project changes, NMAKE directs the C/C++ compiler to recompile the changed file, and all affected compiling and linking steps are performed. The MAKEFILE file is almost identical to those provided in the CDK subdirectories of the Professional Edition of Visual Basic for Windows 3.

Source code for MAKEFILE

```
#--------------------------------------------------------------------
# Custom control makefile
#--------------------------------------------------------------------

.SUFFIXES:  .c .def .VBX .h .lnk .map .obj .rc .res .sym

PRODUCT     = VBINI
DEBUG       = 1
#C6         =

Default: $(PRODUCT).VBX
```

(continued)

MAKEFILE *continued*

```
#-------------------------------------------------------------------
# Tools required
#-------------------------------------------------------------------

CC          = cl
CVPACK      = cvpack
LINK        = link
MAPSYM      = mapsym
RC          = rc
SZSCRN      = echo >con

!ifdef C6
OBJS        = ..\libentry.obj
CFLAGS2     = /Gw -Asnw
!else
CFLAGS2     = /GD -AS
RCFLAGS     = -d RC31
RCFLAGS2    = -30
!endif


#-------------------------------------------------------------------
# Flags
#-------------------------------------------------------------------
!IF $(DEBUG)
CFLAGS      = /c /W4 /G2cs /Zip /BATCH /Od
!ELSE
CFLAGS      = /c /W4 /G2cs /Zp /BATCH /Osge
!ENDIF


LFLAGS      = /co /align:16 /batch /far /li /map /nod /noe /nopackc /w

#-------------------------------------------------------------------
# Default build rules
#-------------------------------------------------------------------
.c.obj:
    $(SZSCRN) Compiling $(<F)
    $(CC) $(CFLAGS) $(CFLAGS2) $<
```

(continued)

MAKEFILE *continued*

```
#------------------------------------------------------------------
# Dependencies
#------------------------------------------------------------------
$(PRODUCT).obj: $(PRODUCT).c $(PRODUCT).h

$(PRODUCT).VBX: $(PRODUCT).obj $(PRODUCT).lnk $(PRODUCT).res→
 $(PRODUCT).def
    $(SZSCRN) Linking $(PRODUCT).VBX...
    $(LINK) /co @$(PRODUCT).lnk
!ifdef C6
    $(SZSCRN) CVPACKing $(PRODUCT).VBX...
    $(CVPACK) $(PRODUCT).VBX
!endif
    $(SZSCRN) RCing $(PRODUCT).VBX...
    $(RC) $(RCFLAGS2) $(PRODUCT).res $(PRODUCT).VBX
    $(SZSCRN) MAPSYMing $(PRODUCT).VBX...
    $(MAPSYM) $(PRODUCT)
    $(SZSCRN) Done Linking $(PRODUCT).VBX


$(PRODUCT).lnk: makefile
    $(SZSCRN) Making <<$(PRODUCT).lnk
    $(OBJS) $(PRODUCT).obj
    $(PRODUCT).VBX $(LFLAGS)
    $(PRODUCT).map
    vbapi.lib libw.lib sdllcew.lib
    $(PRODUCT).def
<<KEEP

$(PRODUCT).res: $(PRODUCT).rc $(PRODUCT).h \
    $(PRODUCT)cd.bmp \
    $(PRODUCT)cu.bmp \
    $(PRODUCT)mu.bmp \
    $(PRODUCT)eu.bmp
    $(SZSCRN) Resource compiling $(PRODUCT).RC
    $(RC) -R $(RCFLAGS) $(RCINCS) $(PRODUCT).rc

cln:
    -del $(PRODUCT).obj
    -del $(PRODUCT).res
    -del $(PRODUCT).lnk
    -del $(PRODUCT).vbx
    -del $(PRODUCT).map
    -del $(PRODUCT).sym
```

The VBINI.DEF File

The VBINI.DEF file provides information for properly linking the module. A DEF file is required when building any application for Windows.

Source code for VBINI.DEF

```
;-----------------------------------------------------------------
; VBini.def - module definition file for VBINI.VBX custom control
;-----------------------------------------------------------------
LIBRARY         VBINI
EXETYPE         WINDOWS
DESCRIPTION     'Visual Basic VBini Custom Control'

CODE            MOVEABLE
DATA            MOVEABLE SINGLE

HEAPSIZE        2048

EXPORTS
        WEP     @1          RESIDENTNAME

SEGMENTS
        WEP_TEXT FIXED
```

The VBINI.RC File

The VBINI.RC file provides instructions to the resource compiler. In this case, the file's main purpose is to embed the control's bitmap files directly into the VBINI.VBX file. These four bitmap files are described in the next section of this chapter.

Source code for VBINI.RC

```
//-----------------------------------------------------------------
// VBini.rc
//-----------------------------------------------------------------

#include "vbini.h"

//-----------------------------------------------------------------
// Control resources for VBINI control model
//-----------------------------------------------------------------
IDBMP_VBINI             BITMAP DISCARDABLE "vbinicu.bmp"
```

(continued)

VBINI.RC *continued*

```
IDBMP_VBINIDOWN       BITMAP DISCARDABLE "vbinicd.bmp"
IDBMP_VBINIMONO       BITMAP DISCARDABLE "vbinimu.bmp"
IDBMP_VBINIEGA        BITMAP DISCARDABLE "vbinieu.bmp"
```

The VBINICU.BMP, VBINICD.BMP, VBINIMU.BMP, and VBINIEU.BMP Files

The four bitmap files VBINICU.BMP, VBINICD.BMP, VBINIMU.BMP, and VBINIEU.BMP provide the buttons that Visual Basic displays in the Toolbox. In Figure 18-1 you can see the VBini tool at the bottom of the Toolbox. You can edit the bitmap files by using any BMP file editing tool, such as Windows Paintbrush or the tools provided in the SDK. To create new icons, I suggest that you copy and rename these files and then edit them. Don't change their sizes, and when you alter their appearances, consider being conservative so that they look like other Toolbox icons.

Figure 18-1.
The Toolbox with the VBini tool added.

On most computer systems, the user will see only the first two bitmaps. The last two bitmaps are for EGA and monochrome systems. For the best effect, stick with the simple black-and-white color scheme of these icons.

The VBINI.H File

The VBINI.H include file is an important piece of this project. When you create your own custom controls, much of your time and energy will go into modifying this file and the main C code file. The properties, events, and other details of the custom control are defined in the VBINI.H file. If you're new to custom control programming, pay a lot of attention to how the parts of this file work. The Control Development Guide that is provided with the Professional Edition of Visual Basic for Windows 3 explains the contents of this file in detail.

Source code for VBINI.H

```
//------------------------------------------------------------------
// VBini.h
//------------------------------------------------------------------


//------------------------------------------------------------------
// Resource information
//------------------------------------------------------------------
// Toolbox bitmap resource ID numbers
//------------------------------------------------------------------
#define IDBMP_VBINI          8000
#define IDBMP_VBINIDOWN      8001
#define IDBMP_VBINIMONO      8003
#define IDBMP_VBINIEGA       8006


#ifndef RC_INVOKED
//------------------------------------------------------------------
// Macro for referencing member of structure
//------------------------------------------------------------------
#define OFFSETIN(struc, field)        ((USHORT)&(((struc *)0)->field))


//------------------------------------------------------------------
// VBini control data and structures
//------------------------------------------------------------------
typedef struct tagVBINI
    {
    HSZ  hszFileName;
    HSZ  hszSection;
    HSZ  hszEntry;
    HSZ  hszString;
    } VBINI;


typedef VBINI FAR * PVBINI;


//------------------------------------------------------------------
// Control procedure
//------------------------------------------------------------------
LONG FAR PASCAL _export VBiniCtlProc(HCTL, HWND, USHORT, USHORT,⤙
  LONG);
```

(continued)

VBINI.H *continued*

```
//-------------------------------------------------------------------
// Property information
//-------------------------------------------------------------------
PROPINFO Property_FileName =
    {
    "FileName",
    DT_HSZ | PF_fGetData | PF_fSetData | PF_fSetMsg | PF_fSaveData,
    OFFSETIN(VBINI, hszFileName),
    NULL
    };

PROPINFO Property_Section =
    {
    "Section",
    DT_HSZ | PF_fGetData | PF_fSetData | PF_fSetMsg | PF_fSaveData,
    OFFSETIN(VBINI, hszSection),
    NULL
    };

PROPINFO Property_Entry =
    {
    "Entry",
    DT_HSZ | PF_fGetData | PF_fSetData | PF_fSetMsg | PF_fSaveData,
    OFFSETIN(VBINI, hszEntry),
    NULL
    };

PROPINFO Property_String =
    {
    "String",
    DT_HSZ | PF_fGetData | PF_fSetData | PF_fSetMsg | PF_fSaveData,
    OFFSETIN(VBINI, hszString),
    NULL
    };

//-------------------------------------------------------------------
// Property list
//-------------------------------------------------------------------
// Define the consecutive indexes for the properties
//-------------------------------------------------------------------
#define IPROP_VBINI_CTLNAME                 0
#define IPROP_VBINI_INDEX                   1
#define IPROP_VBINI_LEFT                    2
#define IPROP_VBINI_TOP                     3
```

(continued)

VBINI.H *continued*

```
#define IPROP_VBINI_TAG                 4
#define IPROP_VBINI_FILENAME            5
#define IPROP_VBINI_SECTION             6
#define IPROP_VBINI_ENTRY               7
#define IPROP_VBINI_STRING              8

PPROPINFO VBini_Properties[] =
    {
    PPROPINFO_STD_CTLNAME,
    PPROPINFO_STD_INDEX,
    PPROPINFO_STD_LEFT,
    PPROPINFO_STD_TOP,
    PPROPINFO_STD_TAG,
    &Property_FileName,
    &Property_Section,
    &Property_Entry,
    &Property_String,
    NULL
    };

//--------------------------------------------------------------------
// Event list
//--------------------------------------------------------------------
// Define the consecutive indexes for the events
//--------------------------------------------------------------------
#define IEVENT_VBINI_CLICK              0

PEVENTINFO VBini_Events[] =
    {
    PEVENTINFO_STD_CLICK,
    NULL
    };

//--------------------------------------------------------------------
// Model structure
//--------------------------------------------------------------------
// Define the control model (using event and property structures)
//--------------------------------------------------------------------
MODEL modelVBini =
    {
    VB_VERSION,                 // Visual Basic version being used
    MODEL_fInvisAtRun,          // MODEL flags
    (PCTLPROC)VBiniCtlProc,     // Control procedures
```

(continued)

VBINI.H *continued*

```
    0,                              // Class style
    0,                              // Default style of Windows
    sizeof(VBINI),                  // Size of VBINI structure
    IDBMP_VBINI,                    // Palette bitmap ID
    "VBini",                        // Default control name
    "VBini",                        // Visual Basic class name
    NULL,                           // Parent class name
    VBini_Properties,               // Property information table
    VBini_Events,                   // Event information table
    IPROP_VBINI_FILENAME,           // Default property
    IEVENT_VBINI_CLICK,             // Default event
    -1                              // Property representing value of ctl
    };

#endif // RC_INVOKED
```

The VBINI.C File

The VBINI.C file is the heart of the custom control project. The code in this file loads the control and processes messages from Windows and Visual Basic when the control is in use. The VBINI.C file calls the Windows API functions *GetPrivateProfileString* and *WritePrivateProfileString* to read and write the string data to the INI file. Again, the Control Development Guide is a good source of information about how to program correctly when creating custom controls. It lists many useful functions that are not demonstrated here.

Source code for VBINI.C

```
//------------------------------------------------------------------
// VBini.c
//------------------------------------------------------------------

#include <windows.h>
#include <vbapi.h>
#include <string.h>
#include "vbini.h"


//------------------------------------------------------------------
// Global variables
//------------------------------------------------------------------
HANDLE hmodDLL;
char FAR szBuf[80];
```

(continued)

VBINI.C *continued*

```
//----------------------------------------------------------------
// Local prototypes
//----------------------------------------------------------------
VOID NEAR GetIniString(HCTL);
VOID NEAR PutIniString(HCTL);


//----------------------------------------------------------------
// VBini control procedure
//----------------------------------------------------------------
LONG FAR PASCAL _export VBiniCtlProc
(
    HCTL    hctl,
    HWND    hwnd,
    USHORT  msg,
    USHORT  wp,
    LONG    lp
)
{
    PVBINI pvbini = NULL;
    LPSTR lpstr;

    switch (msg)
    {
    case VBM_CREATED:
        if (VBGetMode() != MODE_DESIGN)
            return 0;
        break;

    case WM_NCDESTROY:
        pvbini = (PVBINI)VBDerefControl(hctl);
        if (pvbini->hszFileName)
            VBDestroyHsz(pvbini->hszFileName);

        pvbini = (PVBINI)VBDerefControl(hctl);
        if (pvbini->hszSection)
            VBDestroyHsz(pvbini->hszSection);

        pvbini = (PVBINI)VBDerefControl(hctl);
        if (pvbini->hszEntry)
            VBDestroyHsz(pvbini->hszEntry);

        pvbini = (PVBINI)VBDerefControl(hctl);
        if (pvbini->hszString)
            VBDestroyHsz(pvbini->hszString);
```

(continued)

VBINI.C *continued*

```
        break;

    case VBM_METHOD:
        switch (wp)
        {
        case (METH_REFRESH):
            {
            pvbini = (PVBINI)VBDerefControl(hctl);
            lpstr = VBLockHsz(pvbini->hszString);
            if (lstrlen(lpstr))
                {
                VBUnlockHsz(pvbini->hszString);
                PutIniString(hctl);
                }
            else
                {
                VBUnlockHsz(pvbini->hszString);
                GetIniString(hctl);
                }
            return 0;
            }
        }
    }
    return VBDefControlProc(hctl, hwnd, msg, wp, lp);
}

//-------------------------------------------------------------------
// Register custom control; Visual Basic calls this routine when the
// custom control DLL is loaded for use
//-------------------------------------------------------------------
BOOL FAR PASCAL _export VBINITCC
(
    USHORT usVersion,
    BOOL    fRuntime
)
{

    // Avoid warnings on unused (but required) formal parameters
    fRuntime = fRuntime;
    usVersion = usVersion;

    // Register control(s)
    return VBRegisterModel(hmodDLL, &modelVBini);
}
```

(continued)

VBINI.C *continued*

```
//-------------------------------------------------------------------
// Initialize library; this routine is called when the first client
// loads the DLL
//-------------------------------------------------------------------
int FAR PASCAL LibMain
(
    HANDLE  hModule,
    WORD    wDataSeg,
    WORD    cbHeapSize,
    LPSTR   lpszCmdLine
)
{
    // Avoid warnings on unused (but required) formal parameters
    wDataSeg     = wDataSeg;
    cbHeapSize   = cbHeapSize;
    lpszCmdLine  = lpszCmdLine;

    hmodDLL = hModule;

    return 1;
}

//-------------------------------------------------------------------
// Attempt to write a private profile string using
// current properties
//-------------------------------------------------------------------
VOID NEAR PutIniString( HCTL hctl )
{
    PVBINI  pvbini = NULL;
    LPSTR   lpstrFileName;
    LPSTR   lpstrSection;
    LPSTR   lpstrEntry;
    LPSTR   lpstrString;
    BOOL    fSuccess;

    pvbini = (PVBINI)VBDerefControl(hctl);
    lpstrFileName = VBLockHsz(pvbini->hszFileName);

    pvbini = (PVBINI)VBDerefControl(hctl);
    lpstrSection = VBLockHsz(pvbini->hszSection);

    pvbini = (PVBINI)VBDerefControl(hctl);
    lpstrEntry = VBLockHsz(pvbini->hszEntry);
```

(continued)

VBINI.C *continued*

```
    pvbini = (PVBINI)VBDerefControl(hctl);
    lpstrString = VBLockHsz(pvbini->hszString);

    if (lstrlen(lpstrFileName) && lstrlen(lpstrSection) &&
                lstrlen(lpstrEntry) && lstrlen(lpstrString))
        fSuccess = WritePrivateProfileString( lpstrSection,
                    lpstrEntry, lpstrString, lpstrFileName );

    VBUnlockHsz(pvbini->hszFileName);
    VBUnlockHsz(pvbini->hszSection);
    VBUnlockHsz(pvbini->hszEntry);
    VBUnlockHsz(pvbini->hszString);
}

//-------------------------------------------------------------------
// Attempt to get a private profile string using current properties
//-------------------------------------------------------------------
VOID NEAR GetIniString( HCTL hctl )
{
    PVBINI pvbini = NULL;
    LPSTR  lpstrFileName;
    LPSTR  lpstrSection;
    LPSTR  lpstrEntry;

    pvbini = (PVBINI)VBDerefControl(hctl);
    lpstrFileName = VBLockHsz(pvbini->hszFileName);

    pvbini = (PVBINI)VBDerefControl(hctl);
    lpstrSection = VBLockHsz(pvbini->hszSection);

    pvbini = (PVBINI)VBDerefControl(hctl);
    lpstrEntry = VBLockHsz(pvbini->hszEntry);

    GetPrivateProfileString( lpstrSection, lpstrEntry, "",
                            szBuf, sizeof(szBuf), lpstrFileName );

    VBSetControlProperty( hctl, IPROP_VBINI_STRING, (LONG)szBuf );

    VBUnlockHsz(pvbini->hszFileName);
    VBUnlockHsz(pvbini->hszSection);
    VBUnlockHsz(pvbini->hszEntry);
}
```

The INIDEMO Application

The INIDEMO application demonstrates the VBINI.VBX custom control. At runtime the control is invisible, like the standard Timer control. INIDEMO lets you set the VBini control's FileName, Section, Entry, and String properties, and it lets you read or write the initialization string by using the control's *Refresh* method.

When you use the VBini control in your own applications, you generally won't display the control's properties. Often an application will read the required initialization strings as the form loads and will save the current settings as the form unloads. This action is transparent to the user.

When you run the INIDEMO application, I suggest you use it to create a new file, such as the suggested default file of TEST.INI in the current directory, instead of using it to explore the contents of known INI files. If you use INIDEMO to look at a known INI file and you click Write when you mean to click Read, you might overwrite initialization strings. This can have unpredictable results. You can't hurt anything if you stick to the TEST.INI file.

The *Refresh* method is used to both read and write strings in INI files. The VBini control checks the String property to decide which way to transfer the data. If the String property has a string length greater than zero, the *Refresh* method writes to the indicated file, section, and entry. If the String property is empty, the *Refresh* method reads from the file. When you're using VBini controls in your own applications and you want to read a string from a file, be sure to assign an empty string to the String property just before performing the *Refresh* method. Take a look at the cmdRead_Click and cmdWrite_Click subprograms in INIDEMO to see how these properties are set to read and write the strings.

The files for the INIDEMO application are included on the disk packaged with this book. To load the files into the Visual Basic environment, choose the Open Project option from the File menu, and then type *C:\WORKSHOP\INIDEMO.MAK*. This opens the project and enables you to view and modify the forms and code. The following figures, tables, and code give the details of the application's creation.

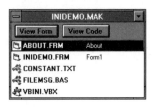

Figure 18-2.
INIDEMO project list.

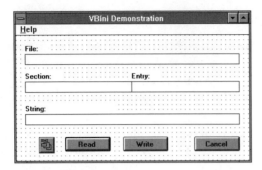

Figure 18-3.
INIDEMO.FRM during development.

INIDEMO.FRM Menu Design Window Entries

Caption	Name	Indentation
&Help	menHelp	0
&Help on INIDemo	menHelpINIDemo	1
&About INIDemo	menAboutINIDemo	1
-	menSep	1
E&xit	menExit	1

INIDEMO.FRM Form and Control Properties

Property	Value
Form	
Caption	VBini Demonstration
Name	Form1
VBini	
Name	VBini1
Command Button	
Caption	Write
Name	cmdWrite
Text Box	
Name	txtString
Text	[none]

(continued)

INIDEMO.FRM Form and Control Properties *continued*

Property	Value
Command Button	
Cancel	True
Caption	Cancel
Name	cmdCancel
Command Button	
Caption	Read
Default	True
Name	cmdRead
Text Box	
Name	txtEntry
Text Box	
Name	txtSection
Text Box	
Name	txtFile
Label	
Caption	String:
Name	Label4
Label	
Caption	Entry:
Name	Label3
Label	
Caption	Section:
Name	Label2
Label	
Caption	File:
Name	Label1

Source code for INIDEMO.FRM

```
Sub cmdCancel_Click ()
    End
End Sub

Sub cmdRead_Click ()
    VBini1.FileName = txtFile.Text
    VBini1.Section = txtSection.Text
    VBini1.Entry = txtEntry.Text
    VBini1.String = ""
    VBini1.Refresh
    txtString.Text = VBini1.String
End Sub

Sub cmdWrite_Click ()
    VBini1.FileName = txtFile.Text
    VBini1.Section = txtSection.Text
    VBini1.Entry = txtEntry.Text
    VBini1.String = txtString.Text
    VBini1.Refresh
End Sub

Sub Form_Load ()
    'Center form
    Left = (Screen.Width - Width) / 2
    Top = (Screen.Height - Height) / 2

    'Default to TEST.INI in current directory
    fullpath$ = LCase$(App.Path)
    If Right$(fullpath$, 1) <> "\" Then
        fullpath$ = fullpath$ + "\"
    End If
    txtFile.Text = fullpath$ + "test.ini"

    'Set defaults for Section, Entry, and String
    txtSection.Text = "Alpha"
    txtEntry.Text = "One"
    txtString.Text = "This is a sample profile string"
End Sub
```

(continued)

INIDEMO.FRM *continued*

```
Sub menAboutINIDemo_Click ()
    'Display About dialog box
    About.Label1.Caption = "INIDEMO"
    About.Show MODAL
End Sub

Sub menExit_Click ()
    End
End Sub

Sub menHelpINIDemo_Click ()
    'Display some Help text
    FileMsg "INIDEMO.MSG", 1
End Sub
```

Figure 18-4.
INIDEMO.FRM in action.

## CHAPTER NINETEEN

PROFESSIONAL EDITION CONTROLS

The Professional Edition of Visual Basic for Windows 3 includes several controls not included in the Standard Edition. These controls add a great deal of flexibility and power to your programming toolbox. The applications in this chapter provide working examples of many of these controls.

The DIALOGS Application

The DIALOGS application demonstrates the Common Dialog control. Common Dialog controls provide an efficient way to display Open, Save As, Print Setup, and several other common dialog boxes by simply changing a few properties and setting the Action property. A Common Dialog control also provides a straightforward mechanism for displaying Help files from a running application. The DIALOGS application demonstrates all of the common dialog boxes and lets you view all the Help files in C:\VB and its subdirectories.

Six commonly used dialog boxes are initiated by setting the Action property of the Common Dialog control. The File Open and File Save As dialog boxes are very similar in appearance and function; they appear exactly the same as the dialog boxes in the Visual Basic environment. You can also use the Common Dialog control to ask the user for a color, to choose a font and its characteristics, and to set up printer output options. Finally, the Common Dialog control can start any Windows Help file, jumping right to the contents or to a keyword.

The five command buttons on the left side of the form let you try out the various dialog boxes. The Click subprograms demonstrate how the Common Dialog control is invoked for each type of dialog box. During Form_Load, all HLP files in the \VB directory and its subdirectories are added to the Combo Box control. Select any Help file in this list, and then click the Help button to activate Help.

The files for the DIALOGS application are included on the disk packaged with this book. To load the files into the Visual Basic environment, choose the Open Project option from the File menu, and then type *C:\WORKSHOP\DIALOGS.MAK*. This opens the project and enables you to view and modify the forms and code. The following figures, tables, and code give the details of the application's creation.

Figure 19-1.
DIALOGS project list.

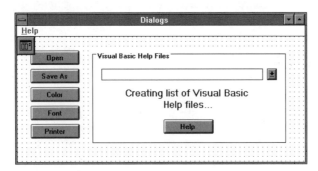

Figure 19-2.
DIALOGS.FRM during development.

DIALOGS.FRM Menu Design Window Entries

Caption	Name	Indentation	Other Information
&Help	menHelp	0	Enabled = False
&Help on Dialogs	menHelpDialogs	1	
&About Dialogs...	menAboutDialogs	1	
-	menSep	1	
E&xit	menExit	1	

DIALOGS.FRM Form and Control Properties

Property	Value
Form	
Caption	Dialogs
Name	Dialogs
Frame	
Caption	Visual Basic Help Files
Name	Frame1
Command Button	
Caption	Help
Name	cmdHelpFile
Combo Box	
Name	Combo1
Text	[none]
Label	
Alignment	2 - Center
Caption	Creating list of Visual Basic Help files...
FontSize	12
Name	Label1
Common Dialog	
Name	CMDialog1
Command Button	
Caption	Printer
Enabled	False
Name	cmdPrinter
Command Button	
Caption	Font
Enabled	False
Name	cmdFont

(continued)

415

DIALOGS.FRM Form and Control Properties *continued*

Property	Value
Command Button	
Caption	Color
Enabled	False
Name	cmdColor
Command Button	
Caption	Save As
Enabled	False
Name	cmdSaveAs
Command Button	
Caption	Open
Enabled	False
Name	cmdOpen

Source code for DIALOGS.FRM

```
Sub cmdColor_Click ()
    NL$ = Chr$(13) + Chr$(10)

    'Set up color
    CMDialog1.Color = GREEN

    'Set up flags
    CMDialog1.Flags = CC_RGBINIT + CC_FULLOPEN

    'Display Color dialog box
    CMDialog1.Action = DLG_COLOR

    'Confirm to user
    MsgBox "Color..." + NL$ + "Hex: " + Hex$(CMDialog1.Color)
End Sub

Sub cmdFont_Click ()
    NL$ = Chr$(13) + Chr$(10)
    TB$ = Chr$(9)

    'Set up flags
    CMDialog1.Flags = CF_WYSIWYG + CF_BOTH + CF_SCALABLEONLY
```

(continued)

DIALOGS.FRM *continued*

```
      'Display Font dialog box
      CMDialog1.Action = DLG_FONT

      'Confirm to user
      F1$ = "Font Name:" + TB$ + CMDialog1.FontName + NL$
      F2$ = "Font Size:" + TB$ + CMDialog1.FontSize + NL$
      F3$ = "Bold:" + TB$ + TB$ + CMDialog1.FontBold + NL$
      F4$ = "Italic:" + TB$ + TB$ + CMDialog1.FontItalic + NL$
      F5$ = "Underline:" + TB$ + CMDialog1.FontUnderLine + NL$
      F6$ = "Strikethru:" + TB$ + CMDialog1.FontStrikeThru + NL$
      MsgBox F1$ + F2$ + F3$ + F4$ + F5$ + F6$
End Sub

Sub cmdHelpFile_Click ()
      CMDialog1.HelpFile = Combo1.List(Combo1.ListIndex)
      CMDialog1.HelpCommand = HELP_CONTENTS
      CMDialog1.Action = DLG_HELP
End Sub

Sub cmdOpen_Click ()
      NL$ = Chr$(13) + Chr$(10)

      'Set up filter
      B$ = "Batch Files (*.BAT)|*.bat"
      t$ = "Text Files (*.TXT)|*.txt"
      A$ = "All Files (*.*)|*.*"
      CMDialog1.Filter = B$ + "|" + t$ + "|" + A$

      'Specify default filter
      CMDialog1.FilterIndex = 3

      'Set up flags
      CMDialog1.Flags = OFN_HIDEREADONLY

      'Display File Open dialog box
      CMDialog1.Action = DLG_FILE_OPEN

      'Confirm to user
      MsgBox "File Open..." + NL$ + CMDialog1.Filename
End Sub

Sub cmdPrinter_Click ()
      NL$ = Chr$(13) + Chr$(10)
      TB$ = Chr$(9)
```

(continued)

417

DIALOGS.FRM *continued*

```
        'Set up flags
        CMDialog1.Flags = PD_ALLPAGES

        'Set page-range numbers
        CMDialog1.Min = 1
        CMDialog1.Max = 100
        CMDialog1.FromPage = 1
        CMDialog1.ToPage = 100

        'Display Print dialog box
        CMDialog1.Action = DLG_PRINT

        'Confirm to user
        P1$ = "Begin Page:" + TB$ + CMDialog1.FromPage + NL$
        P2$ = "End Page:" + TB$ + CMDialog1.ToPage + NL$
        P3$ = "No. Copies:" + TB$ + CMDialog1.Copies + NL$
        MsgBox P1$ + P2$ + P3$
End Sub

Sub cmdSaveAs_Click ()
        NL$ = Chr$(13) + Chr$(10)

        'Set up filter
        B$ = "Batch Files (*.BAT)|*.bat"
        t$ = "Text Files (*.TXT)|*.txt"
        A$ = "All Files (*.*)|*.*"
        CMDialog1.Filter = B$ + "|" + t$ + "|" + A$

        'Specify default filter
        CMDialog1.FilterIndex = 3

        'Set up flags
        CMDialog1.Flags = OFN_HIDEREADONLY

        'Display File Save As dialog box
        CMDialog1.Action = DLG_FILE_SAVE

        'Confirm to user
        MsgBox "Save As..." + NL$ + CMDialog1.Filename
    End Sub

Sub FindDirectories (Directory$)
        'Build list of all subdirectories in specified directory
        Dim D$()
```

(continued)

DIALOGS.FRM *continued*

```
    Fil$ = Dir$(Directory$, ATTR_DIRECTORY)
    Do Until Fil$ = ""
        If Left$(Fil$, 1) <> "." Then
            FullPath$ = Directory$ + Fil$
            If GetAttr(FullPath$) = ATTR_DIRECTORY Then
                n% = n% + 1
                ReDim Preserve D$(n%)
                D$(n%) = FullPath$ + "\"
            End If
        End If
        Fil$ = Dir$
    Loop

    'Search directory for HLP files
    Fil$ = Dir$(Directory$ + "*.HLP")
    Do Until Fil$ = ""
        FullPath$ = Directory$ + Fil$
        Combo1.AddItem FullPath$
        Fil$ = Dir$
    Loop

    'Search each subdirectory
    If n% Then
        For i% = 1 To n%
            FindDirectories D$(i%)
        Next i%
    End If
End Sub

Sub Form_Load ()
    'Center form on screen
    Left = (Screen.Width - Width) / 2
    Top = (Screen.Height - Height) / 2

    'Get form displayed
    Show
    Refresh

    'Search for all VB HLP files
    FindDirectories Left$(App.Path, 2) + "\VB\"
    Combo1.ListIndex = 0

    'Prompt user
    Label1.Caption = ─┐
     "Select Help file from list, and then click to activate Help"
```

(continued)

DIALOGS.FRM *continued*

```
        'Enable controls
        cmdOpen.Enabled = True
        cmdSaveAs.Enabled = True
        cmdColor.Enabled = True
        cmdFont.Enabled = True
        cmdPrinter.Enabled = True
        cmdHelpFile.Enabled = True
        menHelp.Enabled = True
End Sub

Sub menAboutDialogs_Click ()
        'Display About dialog box
        About.Label1.Caption = "DIALOGS"
        About.Show MODAL
End Sub

Sub menExit_Click ()
        'All done
        Unload Dialogs
End Sub

Sub menHelpDialogs_Click ()
        'Display some Help text
        FileMsg "DIALOGS.MSG", 1
End Sub
```

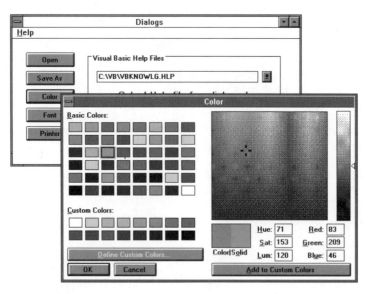

Figure 19-3.
DIALOGS.FRM in action.

The THREED Application

The THREED application demonstrates several of the new three-dimensional controls available in the Professional Edition of Visual Basic 3. Some of the flexible properties of these controls are selectable while the program runs, letting you see immediately the effect they have on the appearance of the controls. For example, you can adjust the border of the 3D Panel control by using a large number of combinations of BevelWidth, BorderWidth, BevelInner, and BevelOuter property settings. These properties can be adjusted at runtime, so you can instantly see the effect on the 3D Panel control's appearance.

The 3D Frame control contains three 3D Option Button controls, which let you select the caption alignment for the frame. Again, you'll see the results instantly when you try these options. Likewise, two 3D Check Box controls let you experiment with the Align property of a small 3D Panel control. Select Panel Align, and then try setting or clearing the Align Top check box. The panel instantly jumps to the top or bottom of the form and resizes itself to match the width of the form.

A Spin Button control is provided to cycle through the nine caption alignment options of the larger 3D Panel control. The caption jumps to each edge, each corner, and the center of the panel.

There are a lot of other properties available with the 3D controls in Visual Basic 3. The THREED application provides only a sampling of what can be done, and it shows what you can expect for the overall appearance of forms based on these new controls. The form's BackColor property is set to gray (&H00C0C0C0&) to match the default color scheme of the 3D controls. You can change these colors if desired.

The files for the THREED application are included on the disk packaged with this book. To load the files into the Visual Basic environment, choose the Open Project option from the File menu, and then type *C:\WORKSHOP\THREED.MAK*. This opens the project and enables you to view and modify the forms and code. The following figures, tables, and code give the details of the application's creation.

Figure 19-4.
THREED project list.

421

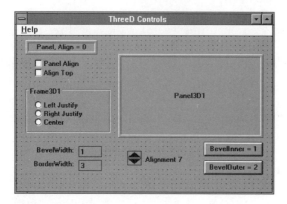

Figure 19-5.
THREED.FRM during development.

THREED.FRM Menu Design Window Entries

Caption	Name	Indentation
&Help	menHelp	0
&Help on ThreeD	menHelpThreeD	1
&About ThreeD...	menAboutThreeD	1
-	menSep	1
E&xit	menExit	1

THREED.FRM Form and Control Properties

Property	Value
Form	
BackColor	&H00C0C0C0&
Caption	ThreeD Controls
Name	ThreeD
3D Check Box	
Caption	Align Top
Name	Check3D2

(continued)

THREED.FRM Form and Control Properties *continued*

Property	Value
3D Check Box	
Caption	Panel Align
Name	Check3D1
Text Box	
BackColor	&H00C0C0C0&
Name	Text2
Text	3
Text Box	
BackColor	&H00C0C0C0&
Name	Text1
Text	1
3D Command Button	
Caption	BevelOuter = 2
Name	Command3D2
Spin Button	
Name	Spin1
3D Panel	
BackColor	&H00C0C0C0&
BevelInner	1 - Inset
Caption	Panel, Align = 0
Name	Panel3D2
3D Command Button	
Caption	BevelInner = 1
Name	Command3D1
3D Frame	
Caption	Frame3D1
Name	Frame3D1

(continued)

THREED.FRM Form and Control Properties *continued*

Property	Value
3D Option Button	
Caption	Center
Name	Option3D3
3D Option Button	
Caption	Right Justify
Name	Option3D2
3D Option Button	
Caption	Left Justify
Name	Option3D1
3D Panel	
BackColor	&H00C0C0C0&
BevelInner	1 - Inset
Caption	Panel3D1
Name	Panel3D1
Label	
Alignment	1 - Right Justify
BackColor	&H00C0C0C0&
Caption	BorderWidth:
Name	Label3
Label	
Alignment	1 - Right Justify
BackColor	&H00C0C0C0&
Caption	BevelWidth:
Name	Label2
Label	
BackColor	&H00C0C0C0&
Caption	Alignment 7
Name	Label1

Source code for THREED.FRM

```
Sub Check3D1_Click (Value As Integer)
    SetPanelAlign
End Sub

Sub Check3D2_Click (Value As Integer)
    SetPanelAlign
End Sub

Sub Command3D1_Click ()
    'Cycle through BevelInner settings
    n% = Panel3D1.BevelInner
    n% = (n% + 1) Mod 3
    Command3D1.Caption = "BevelInner =" + Str$(n%)
    Panel3D1.BevelInner = n%
End Sub

Sub Command3D2_Click ()
    'Cycle through BevelOuter settings
    n% = Panel3D1.BevelOuter
    n% = (n% + 1) Mod 3
    Command3D2.Caption = "BevelOuter =" + Str$(n%)
    Panel3D1.BevelOuter = n%
End Sub

Sub Form_Load ()
    Option3D1.Value = True
End Sub

Sub menAboutThreeD_Click ()
    'Display About dialog box
    About.Label1.Caption = "THREED"
    About.Show MODAL
End Sub

Sub menExit_Click ()
    'All done
    Unload ThreeD
End Sub

Sub menHelpThreeD_Click ()
    'Display some Help text
    FileMsg "THREED.MSG", 1
End Sub
```

(continued)

THREED.FRM *continued*

```
Sub Option3D1_Click (Value As Integer)
    'Set frame alignment to left justify
    Frame3D1.Alignment = 0
End Sub

Sub Option3D2_Click (Value As Integer)
    'Set frame alignment to right justify
    Frame3D1.Alignment = 1
End Sub

Sub Option3D3_Click (Value As Integer)
    'Set frame alignment to center
    Frame3D1.Alignment = 2
End Sub

Sub RangeCheck (n%)
    'Must be in range 1 through 30
    If n% >= 1 And n% <= 30 Then
        Exit Sub
    End If

    'Message to user
    If n% < 0 Or n% > 30 Then
        Beep
        MsgBox "Valid range is 1 through 30."
    End If

    'Bring it into correct range
    If n% < 1 Then n% = 1
    If n% > 30 Then n% = 30
End Sub

Sub SetPanelAlign ()
    'Align at top or bottom
    If Check3D1.Value = True Then
        If Check3D2.Value = True Then
            Panel3D2.Align = 1
            Panel3D2.Caption = "Panel3D, Align = 1 (Top)"
        Else
            Panel3D2.Align = 2
            Panel3D2.Caption = "Panel3D, Align = 2 (Bottom)"
        End If
```

(continued)

426

THREED.FRM *continued*

```
        'Don't align, so move to starting position
        Else
            Panel3D2.Align = 0
            Panel3D2.Caption = "Panel3D, Align = 0"
            Panel3D2.Left = 240
            Panel3D2.Top = 120
            Panel3D2.Width = 1935
        End If
End Sub


Sub Spin1_SpinDown ()
    n% = Panel3D1.Alignment

    'Decrement only to 1
    If n% > 0 Then
        n% = n% - 1
        Label1.Caption = "Alignment" + Str$(n%)
        Label1.Refresh
        Panel3D1.Alignment = n%
        Panel3D1.Refresh
    End If
End Sub


Sub Spin1_SpinUp ()
    n% = Panel3D1.Alignment

    'Increment only to 8
    If n% < 8 Then
        n% = n% + 1
        Label1.Caption = "Alignment" + Str$(n%)
        Label1.Refresh
        Panel3D1.Alignment = n%
        Panel3D1.Refresh
    End If
End Sub


Sub Text1_Change ()
    'Check range and adjust bevel
    n% = Val(Text1.Text)
    RangeCheck n%
    Panel3D1.BevelWidth = n%
End Sub
```

(continued)

427

THREED.FRM *continued*

```
Sub Text2_Change ()
    'Check range and adjust border
    n% = Val(Text2.Text)
    RangeCheck n%
    Panel3D1.BorderWidth = n%
End Sub
```

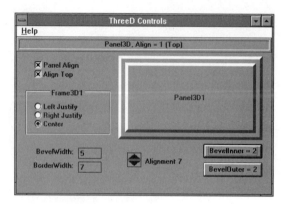

Figure 19-6.
THREED.FRM in action.

The NISTTIME Application

The NISTTIME application demonstrates the new Communications control, which provides easy-to-use serial I/O capabilities. NISTTIME calls up the National Institute of Standards and Technology (that's what NIST stands for) and sets the system clock accurately from the information provided.

The value of the constant PORT, declared in the general-declarations area of NISTTIME.FRM, determines which serial port is used to communicate with your modem. You will need to change the constant if your modem is not plugged into the first communications port.

NOTE: If you live in the Denver, Colorado area, remove the long-distance part of the telephone number (*1-303-*) from the TELEPHONE constant. If you need to dial any special access codes (such as 9 to reach an outside dial tone or 10*xxx* to specify a long-distance carrier), add those digits to the beginning of the TELEPHONE constant.

When this application starts, it first tries to run the Windows Clock application. Look in the Form_Load subprogram to see how the *Shell* function is used to accomplish this. You can start any application in Windows by using this technique.

NISTTIME does not set the date or hour information, so be sure that your system time is reasonably close to the correct time before you run the application. NISTTIME sets the minute and second information to within about a second of the correct time. The first few lines of information from the National Institute of Standards and Technology are as follows. This application simply extracts the minute and second information from the string and leaves the system date and hour in your computer unchanged.

```
National Institute of Standards and Technology
Telephone Time Service
                      D  L D
MJD   YR MO DA HH MM SS ST S UT1 msADV          <OTM>
49097 93-04-20 22:42.39 50 0   .2 045.0 UTC(NIST) *
49097 93-04-20 22:42:40 50 0  -.2 045.0 UTC(NIST) *
...
```

Two timers are used in this application. Timer1 is set to the minimum possible time interval (1 millisecond) and continuously checks for bytes that have arrived over the modem. When a complete time string is detected (ending with an asterisk), the time information is extracted, the system time is updated, and the application unloads itself. As a safety measure, Timer2 is set to an interval of 45 seconds. The Timer2_Timer subprogram hangs up the phone and unloads the application if 45 seconds have elapsed and the connection hasn't succeeded.

The files for the NISTTIME application are included on the disk packaged with this book. To load the files into the Visual Basic environment, choose the Open Project option from the File menu, and then type *C:\WORKSHOP\NISTTIME.MAK.* This opens the project and enables you to view and modify the form and code. The following figures, table, and code give the details of the application's creation.

Figure 19-7.
NISTTIME project list.

Figure 19-8.
NISTTIME.FRM during development.

NISTTIME.FRM Form and Control Properties

Property	Value
Form	
Caption	NIST Time Set
Name	NistForm
Communications	
Interval	1000
Name	Comm1
Timer	
Enabled	False
Interval	1
Name	Timer1
Timer	
Enabled	False
Interval	45000
Name	Timer2
Command Button	
Caption	Cancel
Enabled	False
Name	cmdCancel
Label	
Alignment	2 - Center
Caption	Dialing National Institute of Standards and Technology Telephone Time Service
Name	Label1

Source code for NISTTIME.FRM

```
DefInt A-Z

Const PORT = 1
Const TELEPHONE = "1-303-494-4774"

Dim NistNdx As Integer
Dim NistBuf As String * 10000

Sub cmdCancel_Click ()
    'Cancel this application
    Unload NistForm
End Sub

Sub Form_Load ()
    'Show form and first message
    Show

    'Try to start the Windows Clock application
    On Error Resume Next
    X = Shell("clock.exe", 4)
    On Error GoTo 0

    'Put focus on this application
    SetFocus

    'Set up Communications control parameters
    Comm1.CommPort = PORT
    Comm1.Settings = "1200,N,8,1"
    Comm1.InputLen = 0
    Comm1.DTREnable = True
    Comm1.PortOpen = True

    'Send commands to dial NIST
    Comm1.Output = "ATZ" + Chr$(13)
    Pause 500
    Comm1.Output = "ATQ0V1E1S0=0" + Chr$(13)
    Pause 500
    Comm1.Output = "ATDT" + TELEPHONE + Chr$(13)
    Pause 2000

    'Activate timers
    Timer1.Enabled = True
    Timer2.Enabled = True
```

(continued)

NISTTIME.FRM *continued*

```
    'Next message
    Label1.Caption = "Attempting to connect"

    'Enable Cancel button
    cmdCancel.Enabled = True
End Sub

Sub Form_Unload (Cancel As Integer)
    'Update message for user
    Label1.Caption = "Hanging up"

    'This usually hangs up phone
    Comm1.DTREnable = False

    'This ensures it hangs up
    Pause 1500
    Comm1.Output = "+++"
    Pause 1500
    Comm1.Output = "ATH0" + Chr$(13)

    'Close down communications
    Comm1.PortOpen = False
End Sub

Sub Pause (millisec)
    'Determine end time of delay
    EndOfPause# = Timer + millisec / 1000

    'Twiddle away the time
    Do
        X% = DoEvents()
    Loop While Timer < EndOfPause#
End Sub

Sub SetTime (a$)
    'Extract current hour from system
    Ho = Hour(Now)

    'Extract minute and second from NIST string
    Mi = Val(Mid$(a$, 22, 2))
    Se = Val(Mid$(a$, 25, 2))

    'Construct new time
    TimeNow# = TimeSerial(Ho, Mi, Se)
```

(continued)

NISTTIME.FRM *continued*

```
    'Set system clock
    Time$ = Format$(TimeNow#, "hh:mm:ss")
End Sub

Sub Timer1_Timer ()
    Static ConnectFlag

    'Check for incoming bytes
    If Comm1.InBufferCount = 0 Then
        Exit Sub
    Else
        Tmp$ = Comm1.Input
        Bytes = Len(Tmp$)
        If Bytes + NistNdx >= 10000 Then
            Label1.Caption = "Hanging Up"
            Timer1.Enabled = False
            Timer2.Enabled = False
            Unload NistForm
        Else
            Mid$(NistBuf, NistNdx + 1, Bytes) = Tmp$
            NistNdx = NistNdx + Bytes
        End If
    End If

    'Check for sign that we've connected
    If ConnectFlag = False Then
        If InStr(NistBuf, "National") Then
            Label1.Caption = "Connected... setting clock"
            ConnectFlag = True
        End If
    End If

    'Check for time marks
    p1 = InStr(NistBuf, "*")
    p2 = InStr(p1 + 1, NistBuf, "*")

    'Time received if two time marks found
    If p2 > p1 Then
        SetTime Mid$(NistBuf, p1, p2 - p1 + 1)
        Unload NistForm
    End If
End Sub
```

(continued)

NISTTIME.FRM *continued*

```
Sub Timer2_Timer ()
    'Safety timeout if no connection
    Beep
    Unload NistForm
End Sub
```

Figure 19-9.
NISTTIME.FRM in action.

The ANIMATE Application

The ANIMATE application demonstrates the Animated Button control. This control contains a sequence of bitmap or icon images that can create a form of animation.

On the left side of the form is an Animated Button control displaying the new-moon icon, which is one of a sequence of moon-phase icons in the C:\VB\ICONS\MISC directory. All eight of these icons are loaded into this control and are shown when you click on the control. The Cycle property is set to *2 - 2-state 1/2 & 1/2*, which causes half of the images to be shown each time the control is clicked. The moon image smoothly changes from new to full and back again each time the control is clicked.

The Animated Button control on the right side of the form contains a sequence of bitmap images to create a rain shower. These images were created by using Windows Paintbrush, with each image displaying the rain drops a little further down from the cloud. You can load any sequence of bitmaps or icon images you desire. This control's Cycle property is set to *1 - By Frame*, which causes the next image in the sequence to display with each Click event. You can see how this works by clicking on the control and watching each image appear.

You can use a special property named, appropriately enough, SpecialOp to programmatically click the Animated Button control. When enabled, Timer1_Timer sets this property to 1 every tenth of a second, causing the Animated Button control to behave as though the user were clicking the mouse button at this rate. This causes a continuous rain animation to appear. One drawback of this technique is that the menu is effectively disabled while the rain falls because the focus is shifted to the Animated Button control with each Click event. Because of this, the rain stops after 2 seconds, and the menu is reenabled.

The files for the ANIMATE application are included on the disk packaged with this book. To load the files into the Visual Basic environment, choose the Open Project option from the File menu, and then type *C:\WORKSHOP\ANIMATE.MAK.* This opens the project and enables you to view and modify the forms and code. The following figures, tables, and code give the details of the application's creation.

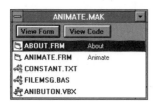

Figure 19-10.
ANIMATE project list.

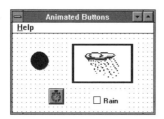

Figure 19-11.
ANIMATE.FRM during development.

ANIMATE.FRM Menu Design Window Entries

Caption	Name	Indentation
&Help	menHelp	0
&Help on Animate	menHelpAnimate	1
&About Animate...	menAboutAnimate	1
-	menSep	1
E&xit	menExit	1

ANIMATE.FRM Form and Control Properties

Property	Value
Form	
Caption	Animated Buttons
Name	Animate
Check Box	
Caption	Rain
Name	chkRain
Timer	
Enabled	False
Interval	100
Name	Timer1
Animated Button	
Cycle	1 - By frame
HideFocusBox	True
Name	AniButton2
PictDrawMode	2 - Stretch to fit
Speed	50
Animated Button	
Cycle	2 - 2-state 1/2 & 1/2
HideFocusBox	True
Name	AniButton1
PictDrawMode	1 - Autosize control
Speed	50

Source code for ANIMATE.FRM

```
Sub chkRain_Click ()
    'Toggle rain action
    If chkRain.Value = CHECKED Then
        Timer1.Enabled = True
    Else
```

(continued)

ANIMATE.FRM *continued*

```
        Timer1.Enabled = False
    End If
End Sub

Sub menAboutAnimate_Click ()
    'Display About dialog box
    About.Label1.Caption = "ANIMATE"
    About.Show MODAL
End Sub

Sub menExit_Click ()
    'All done
    Unload Animate
End Sub

Sub menHelpAnimate_Click ()
    'Display some Help text
    FileMsg "ANIMATE.MSG", 1
End Sub

Sub Timer1_Timer ()
    Static RainCount

    'Simulate a click
    AniButton2.SpecialOp = 1

    'Rain for only two seconds
    RainCount = RainCount + 1
    If RainCount > 20 Then
        RainCount = 0
        Timer1.Enabled = False
        ChkRain.Value = UNCHECKED
    End If
End Sub
```

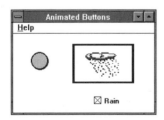

Figure 19-12.
ANIMATE.FRM in action.

The KEYSTAT Application

The KEYSTAT application demonstrates the Key Status control, which can be used to monitor or set the state of the Insert, Num Lock, Caps Lock, and Scroll Lock keys.

Four Key Status controls are displayed on the form, and the Style property of each control is set to one of the monitored keys. These controls check the state of the indicated key at a predetermined time interval and update the displayed state when the key's state changes. You can change the state of these keys in several ways. Pressing the key on the keyboard is the most obvious way, but you can also click the control on the form by using the mouse, or you can toggle the state programmatically. Click the Count command button to see how the program can toggle the key states to count in binary. If your keyboard has lights for these keys, you'll see your keyboard start counting in binary!

The initial state of the keys is recorded when the form loads, and the key states are set back to these states when the program unloads. This technique is handy for any application that manipulates these key states.

The files for the KEYSTAT application are included on the disk packaged with this book. To load the files into the Visual Basic environment, choose the Open Project option from the File menu, and then type *C:\WORKSHOP\KEYSTAT.MAK*. This opens the project and enables you to view and modify the forms and code. The following figures, tables, and code give the details of the application's creation.

Figure 19-13.
KEYSTAT project list.

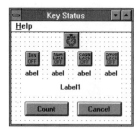

Figure 19-14.
KEYSTAT.FRM during development.

KEYSTAT.FRM Menu Design Window Entries

Caption	Name	Indentation
&Help	menHelp	0
&Help on KeyStat	menHelpKeyStat	1
&About KeyStat...	menAboutKeyStat	1
-	menSep	1
E&xit	menExit	1

KEYSTAT.FRM Form and Control Properties

Property	Value
Form	
Caption	Key Status
Name	Form1
Command Button	
Cancel	True
Caption	Cancel
Name	btnCancel
Command Button	
Caption	Count
Name	btnCount
Timer	
Enabled	False
Interval	1000
Name	Timer1
Key Status	
Autosize	True
Name	InsState
Style	2 - Insert State
TimerInterval	100

(continued)

KEYSTAT.FRM Form and Control Properties *continued*

Property	Value
Key Status	
Autosize	True
Name	ScrollState
Style	3 - Scroll Lock
TimerInterval	100
Key Status	
Autosize	True
Name	CapsState
TimerInterval	100
Key Status	
Autosize	True
Name	NumState
Style	1 - Num Lock
TimerInterval	100
Label	
Alignment	2 - Center
Name	HexLabel
Label	
Alignment	2 - Center
Name	InsLabel
Label	
Alignment	2 - Center
Name	NumLabel
Label	
Alignment	2 - Center
Name	CapsLabel
Label	
Alignment	2 - Center
Name	ScrollLabel

Source code for KEYSTAT.FRM

```
Dim Scroll, Caps, Num, Insert

Sub btnCancel_Click ()
    'All done
    Unload Form1
End Sub

Sub btnCount_Click ()
    'Toggle binary counting
    Timer1.Enabled = Not Timer1.Enabled
End Sub

Sub CapsState_Change ()
    'Update display
    Display
End Sub

Sub Display ()
    'Get current states
    Bit0 = Abs(ScrollState)
    Bit1 = Abs(CapsState)
    Bit2 = Abs(NumState)
    Bit3 = Abs(InsState)

    'Display bits
    ScrollLabel = Str$(Bit0)
    CapsLabel = Str$(Bit1)
    NumLabel = Str$(Bit2)
    InsLabel = Str$(Bit3)

    'Convert pattern to hexadecimal
    HexNum = Bit0 + 2 * Bit1 + 4 * Bit2 + 8 * Bit3

    'Display hexadecimal value
    HexLabel = "H" + Trim$(Hex$(HexNum))
End Sub

Sub Form_Load ()
    'Initialize display
    Show
    Refresh
    Display
```

(continued)

KEYSTAT.FRM *continued*

```
    'Record starting states
    Scroll = ScrollState.Value
    Caps = CapsState.Value
    Num = NumState.Value
    Insert = InsState.Value
End Sub

Sub Form_Unload (Cancel As Integer)
    'Restore starting states
    ScrollState.Value = Scroll
    CapsState.Value = Caps
    NumState.Value = Num
    InsState.Value = Insert
End Sub

Sub InsState_Change ()
    'Update display
    Display
End Sub

Sub menAboutKeyStat_Click ()
    'Show About dialog box
    About.Label1.Caption = "KEYSTAT"
    About.Show MODAL
End Sub

Sub menExit_Click ()
    'All done
    Unload Form1
End Sub

Sub menHelpKeyStat_Click ()
    'Display some Help text
    FileMsg "KEYSTAT.MSG", 1
End Sub

Sub NumState_Change ()
    'Update display
    Display
End Sub

Sub ScrollState_Change ()
    'Update display
    Display
End Sub
```

(continued)

KEYSTAT.FRM *continued*

```
Sub Timer1_Timer ()
    'Get current states
    Bit0 = Abs(ScrollState.Value)
    Bit1 = Abs(CapsState.Value)
    Bit2 = Abs(NumState.Value)
    Bit3 = Abs(InsState.Value)

    'Combine bits to form single number
    n% = Bit0 + 2 * Bit1 + 4 * Bit2 + 8 * Bit3

    'Increment count, in range 0 through 15
    n% = (n% + 1) Mod 16

    'Set new states
    ScrollState.Value = (1 = (n% And 1))
    CapsState.Value = (2 = (n% And 2))
    NumState.Value = (4 = (n% And 4))
    InsState.Value = (8 = (n% And 8))
End Sub
```

Figure 19-15.
KEYSTAT.FRM in action.

The SOUNDS Application

The SOUNDS application demonstrates the new Multimedia MCI (Media Control Interface) control. The MCI control can control a wide variety of multimedia devices, such as sound boards, CD-ROM drives, MIDI sequencers, audio CD players, videodisc players, and videotape recorders. The SOUNDS application plays WAV files in any directory on any drive. You must have sound-board capability for this application to work.

The MCI control is configured as a group of buttons, very similar in operation and concept to those found on the front of a typical VCR. These buttons can be displayed for the user to click and control the media directly, or you can use them programmatically. Depending on the particular multimedia device, some or all of these buttons are used.

The SOUNDS form lets you select any directory on any drive. If any WAV files are located in the selected directory, the first one found is played, and its name is displayed. Click the Again button to replay the file, or click >> and << to play all the WAV files in the directory.

The files for the SOUNDS application are included on the disk packaged with this book. To load the files into the Visual Basic environment, choose the Open Project option from the File menu, and then type *C:\WORKSHOP\SOUNDS.MAK*. This opens the project and enables you to view and modify the forms and code. The following figures, tables, and code give the details of the application's creation.

Figure 19-16.
SOUNDS project list.

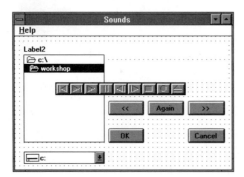

Figure 19-17.
SOUNDS.FRM during development.

SOUNDS.FRM Menu Design Window Entries *continued*

Caption	Name	Indentation
&Help	menHelpTop	0
&Help on Sounds	menHelpSounds	1
&About Sounds...	menAboutSounds	1
-	menSep	1
E&xit	menExit	1

SOUNDS.FRM Form and Control Properties

Property	Value
Form	
Caption	Sounds
Name	Sounds
Drive List Box	
Name	Drive1
Command Button	
Caption	Again
Name	cmdAgain
Multimedia MCI	
Enabled	False
Name	MMControl1
Visible	False
Command Button	
Caption	OK
Name	cmdOK
Directory List Box	
Name	Dir1

(continued)

SOUNDS.FRM Form and Control Properties *continued*

Property	Value
Command Button	
Caption	>>
Name	cmdNext
Command Button	
Caption	<<
Name	cmdPrevious
Command Button	
Caption	Cancel
Name	cmdCancel
Label	
Caption	Label2
Name	Label2
Label	
Alignment	2 - Center
FontSize	13.5
Name	Label1

Source code for SOUNDS.FRM

```
Dim SoundList() As String
Dim Extension As String
Dim SoundIndex As Integer
Dim SoundCount As Integer

Sub cmdAgain_Click ()
    'Close any previous WAV file
    MMControl1.Command = "Close"

    'Play it again, Sam
    PlayIt
End Sub
```

(continued)

SOUNDS.FRM *continued*

```
Sub cmdCancel_Click ()
    'Force exit via menu Exit
    menExit_Click
End Sub

Sub cmdNext_Click ()
    'Close any previous WAV file
    MMControl1.Command = "Close"

    'Increment list index
    If SoundIndex < SoundCount Then
        SoundIndex = SoundIndex + 1
    End If

    'Play WAV file
    PlayIt
End Sub

Sub cmdOK_Click ()
    'OK button works like Dir double click
    Dir1.Path = Dir1.List(Dir1.ListIndex)
    Dir1_Change
End Sub

Sub cmdPrevious_Click ()
    'Close any previous WAV file
    MMControl1.Command = "Close"

    'Decrement list index
    If SoundIndex > 1 Then
        SoundIndex = SoundIndex - 1
    End If

    'Play WAV file
    PlayIt
End Sub

Sub Dir1_Change ()
    'Close any previous WAV file
    MMControl1.Command = "Close"

    'Grab current directory path from list
    Directory = Dir1.List(-1)
```

(continued)

SOUNDS.FRM *continued*

```
    'Display directory
    Label2.Caption = Directory

    'If not root directory, add backslash to path
    If Right$(Directory, 1) <> "\" Then
        Directory = Directory + "\"
    End If

    'Determine whether directory contains any WAV files
    If Dir$(Directory + Extension) = "" Then
        SoundCount = 0
        ReDim SoundList(0)

        'Replace displayed filename
        Label1.Caption = "Select directory..."

        'Quit subprogram
        Exit Sub
    End If

    'Get name of first WAV file in directory
    SoundCount = 1
    ReDim SoundList(SoundCount)
    SoundList(SoundCount) =⤷
     LCase$(Directory + Dir$(Directory + Extension))

    'Find rest of WAV files in directory
    Do
        NextWave$ = Dir$
        If NextWave$ = "" Then Exit Do
        SoundCount = SoundCount + 1
        ReDim Preserve SoundList(SoundCount)
        SoundList(SoundCount) = LCase$(Directory + NextWave$)
    Loop

    'Play first WAV file in directory
    SoundIndex = 1
    PlayIt
End Sub

Sub Drive1_Change ()
    'Drive selected
    Dir1.Path = Drive1.Drive
End Sub
```

(continued)

SOUNDS.FRM *continued*

```
Sub Form_Load ()
    'Center form
    Left = (Screen.Width - Width) / 2
    Top = (Screen.Height - Height) / 2

    'Initialize for WAV files
    Extension = "*.WAV"

    'Set MCI control properties
    MMControl1.Notify = False
    MMControl1.Wait = True
    MMControl1.Shareable = False
    MMControl1.DeviceType = "WaveAudio"

    'Force check of starting directory
    Dir1_Change
End Sub

Sub Form_Unload (Cancel As Integer)
    'Close MCI control
    MMControl1.Command = "Close"
End Sub

Sub menAboutSounds_Click ()
    'Display About dialog box
    About.Label1.Caption = "SOUNDS"
    About.Show MODAL
End Sub

Sub menExit_Click ()
    'All done
    Unload Sounds
End Sub

Sub menHelpSounds_Click ()
    'Display some Help text
    FileMsg "SOUNDS.MSG", 1
End Sub

Sub PlayIt ()
    'Extract filename from path
    Fil$ = SoundList(SoundIndex)
    Do
        n% = InStr(Fil$, "\")
        If n% = 0 Then Exit Do
        Fil$ = Mid$(Fil$, n% + 1)
    Loop
```

(continued)

SOUNDS.FRM *continued*

```
        'Display current filename
        Label1.Caption = Fil$

        'Play WAV file
        MMControl1.FileName = SoundList(SoundIndex)
        MMControl1.Command = "Open"
        MMControl1.Command = "Play"
    End Sub
```

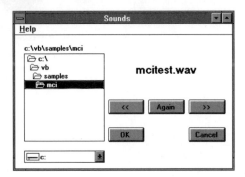

Figure 19-18.
SOUNDS.FRM in action.

The MASKEDIT Application

The MASKEDIT application demonstrates the Masked Edit control. The Masked Edit control is very similar to the Text Box control, except that it provides a straightforward way to add character validation to data entry fields.

The options listed on the right side of the form let you experiment with a variety of input mask styles. The entry fields on the left change immediately when you select options. The Masked Edit controls on this form provide a sampling of the types of data input validation masks that can be set up.

The files for the MASKEDIT application are included on the disk packaged with this book. To load the files into the Visual Basic environment, choose the Open Project option from the File menu, and then type *C:\WORKSHOP\MASKEDIT.MAK*. This opens the project and enables you to view and modify the forms and code. The following figures, tables, and code give the details of the application's creation.

Figure 19-19.
MASKEDIT project list.

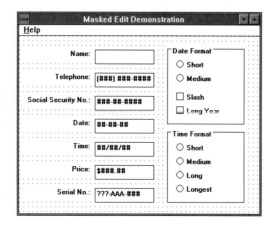

Figure 19-20.
MASKEDIT.FRM during development.

MASKEDIT.FRM Menu Design Window Entries

Caption	Name	Indentation
&Help	menHelp	0
&Help on MaskEdit	menHelpMaskEdit	1
&About MaskEdit...	menAboutMaskEdit	1
-	menSep	1
E&xit	menExit	1

MASKEDIT.FRM Form and Control Properties

Property	Value
Form	
Caption	Masked Edit Demonstration
Name	MaskEdit
Frame	
Caption	Time Format
Name	Frame2
Option Button	
Caption	Longest
Name	Option6
Option Button	
Caption	Long
Name	Option5
Option Button	
Caption	Medium
Name	Option4
Option Button	
Caption	Short
Name	Option3
Frame	
Caption	Date Format
Name	Frame1
Option Button	
Caption	Medium
Name	Option2
Check Box	
Caption	Long Year
Name	Check2

(continued)

MASKEDIT.FRM Form and Control Properties *continued*

Property	Value
Check Box	
Caption	Slash
Name	Check1
Option Button	
Caption	Short
Name	Option1
Masked Edit Box	
Mask	???-AAA-###
MaxLength	11
Name	MaskedEdit7
Masked Edit Box	
Mask	$###.##
MaxLength	7
Name	MaskedEdit6
Masked Edit Box	
Mask	##/##/##
MaxLength	8
Name	MaskedEdit5
Masked Edit Box	
Name	MaskedEdit1
Masked Edit Box	
Mask	(###) ###-####
MaxLength	14
Name	MaskedEdit2
Masked Edit Box	
Mask	###-##-####
MaxLength	11
Name	MaskedEdit3

(continued)

MASKEDIT.FRM Form and Control Properties *continued*

Property	Value
Masked Edit Box	
Mask	##-##-##
MaxLength	8
Name	MaskedEdit4
Label	
Alignment	1 - Right Justify
Caption	Serial No.:
Name	Label7
Label	
Alignment	1 - Right Justify
Caption	Price:
Name	Label6
Label	
Alignment	1 - Right Justify
Caption	Time:
Name	Label5
Label	
Alignment	1 - Right Justify
Caption	Name:
Name	Label4
Label	
Alignment	1 - Right Justify
Caption	Date:
Name	Label3
Label	
Alignment	1 - Right Justify
Caption	Social Security No.:
Name	Label2

(continued)

MASKEDIT.FRM Form and Control Properties *continued*

Property	Value
Label	
Alignment	1 - Right Justify
Caption	Telephone:
Name	Label1

Source code for MASKEDIT.FRM

```
Sub Check1_Click ()
    SetDateMask
End Sub

Sub Check2_Click ()
    SetDateMask
End Sub

Sub Form_Load ()
    Show
    MaskedEdit1.SetFocus
    Option1.Value = True
    Option3.Value = True
End Sub

Sub menAboutMaskEdit_Click ()
    'Show About dialog box
    About.Label1.Caption = "MASKEDIT"
    About.Show MODAL
End Sub

Sub menExit_Click ()
    'All done
    Unload MaskEdit
End Sub

Sub menHelpMaskEdit_Click ()
    'Display some Help text
    FileMsg "MASKEDIT.MSG", 1
End Sub

Sub Option1_Click ()
    SetDateMask
End Sub
```

(continued)

MASKEDIT.FRM *continued*

```
Sub Option2_Click ()
    SetDateMask
End Sub

Sub Option3_Click ()
    SetTimeMask
End Sub

Sub Option4_Click ()
    SetTimeMask
End Sub

Sub Option5_Click ()
    SetTimeMask
End Sub

Sub Option6_Click ()
    SetTimeMask
End Sub

Sub SetDateMask ()
    'Check for / or -
    If Check1.Value = CHECKED Then
        Sep$ = "/"
    Else
        Sep$ = "-"
    End If

    'Check for short or long year
    If Check2.Value = CHECKED Then
        Yr$ = "####"
    Else
        Yr$ = "##"
    End If

    'Check for medium or long date
    If Option1.Value = True Then
        Ml$ = "##"
    Else
        Ml$ = "???"
    End If

    'Build date mask
    MaskedEdit4.Mask = "##" + Sep$ + Ml$ + Sep$ + Yr$
End Sub
```

(continued)

MASKEDIT.FRM *continued*

```
Sub SetTimeMask ()
    'Short mask
    If Option3.Value = True Then
        MaskedEdit5.Mask = "##:##"
    End If

    'Medium mask
    If Option4.Value = True Then
        MaskedEdit5.Mask = "##:## ??"
    End If

    'Long mask
    If Option5.Value = True Then
        MaskedEdit5.Mask = "##:##:##"
    End If

    'Longest mask
    If Option6.Value = True Then
        MaskedEdit5.Mask = "##:##:## ??"
    End If
End Sub
```

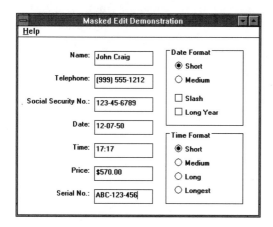

Figure 19-21.
MASKEDIT.FRM in action.

The SYSGAUGE Application

The SYSGAUGE application demonstrates several styles of the Gauge control. Three types of gauges are displayed, to provide a sampling of the types of Gauge controls that can be used.

GetFreeSystemResources is an API in the User DLL that returns information about available resources at the moment the function is called. Depending on the value of the parameter passed to *GetFreeSystemResources*, the returned value is the number of bytes of available System, GDI, or User resources. In each case, the returned value is a percentage ranging from 0 through 100, which makes these values ideal for demonstrating gauges. After the application is up and running, try running and stopping other Windows-based applications to see the resource amounts change.

The dial gauge's Style property is set to *3 - 'Full' Needle*. The thermometer-type gauge's Style property is set to *1 - Vertical Bar*, and the homemade blue-on-yellow gauge's Style property is set to *0 - Horizontal Bar*. The bar-style gauges are very flexible because the exact shape, position, and color of the bar are controlled through property settings, and any bitmap can serve as the background image.

The files for the SYSGAUGE application are included on the disk packaged with this book. To load the files into the Visual Basic environment, choose the Open Project option from the File menu, and then type *C:\WORKSHOP\SYSGAUGE.MAK*. This opens the project and enables you to view and modify the forms and code. The following figures, tables, and code give the details of the application's creation.

Figure 19-22.
SYSGAUGE project list.

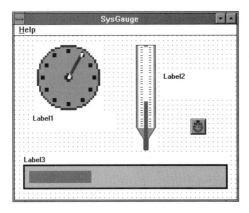

Figure 19-23.
SYSGAUGE.FRM during development.

SYSGAUGE.FRM Menu Design Window Entries

Caption	Name	Indentation
&Help	menHelp	0
&Help on SysGauge	menHelpSysGauge	1
&About SysGauge...	menAboutSysGauge	1
-	menSep	1
E&xit	menExit	1

SYSGAUGE.FRM Form and Control Properties

Property	Value
Form	
Caption	SysGauge
Name	SysGauge

(continued)

SYSGAUGE.FRM Form and Control Properties *continued*

Property	Value
Gauge	
Autosize	True
BackColor	&H0000FFFF&
ForeColor	&H00FF0000&
InnerBottom	3
InnerLeft	1
InnerRight	3
InnerTop	1
Max	100
Name	Gauge3
NeedleWidth	1
Value	33
Gauge	
Autosize	True
BackColor	&H00FFFFFF&
ForeColor	&H000000FF&
InnerBottom	40
InnerLeft	13
InnerRight	15
InnerTop	5
Max	100
Name	Gauge2
NeedleWidth	1
Style	1 - Vertical Bar
Value	33
Timer	
Interval	500
Name	Timer1

(continued)

SYSGAUGE.FRM Form and Control Properties *continued*

Property	Value
Gauge	
Height	1695
InnerBottom	5
InnerLeft	5
InnerRight	5
InnerTop	5
Max	100
Name	Gauge1
NeedleWidth	4
Style	3 - 'Full' Needle
Value	33
Shape	
BackColor	&H0000FFFF&
BorderWidth	3
FillColor	&H0000FFFF&
FillStyle	0 - Solid
Name	Shape1
Label	
Name	Label3
Label	
Name	Label2
Label	
Name	Label1

Source code for SYSGAUGE.FRM

```
Declare Function GetFreeSystemResources Lib "User"→
 (ByVal fuSysResource As Integer) As Integer

Sub menAboutSysGauge_Click ()
    'Display About dialog box
    About.Label1.Caption = "SYSGAUGE"
```

(continued)

461

SYSGAUGE.FRM *continued*

```
     About.Show MODAL
End Sub

Sub menExit_Click ()
     'All done
     Unload SysGauge
End Sub

Sub menHelpSysGauge_Click ()
     'Display some Help text
     FileMsg "SYSGAUGE.MSG", 1
End Sub

Sub Timer1_Timer ()
     Static R1Last%, R2Last%, R3Last%

     'Build message strings
     M0$ = "Percentage free space for "
     M1$ = M0$ + "System resources: "
     M2$ = M0$ + "GDI resources: "
     M3$ = M0$ + "User resources: "

     'Get percentage of resources from system
     R1% = GetFreeSystemResources(0)
     R2% = GetFreeSystemResources(1)
     R3% = GetFreeSystemResources(2)

     'Update first gauge only when value changes
     If R1% <> R1Last% Then
         Gauge1.Value = R1%
         Label1.Caption = M1$ + Str$(R1%)
         R1Last% = R1%
     End If

     'Update second gauge only when value changes
     If R2% <> R2Last% Then
         Gauge2.Value = R2%
         Label2.Caption = M2$ + Str$(R2%)
         R2Last% = R2%
     End If
```

(continued)

SYSGAUGE.FRM *continued*

```
    'Update third gauge only when value changes
    If R3% <> R3Last% Then
        Gauge3.Value = R3%
        Label3.Caption = M3$ + Str$(R3%)
        R3Last% = R3%
    End If
End Sub
```

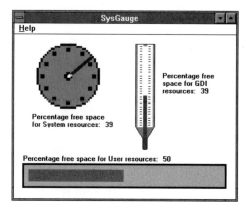

Figure 19-24.
SYSGAUGE.FRM in action.

INDEX

Note: Italicized page numbers refer to figures.

Special Characters

¬ (line continuation character), *xi*

A

ABOUTDEM application
  ABOUTDEM.FRM file, 49, 53–56
  ABOUTDEM.MAK file, 48
  ABOUT.FRM file, 48–53
  overview, 47
  project list, *48*
ABOUTDEM.FRM file
  control properties, 55
  editing, 53–55
  form during development, *54*
  form properties, 55
  Menu Design Window entries, 54
  overview, 49
  source code, 55
ABOUTDEM.MAK file, 48
About dialog box
  adding to projects, 56
  creating with ABOUT.FRM, 47, 48–52
  creating with ABOUTPAS.FRM, 95–98
ABOUT.FRM file
  adding to projects, 56
  control properties, 49–51
  form during development, *49*
  form in action, *56*
  form properties, 49
  overview, 48–49
  source code, 52–53
ABOUTPAS.FRM file
  control properties, 96–97
  form in action, *98*
  form properties, 96
  overview, 95–96
  source code, 98
Access, Microsoft, 355, 356, 357
ACODE.MDB file, 357

Add File command, 56
analog clock, displaying with VBCLOCK, 218–29
ANIMATE application
  ANIMATE.FRM file, 434–37
  overview, 434–35
  project list, *435*
Animated Button controls, 434
ANIMATE.FRM file
  control properties, 436
  form during development, *435*
  form in action, *437*
  form properties, 436
  Menu Design Window entries, 435
  overview, 434–35
  source code, 436–37
API functions. *See* Windows 3.1 API functions
application programming interface (API), 103–4, 365, 366, 369
applications. *See also* projects
  ABOUTDEM, 47–55
  ANIMATE, 434–37
  AREACODE, 357–64
  BITS, 385–91
  COLORBAR, 231–33
  DIALOGS, 413–20
  DRAGDROP, 169–74
  EDITBOX, 122–31
  FILECOMP, 316–23
  FILEFACT, 281–91
  FILEMSG, 56–58
  FILESHOW, 90–95
  FLASHWIN, 366–69
  FLOOD, 241–45
  FRACTION, 265–80
  GETFILE, 65–71
  GRAFSAMP, 374–80
  GRIDGRAF, 291–301

John Clark Craig

Since 1980, John Clark Craig has written several books on computer programming, including *The Microsoft Visual Basic for MS-DOS Workshop* (Microsoft Press, 1993), *Microsoft QuickC Programmer's Toolbox* (Microsoft Press, 1990), and *Microsoft QuickBASIC Programmer's Toolbox* (Microsoft Press, 1988). He also made substantial contributions to the first and second editions of *Microsoft Mouse Programmer's Reference* (Microsoft Press, 1989, 1991). Craig lives with his family in Castle Rock, Colorado.

The manuscript for this book was prepared and submitted to Microsoft Press in electronic form. Text files were formatted and processed using Microsoft Word.

Principal proofreader/copy editor: Shawn Peck
Principal editorial compositor: Cheryl Whiteside
Principal typographers: Carolyn Magruder and Lisa Iversen
Interior text designer: Kim Eggleston
Principal illustrator: Lisa Sandburg
Cover designer: Rebecca Geisler
Cover color separator: Walker Graphics
Indexer: Julie Kawabata

Text composition by Microsoft Press in Baskerville with display type in Helvetica bold, using Aldus PageMaker 4.0. Composed pages were delivered to the printer as electronic prepress files.

Printed on recycled paper stock.

Essential Resources from Microsoft Press

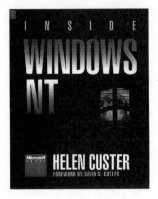

Inside Windows NT™

Helen Custer
Foreword by David N. Cutler

Inside Windows NT is the definitive guide to the Microsoft Windows NT operating system—Microsoft's highly portable, next-generation, 32-bit Windows operating system. It explains the philosophy and design goals behind the creation of Windows NT, details the architectural models on which Windows NT is based, and explains the result: what the operating system is, how it works, and what it offers. Written by a member of the Windows NT design team, this is the official look at the Windows NT system and a must-buy book for all system software designers and computer professionals.

416 pages, softcover $24.95 ($32.95 Canada)   ISBN 1-55615-481-X

Windows™ NT Answer Book

Jim Groves
With a Foreword by Paul Maritz

Here is an authoritative, fact-filled guide with honest, straightforward answers to your questions about the Microsoft Windows NT operating system. The question-and-answer format provides accessible coverage of all relevant topics to help you decide whether the Windows NT system is right for your computing environment. And if you've already decided to move to the Windows NT operating system, this book provides practical advice on installing Windows NT and conceptual advice on implementing Windows NT in your business.

224 pages, softcover $16.95 ($21.95 Canada)   ISBN 1-55615-562-X

Programming Windows™ 3.1, 3rd ed.

Charles Petzold

"If you're going to program for Windows, buy this book.
It will pay for itself in a matter of hours."   **Computer Language**

The programming classic for both new Windows 3.1 programmers and owners of previous editions. It's packed with indispensable reference data, tested programming advice, keen insight, and page after page of sample programs. This edition includes one disk that contains the source code and associated files from the book.

1008 pages, softcover with one 1.44-MB 3.5-inch disk
$49.95 ($67.95 Canada)   ISBN 1-55615-395-3

In-depth References

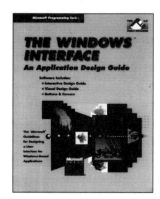

The Windows™ Interface: An Application Design Guide
Microsoft Corporation

The Microsoft guidelines for creating well-designed, visually and functionally consistent user interfaces—an essential reference for all programmers and designers working in Windows. Software includes a Visual Design Guide, an Interactive Style Guide, and Cursors and Buttons.
248 pages, softcover with two 1.44-MB 3.5" disks
$39.95 ($54.95 Canada)   ISBN 1-55615-439-9

The Microsoft® Windows™ 3.1 Developer's Workshop
Dr. John Butler, Bob Chiverton, John Clark Craig,
William S. Hall, Ray Patch, and Alok Sinha

This is a winning collection of articles on significant Windows 3.1 programming issues—from the best programming minds in the business. The book covers internationalizing software for Windows ■ programming Windows for Pen Computing ■ the GDI device transform ■ NetBIOS programming ■ developing virtual device drivers ■ Visual Basic as a professional tool. The accompanying disk contains all the source code and executable (EXE) files in the book.
350 pages, with one 1.44-MB 3.5" disk
$34.95 ($47.95 Canada)   ISBN 1-55615-480-1

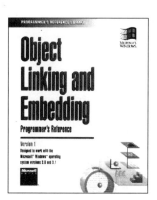

Object Linking and Embedding Programmer's Reference
Microsoft Corporation

Object Linking and Embedding (OLE) is a powerful way to extend the functionality of your applications. This *Programmer's Reference*, critical to programmers in developing Windows-based applications, is both a tutorial and the application programming interface reference for OLE. The first half of the book lays the foundation for programming with OLE, describing the creation of OLE client and server applications. The second half offers a comprehensive and detailed reference to such topics as callback functions and data structures, DLL functions, the registration database, and error codes.
448 pages $27.95 ($37.95 Canada)   ISBN 1-55615-539-5

IMPORTANT— READ CAREFULLY BEFORE OPENING SOFTWARE PACKET(S). By opening the sealed packet(s) containing the software, you indicate your acceptance of the following Microsoft License Agreement.

MICROSOFT LICENSE AGREEMENT
(Book Companion Disks)

This is a legal agreement between you (either an individual or an entity) and Microsoft Corporation. By opening the sealed software packet(s) you are agreeing to be bound by the terms of this agreement. If you do not agree to the terms of this agreement, promptly return the unopened software packet(s) and any accompanying written materials to the place you obtained them for a full refund.

MICROSOFT SOFTWARE LICENSE

1. GRANT OF LICENSE. Microsoft grants to you the right to use one copy of the Microsoft software program included with this book (the "SOFTWARE") on a single terminal connected to a single computer. The SOFTWARE is in "use" on a computer when it is loaded into the temporary memory (i.e., RAM) or installed into the permanent memory (e.g., hard disk, CD-ROM, or other storage device) of that computer. You may not network the SOFTWARE or otherwise use it on more than one computer or computer terminal at the same time.

2. COPYRIGHT. The SOFTWARE is owned by Microsoft or its suppliers and is protected by United States copyright laws and international treaty provisions. Therefore, you must treat the SOFTWARE like any other copyrighted material (e.g., a book or musical recording) except that you may either (a) make one copy of the SOFTWARE solely for backup or archival purposes, or (b) transfer the SOFTWARE to a single hard disk provided you keep the original solely for backup or archival purposes. You may not copy the written materials accompanying the SOFTWARE.

3. OTHER RESTRICTIONS. You may not rent or lease the SOFTWARE, but you may transfer the SOFTWARE and accompanying written materials on a permanent basis provided you retain no copies and the recipient agrees to the terms of this Agreement. You may not reverse engineer, decompile, or disassemble the SOFTWARE. If the SOFTWARE is an update or has been updated, any transfer must include the most recent update and all prior versions.

4. DUAL MEDIA SOFTWARE. If the SOFTWARE package contains both 3.5" and 5.25" disks, then you may use only the disks appropriate for your single-user computer. You may not use the other disks on another computer or loan, rent, lease, or transfer them to another user except as part of the permanent transfer (as provided above) of all SOFTWARE and written materials.

5. SAMPLE CODE. If the SOFTWARE includes Sample Code, then Microsoft grants you a royalty-free right to reproduce and distribute the sample code of the SOFTWARE provided that you: (a) distribute the sample code only in conjunction with and as a part of your software product; (b) do not use Microsoft's or its authors' names, logos, or trademarks to market your software product; (c) include the copyright notice that appears on the SOFTWARE on your product label and as a part of the sign-on message for your software product; and (d) agree to indemnify, hold harmless, and defend Microsoft and its authors from and against any claims or lawsuits, including attorneys' fees, that arise or result from the use or distribution of your software product.

DISCLAIMER OF WARRANTY

The SOFTWARE (including instructions for its use) is provided "AS IS" WITHOUT WARRANTY OF ANY KIND. MICROSOFT FURTHER DISCLAIMS ALL IMPLIED WARRANTIES INCLUDING WITHOUT LIMITATION ANY IMPLIED WARRANTIES OF MERCHANT- ABILITY OR OF FITNESS FOR A PARTICULAR PURPOSE. THE ENTIRE RISK ARISING OUT OF THE USE OR PERFORMANCE OF THE SOFTWARE AND DOCUMENTATION REMAINS WITH YOU.

IN NO EVENT SHALL MICROSOFT, ITS AUTHORS, OR ANYONE ELSE INVOLVED IN THE CREATION, PRODUCTION, OR DELIVERY OF THE SOFTWARE BE LIABLE FOR ANY DAMAGES WHATSOEVER (INCLUDING, WITHOUT LIMITATION, DAMAGES FOR LOSS OF BUSINESS PROFITS, BUSINESS INTERRUPTION, LOSS OF BUSINESS INFORMATION, OR OTHER PECUNIARY LOSS) ARISING OUT OF THE USE OF OR INABILITY TO USE THE SOFTWARE OR DOCUMENTATION, EVEN IF MICROSOFT HAS BEEN ADVISED OF THE POSSIBILITY OF SUCH DAMAGES. BECAUSE SOME STATES/COUNTRIES DO NOT ALLOW THE EXCLUSION OR LIMITATION OF LIABILITY FOR CONSEQUENTIAL OR INCIDENTAL DAMAGES, THE ABOVE LIMITATION MAY NOT APPLY TO YOU.

U.S. GOVERNMENT RESTRICTED RIGHTS

The SOFTWARE and documentation are provided with RESTRICTED RIGHTS. Use, duplication, or disclosure by the Government is subject to restrictions as set forth in subparagraph (c)(1)(ii) of The Rights in Technical Data and Computer Software clause at DFARS 252.227-7013 or subparagraphs (c)(1) and (2) of the Commercial Computer Software — Restricted Rights 48 CFR 52.227-19, as applicable. Manufacturer is Microsoft Corporation, One Microsoft Way, Redmond, WA 98052-6399.

If you acquired this product in the United States, this Agreement is governed by the laws of the State of Washington.

Should you have any questions concerning this Agreement, or if you desire to contact Microsoft Press for any reason, please write: Microsoft Press, One Microsoft Way, Redmond, WA 98052-6399.

5.25-inch disk for Microsoft® Visual Basic™ Workshop, Windows Edition

You can order the enclosed disk in 5.25-inch format (one 1.2-MB disk)—free of charge. Include only shipping charges of $5.00 per disk. To order, request item number **097-000-927**. Send your name, address (no P.O. Boxes please), and daytime phone number along with your check or money order for shipping (U.S. funds only) to: Microsoft Press, Attn: Microsoft VB Workshop disk, P.O. Box 3011, Bothell, WA 98041-3011. Allow 2–3 weeks for delivery. Offer valid in the U.S. only.